BORDER INSECURITY

WHY BIG MONEY, FENCES,
AND DRONES AREN'T
MAKING US SAFER

SYLVIA LONGMIRE

palgrave
macmillan

BORDER INSECURITY
Copyright © Sylvia Longmire, 2014.
All rights reserved.

First published in 2014 by PALGRAVE MACMILLAN® in the United
States—a division of St. Martin's Press LLC, 175 Fifth Avenue, New York, NY
10010.

Where this book is distributed in the UK, Europe and the rest of the world,
this is by Palgrave Macmillan, a division of Macmillan Publishers Limited,
registered in England, company number 785998, of Houndmills, Basingstoke,
Hampshire RG21 6XS.

Palgrave Macmillan is the global academic imprint of the above companies
and has companies and representatives throughout the world.

Palgrave® and Macmillan® are registered trademarks in the United States,
the United Kingdom, Europe and other countries.

ISBN 978-1-137-27890-6

Library of Congress Cataloging-in-Publication Data
Longmire, Sylvia.
    Border insecurity : why big money, fences, and drones aren't making us
safer / Sylvia Longmire.
  pages   cm
    ISBN 978-1-137-27890-6 (hardback)
    1. Border security—United States. 2. Border security—Government
policy—United States. 3. United States—Emigration and immigration—
Government policy. 4. Immigration enforcement—United States. 5. Illegal
aliens—United States. 6. Drug control—United States. 7. Terrorism—
Prevention—United States. 8. National security—United States. I. Title.
JV6483.L66   2014
363.28'50973—dc23

                                                              2013035870

A catalogue record of the book is available from the British Library.

Design by Letra Libre, Inc.

First edition: April 2014

10 9 8 7 6 5 4 3 2 1

Printed in the United States of America.

For J/J/P

CONTENTS

INTRODUCTION

There is a perception that the border is worse now than it ever has been.
That is wrong. The border is better now than it ever has been.[1]

—Janet Napolitano, former DHS Secretary, March 2011

Living and conducting business in a Texas border county is tantamount
to living in a war zone in which civil authorities, law enforcement agen-
cies as well as citizens are under attack around the clock.[2]

—*Texas Border Security: A Strategic Military*
Assessment, September 2011

One billion dollars is a lot of money. It can buy forty private islands or twenty-five private jets; it's more than the annual gross domestic product of several small island countries. It's also the amount of tax dollars the US Department of Homeland Security (DHS) spent over the course of five years on an invisible electronic border fence that never worked.

For over a decade, US government officials, politicians, and law enforcement officers have been arguing about how best to secure our borders and how good (or bad) of a job has been done so far, spending—and wasting—more and more money along the way. During that time, the US government spent over $90 billion on border security efforts without having a truly objective way to measure success—or acknowledge failure. Border security is in the eye of the beholder; ask ten different people on Capitol Hill what a secure border looks like and you'll get ten different answers. Nowhere in the Library of Congress or in the history of American legislation will you find the exact parameters for a secure border, much less a clear path for how to achieve one.

There have been some half-hearted attempts by DHS officials and members of Congress to define what border security means, but none has gained any traction. In February 2011, US Border Patrol Chief Michael Fisher told Congress, "Border security means public safety and the sense in the community that the border is being reasonably and effectively managed."[3] A

Homeland Security News Wire report from April 2011 stated, "Government officials have repeatedly used the phrase establishing 'operational control' when describing their goal or vision for the border, yet this term has no clearly agreed upon definition." And Fisher has even said, "Operation control is not, in and of itself, a measure of border security."[4]

There is absolutely no excuse whatsoever to spend billions of dollars on border security every year without having a concrete definition of success or failure. This is what I believe border security should mean for our nation:

> Border security is the act of denying our enemies the means to enter the United States to do us harm. This is achieved by identifying and prioritizing border crossers based on the level of threat they pose to our national security, and focusing our resources on either preventing their initial entry or apprehending them before they can commit criminal or violent acts on US soil.

This definition I suggest is not to say illegal immigrants should be completely ignored or allowed free access to the United States. It merely follows a line of thinking that emphasizes the word "security" by prioritizing threats over migration policy. In that vein, this is what a secure border should look like:

> Our borders will be considered secure when US citizens can reasonably expect that our enemies cannot penetrate them without resorting to extraordinary means for which there are no existing countermeasures.

This definition takes into account the fact that we, or any other country in the world, will never be able to keep 100 percent of everyone and everything from crossing a border without detection. It also allows some leeway without making Americans think we need our own version of the Berlin Wall. But before we can appreciate the enormity of the task that is securing not just one, but two large land borders, we need to take a step back—or up—to understand how we arrived here.

Any human being with an Internet connection or access to a library can see what an incredible sight the Earth is from space. The oceans are a glittering sapphire blue, land masses all blend together, and the clouds are like veils, hiding and revealing mountain ranges, deserts, ice caps, and grasslands. Zooming in, we can start to see some natural features, like the Himalayan mountain range, the Sahara desert, and the Amazon River basin. Some of these natural features form part of national borders, like the Rhine River in

Europe, the Rio Grande between Mexico and the United States, and the Pyrenees mountain range between France and Spain. But only from this distance of tens of thousands of vertical miles can we really understand how artificial our manmade borders are.

The concept of geographical boundaries and borders goes back to at least biblical times and ancient Greece. In the King James Bible's Book of Exodus, Moses says to the Egyptian Pharaoh, "Let my people go, so that they may worship me. And if thou refuse to let them go, behold, I will smite all thy borders with frogs." The Roman Empire, which dated back to the time of the Republic in 510 BC, spanned an enormous amount of territory over the course of centuries, defined by a combination of natural frontiers and manmade boundaries. Hadrian's Wall, probably the most well known of the Roman fortifications, was an impressive example of border security. Built in AD 122 and stretching seventy-three miles from the Irish Sea to the North Sea, it was the most heavily fortified defensive structure in the entire Roman Empire and cut the isle of Great Britain in two. Borders have tended to be fluid but still defined by a civilization's armies, people, and cultures.

Formal political borders are a relatively recent historical phenomenon, and even determining what was the world's first country or first nation-state can be difficult. Along with the creation of borders came an entire host of issues, both good and bad: the ability to trade with countries outside those borders, the ability to earn income through tariffs collected at the borders, the potential need for a border security mechanism, and the inevitable creation of black markets that would seek to exploit national border weaknesses.

Our northern border with Canada, formally known as the International Boundary, stretches over 5,500 miles and is the longest land border between two countries in the world. Like so many other borders, it was created through a series of treaties and conventions, using two lines of latitude and several bodies of water as guides.

Our southern border with Mexico was initially established in 1848 with the Treaty of Guadalupe Hidalgo, and was finalized five years later with the Gadsden Purchase. Over three hundred thousand Mexican nationals were left in such present-day states like California, Colorado, and New Mexico, which comprised the Purchase and cost Mexico 55 percent of its national territory. Much of this population returned to Mexico, but many stayed. Border towns sprang up, businesses thrived, and cross-border communities like El Paso-Ciudad Juárez and San Ysidro-Tijuana expanded. Residents came and went between the countries for decades with relative ease. It was less "border" and more "borderlands," and an entire Mexican-American subculture emerged from the proximity and interdependence of our two nations.

Then three things happened in the span of less than forty years that would forever change our national view of the US-Mexico border: the Bracero Program, which allowed over four million Mexicans to temporarily and legally work in the United States, came to an end in 1964, which spurred the growth of illegal immigration from Mexico to the United States; President Richard Nixon officially declared the "War on Drugs" in 1971, which cracked down on drug trafficking across the border and eventually led to the present-day criminal insurgency in Mexico; and on September 11, 2001, al-Qa'ida caused a worldwide security shift when it flew two airplanes into the World Trade Center's twin towers, a third into the Pentagon, and a fourth that was possibly destined for the White House into a Pennsylvania field.

Terrorism, transnational crime, and illegal immigration are now the three main issues—and controversies—surrounding US border security efforts, and they largely explain why securing our borders has become more important now than at any time in our history. But addressing these issues isn't as simple as building a Hadrian's Wall along our International Boundary with Canada or a Great Wall between Mexico and the United States. We're not being invaded by the barbarians of the second century or the conventional armies of World War I and II. As intangible as communism and capitalism are, the former Soviet Union and Eastern Bloc countries were able to keep the two more or less separated with the Berlin Wall, but we're no longer facing a threat that can be easily identified with satellites or sonar or radar, or defeated with tanks or soldiers or missiles. The survival of al-Qa'ida, the growth of Hezbollah, and the continual expansion of Mexican cartels within the United States are testaments to that.

The drug-toting and terrorist barbarians of the twenty-first century are attempting to enter—and often succeed in entering—our country across our land borders, and through our airports and seaports that also serve as national borders. They use subterfuge, coercion, intimidation, bribery, and disguise. They can hide among us in plain sight for months, or even years. They use our laws against us. In some cases, they want to avoid all contact with our government. In other cases, they want to obliterate government at all levels. Some of them rely almost completely on our society's need for pleasure, escape, and instant gratification through the use of mind-altering substances to fund their intense monetary greed. Others want to annihilate our society.

And most border crossers are not barbarians at all. They're ordinary people like us, with parents, grandparents, children, and siblings. Many of them are very poor. Many are also hard workers and dreamers, who believe that if they just make it a few hundred or thousand miles north to the Promised Land that is the United States, they can work hard and create a good life.

Far from being a threat to our national security, these "invaders" form an integral, if illicit, part of our workforce. Yet they live and work in an underground world, ever watchful for the government agents they hope will never discover their existence.

Securing a border doesn't mean keeping 100 percent of everyone and everything from coming across it. That is physically impossible, and trying to do so would bankrupt many countries, from both the attempt to create barriers and from the loss of cross-border trade and cultural exchange. First and foremost, we have to prevent our enemies from entering our country without our knowledge. Inherent to this process is not only determining who our enemies are, but being able to clearly differentiate them from people who merely wish to come to the United States for benevolent reasons. Terrorists, associates of terrorists groups, and those who actively support terrorism are our enemies. Drug traffickers, human traffickers and smugglers, and violent criminals are our enemies. We must focus the vast majority of our border security apparatus on preventing these individuals from even attempting to enter our country.

Immigrants, however, are *not* our enemies, regardless of whether they arrived in the United States legally or not. Yes, those who cross our borders without inspection are violating our laws and must be dealt with in a manner that preserves both the integrity of our legal system and their dignity. However, they do not compromise the fundamental security of our nation. This concept is completely separate from the highly controversial debates over illegal immigrants "stealing" American jobs, or being granted in-state tuition at universities, or having access to taxpayer-funded free health care in emergency rooms. That topic is for another book. Apprehending terrorists and violent criminals—the true threats to our national security emanating from our borders—must take precedence over detaining non-terrorist and non-criminal border crossers (that is, economic migrants) if we are effectively going to leverage our limited resources to this end. Only when we can efficiently differentiate true threats from benevolent border crossers and prevent them from entering the United States can we achieve a secure border.

Unfortunately, we aren't even close to making that happen. Thousands of Hezbollah members and supporters have legally immigrated to the United States and raise millions of dollars to send back to their homelands every year. The 9/11 hijackers and the Christmas Day "underwear bomber" all had valid US visas issued at US consulates and traveled legally to the United States on legitimately purchased plane tickets. Members and associates of Mexican drug cartels have a presence in over 1,000 US cities[5] and are responsible for providing 90 percent of the illegal drugs consumed by Americans on a daily basis. Millions of immigrants from all over the world enter the United States illegally from Mexico every year, and while most of them are simply looking for work, hundreds, if not thousands, come every year from "specially designated countries" that sponsor, promote, or are somehow associated with terrorism. Each year, the number of media reports about armed confrontations between drug traffickers and law enforcement officers on US soil increases.

What are we doing wrong? Why do our borders appear less and less secure every year, despite reassurances from our government? The fundamental problem on which many border security failures rest is that border security is not a national priority. DHS and the White House may say otherwise, but in this case, silence is much louder than words. Cartel violence in Mexico and concerns about border violence "spillover" began in earnest in roughly 2007, the year after former Mexican President Felipe Calderón was inaugurated and deployed thousands of troops to various parts of Mexico. Not once in any State of the Union address since this turning point in the drug war has a US president mentioned Mexico or its growing criminal insurgency in any way, shape, or form. In the speeches between 2007 and 2013, the issue of border security—being mentioned only in direct reference to illegal immigration—warranted exactly nine sentences total.

Virtually everyone in America agrees that terrorism is a major threat to our national security, and as a result, counterterrorism policies and strategies are top priorities for the current administration. Politicians may vary in their opinions about how to achieve the best strategy—clearly displayed in debates over the Patriot Act and interrogation methods—but they all agree we need to prevent terrorists from killing Americans at home and abroad.

Unfortunately, the message Congress is sending of how big a role border security should play in our national security strategy is mixed. With a lack of strong leadership at the national level with regards to border security, congressmen and elected officials at all levels are left to decide for themselves—and loudly voice their opinions about—how (in)secure they think our borders really are. Our president, the DHS secretary, members of Congress, border city mayors, border sheriffs, and police chiefs can't agree on anything—if border violence spillover is happening, if the border fence is good or bad, if more or less border fence is needed, if there are enough Border Patrol agents assigned to the southwest border, if they have enough resources, if terrorists and cartels are working together . . . The list goes on and on. As a result, our country is at a political stalemate with regard to border security. Terrorism supporters, drug traffickers, violent criminals, and illegal immigrants keep crossing; meanwhile, our government plods along with no clear strategy for prioritizing threats or managing economic migration.

As dire as the situation sounds, there are some things we're getting right, and advancing technology has helped our border agencies in significant ways. Portable X-ray and gamma ray scanners allow US Customs and Border Protection (CBP) agents to peer inside vehicles and trains with hidden compartments. New seismic detectors are helping US Immigration and Customs Enforcement (ICE) find underground cross-border tunnels being used by smugglers to move drugs north and bulk cash south. Unmanned aerial vehicles (UAVs), sometimes referred to as drones, can fly silently over the border with tools like infrared scanners, identifying drug traffickers and illegal immigrants for responding Border Patrol agents.

But will technology determine the future of border security? It's tempting to imagine a world where border crossers don't have to wait for hours in line every day just to be inspected at a US land border port of entry. Maybe one day, all international travelers will use biometric cards, retina scans, or implanted nanotechnology to verify their identification at border crossings or airports to pass inspection within minutes. Maybe sensors or automatic cameras will be developed that can immediately and accurately distinguish differences between armed individuals or people hauling drug loads and unarmed immigrants. Most important is visualizing the possibility that these kinds of border technologies can one day be created and deployed at low cost, with minimal invasion of privacy and maximum respect for civil liberties.

As ideal as all that sounds, those kinds of systems still can't guarantee a 100 percent secure border, mainly because terrorists and smugglers always manage to stay just one step ahead of the good guys. Radio frequency identification chips have been hacked. GPS locator implants used by VIPs at high risk of kidnapping by cartels have been surgically (or otherwise) removed. Sensors can go bad or be tricked. And the officials who are supposed to be the "good guys" can sometimes be bought for the right price.

If we can't secure 100 percent of our border, what percentage is acceptable? The actual percentage of our southwest border under some level of operational control—meaning agents can respond to an incursion in some way within a reasonable amount of time—by the Border Patrol is 44 percent, and only 2 percent of our northern border fit that bill by 2010. In 2011, the US Border Patrol reported to the Government Accountability Office that nearly two-thirds of the 1,120 southwest border miles that had not yet achieved operational control (the other 56 percent) were reported at the "monitored" level. That meant that across these miles, the probability of detecting illegal cross-border activity was high, but responding was not. They did add the caveat that agents' ability to respond was defined by accessibility to the area or availability of resources. The remaining miles were reported at "low-level monitored," meaning that resources or infrastructure inhibited detection or interdiction of cross-border illegal activity. Border Patrol reported that these two levels of control were "not acceptable for border security."[6]

In addition, a report by the Federal Research Division of Library of Congress has stated, "There seems to be general agreement among law enforcement officials that only a maximum of 10 percent of the marijuana being smuggled into the United States is intercepted."[7] Knowing that our border will always have gaps and many people and illegal drugs will continue to get through, what percentages of operational control and drug seizures can we live with and still say our borders are secure?

Throughout human history, all border crossings have had one thing in common—people. From Roman soldiers to Israeli Border Police to American CBP inspectors, these individuals' governments relied on them to use their judgment and instincts to identify border crossers with bad intentions. It was the people on the front lines who noticed if someone's carotid artery was pulsing too strongly, or they were wearing the wrong kind of clothes, spoke with the wrong accent, or had documentation that just looked "off." Regardless of how advanced technology becomes, the success of any attempt to secure any border boils down to the capabilities of human beings.

The American men and women involved in border security, from law enforcement officers to intelligence analysts, need to hear and believe that their efforts are not in vain. They need to know that what they do has an impact on all US citizens and residents. What they, and Americans in general, don't need is a blurry finish line that never gets any closer. Those individuals on our front lines should have our government's full and united support in their endeavors.

Americans should understand that, while making a border 100 percent secure is an impossible task, it *is* possible to identify who our enemies really are, and to develop a strategy that ensures we focus our limited resources on preventing those enemies from entering our country unnoticed. Our southwest border is not nearly as safe as it could be, but not every mile of its two thousand-mile span is a war zone, either. The better we understand the concept of border security and all the moving parts involved, the better we can hold our leaders accountable when they spend our tax dollars on resources that aren't needed, fail to spend them on resources that are critical, and engage in fear-mongering or hollow reassurances designed to placate voters.

We cannot allow Hezbollah or drug cartels to make one more dollar within our own borders to support their cause or line their pockets. We also cannot continue to work within a broken immigration system that fails to adequately prioritize illegal border crossers who truly pose a danger to our country over those who are simply looking for work. There is no one-size-fits-all answer for these problems. Our borderlands and the people who live there are not homogenous along the two thousand-mile length of Mexico or the 5,500-mile length of Canada. What works in southern California probably won't work in south Texas, and what works in the Great Lakes region probably won't work in northern Montana.

Taking all these challenges into account while devising a proper strategy to stop our enemies from crossing our borders takes time, a herculean effort, and money. *Border Insecurity* is a first step toward understanding that securing our borders must be a national priority.

CHAPTER 1

ENEMIES AT THE GATE

In Mexico you have death very close. That's true for all human beings because it's a part of life, but in Mexico, death can be found in many things.

—Gael García Bernal, Mexican actor and film director

Something happened here. It's as if Mexicans subconsciously decided that their drug-related violence is a condition to be lived with and combated but not something to define them any longer.

—Thomas L. Friedman, *New York Times* op-ed columnist, February 2013

It's not common for a man involved in the drug business to reach his forties, but somehow "Miguel" managed to do it. On this day in August 2013, he's speaking to me from an undisclosed location, possibly southern California, based on the context of our conversation, or possibly somewhere in Mexico, based on his phone number. Wherever he's living, it's a quiet existence and a happy situation for him, compared to his former life. Miguel "retired" from the drug trafficking business after serving a fifteen-year prison sentence for manslaughter and federal drug trafficking charges.

"A lot of times you grow into it, you know? A lot of guys that are getting into it that are older, they're going through rough times and they need money, and they have a *compadre* who says, *Hey man, I can help you out; let's just do this*. And they say, *Oh, okay*," Miguel explained. "But I tell you what, once you get a taste of that money, there's no way they're going to want to stop."[1]

In Miguel's case, he got involved in the drug trade when he was just a kid growing up in the bad part of town. "I started in the neighborhood. In the United States, the majority of people who start [dealing] do it as kids, doing little favors here and there, seeing the homeboys doing this and that, driving good cars. You want to get involved, you know? Some get involved for the money, and for some it's just the adrenaline rush. Mostly the money," he said with a chuckle.[2] And in Miguel's heyday of the 1980s and 1990s, there was plenty of money to be made in the illegal drug trade in the United States.

Methamphetamine was Miguel's product, and he was dealing in it before the drug's popularity exploded after the new millennium. "You could say I was a meth pioneer," he told me. "Back in the early 1990s, you didn't hear about meth being such a problem. We were one of the first crews that was manufacturing." While most of Miguel's business was in the United States, his crew would occasionally reach out to the Mexican side of the border to procure precursor chemicals required for making, or "cooking," the synthetic drug.

I asked Miguel what he liked the most about being a meth trafficker. He laughed. "The money! The power! I was, what, nineteen or twenty years old? I could go to certain car dealers and work with people that I knew and be like, *Hey, I'll have that, I'll take that.* And they'd say, *Oh, sure!* I was pretty mature for my age, and there were older people who would treat me like I was their equal."[3]

I asked Miguel if he was concerned about getting caught, and his response surprised me. Because he was so young and relatively well off at the time, I thought he would tell me he felt a bit invincible, but that wasn't the case. "I was realistic," he said. "I knew at a young age, when I started getting involved in crime, that eventually I was going to end up in prison or I was going to die. I never thought I would be here and be able to say, *I'm retired, I'm not going to do this anymore.* I didn't think I was going to make it to thirty-five years old. I just never looked that far ahead."

"Violence is not good for business at all," Miguel continued. "But you can't let other people get over on you because then they're going to see it as a weakness. Even in the legitimate world, if you have a business . . . and it's the same in the underworld . . . you have to have something called *palabra* (keeping your word). Because if not, you're going to get dealt with. In the 'real' world, people look down on drug traffickers. But when they make a deal and shake on something, they don't respect it. They don't fear consequences, and they don't think, *Man, this guy might come to me and do something if I don't go through with whatever contract we made.* You don't understand how frustrating that is to me."[4]

Miguel thinks generational differences are a part of why loyalty in the business is disappearing. The other part is, he says, "No one wants to do prison time. Prison used to be fun, you know? Now it's much harsher." But even after serving a fifteen-year sentence, Miguel says he's not bitter. "I've told a lot of [police] officers this. I say, *Look, you're a cop, and it's my job to be a criminal. Now, if you catch me, guess what? You were better at it than I was.*"[5]

I wondered how a person could go from working as a drug trafficker to serving a decade and a half in prison to leading a relatively normal life. I asked Miguel if he knew the whereabouts of his original crew. They grew up together, so the ones who are still around keep in touch. Some are serving long prison sentences, and others have been killed over the years. Miguel told me this very matter-of-factly, since this is just a fact of life in his world. As for him, he said he's making a living. He likes construction because he can see buildings coming together, so he does a lot of remodeling work. Miguel is his own master, though. "I don't like to bust my ass so someone else can make money off of me, so I do my own little thing down here," he said. "I'm getting by."[6]

Miguel is just one of a countless number of human tools Mexican cartels have used to distribute their illegal product in the United States. As groups, these men and women form the cartels and other criminal groups we know today in Mexico, and collectively they are one of the biggest national security threats our country is facing. Violent drug traffickers are the primary reason we need enhanced border security measures—not terrorists, who usually come here on airplanes using legal documents, and not economic migrants, who come here looking for work. Cartel members are increasingly difficult for law enforcement agencies to find and have no problem killing and kidnapping each other on US soil. The horrors they commit in Mexico on a daily basis should serve as a wake-up call to US officials who believe this is simply a criminal problem to which they've dedicated adequate resources.

The phenomenon of extreme violence in Mexico is relatively recent, but Mexican cartels have been in the drug smuggling business for decades. The cartels started out very much like the Italian Mafia and flourished, here in the United States, as family businesses. Drug smuggling began in earnest in Mexico after Chinese migrant railroad workers brought opium poppies across the Pacific Ocean in the 1860s. The Chinese got involved in the opium and heroin trade, smuggling sizeable amounts from Tijuana into southern California and making handsome profits. After the turn of the century, smaller Mexican criminal groups decided there were plenty of profits to go around and started to move in on Chinese territory.

Since the 1920s, Mexican smuggling groups have been able to adapt to shifting American tastes for narcotics. The Mexican drug trade began to coalesce in the 1960s in the state of Sinaloa, located in the northwestern part of Mexico, along the Gulf of California. The heart of what's called "The Golden

Triangle," the mountains of Sinaloa and surrounding areas have the perfect conditions for growing opium poppies and marijuana. At first, local farmers grew enough to supply domestic needs, but after awhile, families started to leave rural areas to seek other opportunities or set up camp in the city of Culiacán—now known as the "cradle of drug trafficking" in Mexico. By the 1960s, authorities estimated there were approximately three hundred clandestine airfields in northern Mexico, transporting heroin and marijuana to the United States.[7]

The emergence of true *capos,* or drug lords, began in the 1970s. Pedro Áviles Pérez is known as the "pioneer of drug trafficking" in Mexico, and ran the first large organization that could be considered a cartel[8] by today's standards. Several famous traffickers cut their teeth under his tutelage, including the most wanted man in Mexico, Sinaloa Federation leader Joaquin "El Chapo" Guzmán.

In the mid-1970s, South American governments implemented Operation Condor, a military counterdrug mission that resulted in several deadly confrontations between traffickers and soldiers. As a result, Áviles's trusted lieutenants starting moving out of Culiacán and into Guadalajara and other Mexican cities. When Áviles was killed in a shootout with federal police in 1978, Miguel Ángel Félix Gallardo emerged as the leader of these lieutenants and became known as "The Godfather" of Mexican drug trafficking. He was joined by two other *capos* at the top of the narco food chain: Ernesto Fonseca Carrillo and Rafael Caro Quintero.

Over the next decade, the three men and their people established strong ties with corrupt Mexican politicians and officials, which allowed the organization to flourish. But more importantly, they set up arrangements to transport cocaine for Colombian drug cartels through Mexico into the United States. The Guadalajara cartel, as it was known, started out as the hired help. However, as their expertise improved, they began to demand payment not only in cash, but in product. This expansion into the cocaine trade raised the organization to a whole new level of profit making.

It didn't last forever. The cartel's leadership learned that a DEA agent named Enrique "Kiki" Camarena had infiltrated their organization and had him kidnapped, tortured, and executed. The manhunt for Camarena's killer was on, and Fonseca Carrillo and Caro Quintero were arrested in 1985, only two months after Camarena was murdered. By 1987, Félix Gallardo knew his days as a free man were limited. He finally moved out of Culiacán and into Guadalajara, rounded up his trusted brigade at an Acapulco resort, and divided up his empire into several pieces. This would make it harder for the Mexican government to bring down the entire organization at once. It was a smart move, as Félix Gallardo was arrested in 1989 and is currently serving a forty-year sentence in Mexico's Altiplano maximum security prison.

These are the "old school" cartels—friend- and family-run under the traditional organized crime model. All of them still exist today, more familiar as the Tijuana cartel (Arellano Félix Organization, or AFO), the Juárez cartel (Vicente Carrillo Fuentes Organization, or VCFO), the Sinaloa Federation, and the Gulf cartel (Cartel del Golfo, or CDG). Because of this history and tradition, these cartels have more or less followed the unwritten rules of the Mafia—that is, business is business, keep things under the radar, and stay away from spouses, children, and innocents.

Then something changed. Osiel Cárdenas Guillén was firmly in charge of the CDG in the late 1990s after taking the cartel's reins by murdering his predecessor, Salvador Gómez, and in the process earning himself the nickname "El Mata Amigos"—the friend killer. He's known to be secretive and paranoid, to the point of creating his own private army of mercenaries known as Los Zetas to protect his turf and operations from a myriad of rivals.

In 1997, Cárdenas commanded one of his most trusted subordinates, Arturo "Z-1" Guzmán Decena, to recruit a paramilitary squad for him. Guzmán was a former special forces soldier, so he knew where to look. Within a couple of years, he had recruited thirty-one men, most with military backgrounds and several with special forces–type training, into Cárdenas's private army. Their mission for several years was mainly to protect Cárdenas and his operations through enforcement tactics—meaning the use of threats, assaults, kidnappings, torture, and executions against anyone who crossed the CDG or failed to live up to Cárdenas's expectations.

This worked well enough for a few years, until Cárdenas was arrested in 2003 after a shootout with the Mexican military. While he more or less ran the CDG from a Mexican prison, Los Zetas started to operate under the premise of *when the cat is away, the mice will play*. In 2004, the city of Nuevo Laredo became ground zero for the battle over territory between the Federation and the Gulf cartel. Los Zetas were dispatched to take care of CDG business, and in the process, introduced beheadings, dismemberments, and the narco style of urban guerrilla warfare to the drug war. Most media reports and many journals and books point to the December 2006 inauguration of former President Felipe Cálderon as the beginning of today's drug war in Mexico. However, as neat and tidy as that date is, the *real* start of the brutality we see today along the border and beyond occurred two years earlier in Nuevo Laredo.

Since that time, the cartels have been playing a game of keeping up with the Joneses. Beheadings have become more common, almost to the point of being de rigueur. To keep the attention of the media—and more importantly, to keep rivals and the police terrified—cartels have had to amp up the impact of each new killing. For example, in January 2010, the body of a Juárez cartel member was cut up into pieces and left in different parts of the town of Los Mochis in northwestern Sinaloa state. His torso was found in a plastic container in one location; elsewhere another box contained his arms, legs, and skull. Hernandez's face was skinned from his skull, sewn onto a soccer ball, and left in a plastic bag near City Hall. The killers—most likely affiliated with the Federation—left a note for their Juárez cartel rivals that read, "Happy New Year, because this will be your last."[9]

Los Zetas isn't the newest violent group to appear on the drug war scene, although they did break off from the Gulf cartel in 2010 to become an independent trafficking organization. La Familia Michoacana (LFM) burst onto the stage in 2006 in more ways than one—specifically by rolling several severed heads onto the dance floor of a nightclub in Uruapan. The twenty or so LFM members left a note, written on cardboard: "The family doesn't kill for money. It doesn't kill women. It doesn't kill innocent people, only those who deserve to die. Know that this is divine justice."[10]

The next six years were witness to an unprecedented number of splits and alliances between cartels. Joaquin "El Chapo" Guzmán and Vicente Carrillo Fuentes parted ways for good in 2007 after breaking up and making up three years earlier, and thus began the war over the Ciudad Juárez plaza that would earn it the nickname of "Murder City." The Beltrán Leyva Organization, an older family-run organization that aligned with Guzmán from the beginning, split off from the Federation in 2008, disappeared for a couple of years after several high-profile arrests, and is experiencing a resurgence in northern Sonora state. Both Los Zetas and the Gulf cartel underwent internal splits in 2012 and 2013 as a result of losing leadership. The ultimate outcome of more players entering the game and continuing shifts in alliances is a nationwide death toll that increases every year.

Mexican cartels are responsible for the US import of four different kinds of illegal drugs: marijuana, cocaine, heroin, and methamphetamine (meth). Marijuana accounts for the largest volume of drugs coming across the border, but cocaine is the biggest moneymaker, with meth not far behind. In fiscal year 2012, US Customs and Border Protection (CBP) seized over 3.1 million pounds of illegal drugs along our southwest border, with more than half of that amount seized in Texas alone.[11] Those drugs are not evenly distributed among ports of entry, and some kinds are more common than others. In fiscal year 2011, marijuana accounted for roughly 99 percent of all illegal drugs seized by US Border Patrol in between southwest border ports of entry.[12] US agents will more commonly see large bundles of marijuana in south Texas and carried by human "mules" in the Arizona desert, whereas CBP inspectors are more likely to see smaller cocaine, heroin, and methamphetamine packages tightly wedged in hidden vehicle compartments in places like the San Ysidro and Otay Mesa ports of entry south of San Diego.

There is virtually no limit to the ways in which cartels can smuggle drugs into the US by land, sea, and air. The most commonly used methods today are still the most traditional—hiding larger packages of drugs in cars going through ports of entry, strapping smaller bundles under loose clothing, or hauling bales of dope in pickup trucks or on the backs of human mules in the vast terrain between the ports. "Go-fast" speedboats and commercial and small single-engine aircraft were once favorites for smugglers, but cartels have put their own stamp on all these methods in recent years.

When moving drugs over land becomes too burdensome, cartels move underground. In September 2012, the Department of Homeland Security (DHS) Office of the Inspector General announced that there had been an 80 percent increase in drug tunnel activity since 2008,[13] and more than 160 of these cartel-operated tunnels have been discovered since 1990. Ninety-nine of them have been found just in the Border Patrol's Tucson sector in Arizona.[14] In a report that addressed CBP's strategy to deal with cross-border tunnels, the Office indicated that almost $170,000 worth of illegal drugs have

A drug tunnel near Otay Mesa, California. Photo courtesy of CBP.

been recovered from traffickers using tunnels, and that 42 percent of the structures that have been found are defined as "sophisticated," meaning they are "elaborately constructed and may use shoring, ventilation, electricity, and rail systems."[15] Sometimes the tunnels are also used to transport firearms and bulk cash south into Mexico.

The construction of hidden compartments in vehicles has become something of an art form for cartels, who commission specialists for a cost of as much as tens of thousands of dollars. However, our technology and agent expertise have improved, so the telltale signs of compartments have become a bit more apparent. One way smugglers have tried to discourage agents from looking too closely at vehicle cargo is by stashing illegal drugs in toxic waste. Some of the hazardous materials CBP agents have either come across or anticipate encountering include oil, drilling fluids, and wastewater used in gas and oil wells, among "other substances found in industrial transportation vehicles." In a nasty process, contractors have to drain tankers of chemicals before going in and physically extracting contraband from their innards.[16]

Sometimes cartels avoid the use of cars and trucks altogether at the ports of entry. In April 2013, US Drug Enforcement Administration (DEA) agents in Hidalgo County, Texas, received a tip that some construction equipment might contain a load of illegal drugs hidden inside. When agents found the huge Terex TXC140 LC-1 excavator on the back of a flatbed truck, they called in the experts. A drug detection dog alerted on the excavator, and agents took to it with a blowtorch. Inside the excavator's arm, agents found two hundred bundles of marijuana, and the two men who were escorting the load were brought up on drug charges.[17]

These are just a handful of endless examples of smuggler ingenuity. Cartels have been using drug submarines for many years—and with increasing frequency—to haul multi-ton loads of cocaine from South America into Mexican waters. They are also relying more heavily on small open panga boats to move drug shipments up the California coast. Law enforcement agents in the state are growing alarmed at the increasing volume of drugs being transported by smugglers this way, as well as the difficulty in detecting the small vessels. In 2008, CBP recorded forty-five panga incidents, 230 apprehensions, and the seizure of 3,800 pounds of marijuana in between San Diego and Santa Barbara, California. In 2012, those numbers for the same area shot up to 205 panga incidents and over 120,000 pounds of marijuana seized.[18]

Mexican cartels go through a lot of trouble to move drug loads across an increasingly fortified border. The blood, sweat, and tears required to smuggle these drugs successfully into the US are the biggest reason for the premium

Traffickers used this case of Coke bottles with false bottoms to smuggle a different kind of coke into the United States.

placed on the price of drugs on US streets. Because they're such valuable commodities, drug loads and cartel operations require a great degree of protection—more so from detection by US authorities than those in Mexico. While the primary cartel strategy used to be one of avoidance, they've resorted to confrontation more frequently in the last few years.

These days, the city of Matamoros in the extreme northeast corner of Mexico's Tamaulipas state is a hot spot for cartel-related violence. Located directly across the border from Brownsville, Texas, it's the birthplace of the Gulf cartel. But Matamoros wasn't like this in 1999. Osiel Cárdenas Guillen ensured the cartel was a force to be reckoned with in northeast Mexico, and Matamoros was relatively tranquil as a result. It was in this context that DEA agent Joe DuBois and FBI agent Daniel Fuentes found themselves face to face with one of the country's most dangerous killers.

On the afternoon of November 9, 1999, the two American agents were driving through Matamoros in a Ford Bronco. While the vehicle itself was relatively innocuous, it bore diplomatic license plates that announced to the world a potentially delicious target was inside. This was doubly true, as the agents weren't alone. Their passenger, trying very hard not to be seen, was a local Mexican crime reporter. He was working as an informant and showing the agents the locations of cartel members' homes and stash houses in the city.[19]

One of the houses on the tour was Cárdenas' pink fortress, and given the security he surrounded himself with, it didn't take long for someone to notice the drive-by. Shortly after Dubois and Fuentes passed the house, a car and a pickup truck began to follow the Bronco. The agents lost them on a main road, but picked up another tail. They called the municipal police for assistance, but the commander seemed to be stalling on providing any.[20] Other cars joined the chase, and eventually six vehicles surrounded the agents and informant, forcing them to pull over—ironically enough, just blocks away from a police station. Some of the dozen or so armed gunmen that began to emerge from the vehicles wore police uniforms; others just plainly looked trigger-happy. DuBois and Fuentes tried to mentally prepare for the worst.[21]

Eventually, Cárdenas himself emerged from one of the vehicles and approached the Bronco with a gold-plated AK-47 in his hands. The war of words began, with Cárdenas demanding the agents hand over the informant or die. The agents refused and claimed they were dead either way. The tension escalated. At one point, Cárdenas pointed his rifle at Fuentes's head, stating in colorful language that he had no interest in or concerns about the agents' employers. DuBois attempted to reason with him, reminding him of the US government's backlash against the Guadalajara cartel after they kidnapped and murdered undercover DEA agent Enrique "Kiki" Camarena in 1985. Essentially, he wanted Cárdenas to know the US government would bring down its full diplomatic and law enforcement weight like the hammer of God on both him and his organization, wiping them off the narco map if Cárdenas didn't let them go.[22]

Excruciatingly slow seconds ticked by as the gears in the drug lord's head turned. Ultimately, the tactic worked. Cárdenas called off the gunmen and ordered the agents to leave, but not without an explicit warning: "You [expletive] gringos. This is my town, so get the [expletive] out of here before I kill all of you. Don't ever come back." In a telling statement, Fuentes told a narcoterrorism conference in August 2012, "Had that [happened] today, we would've been dead."[23]

Until relatively recently, confrontations like this between cartels and US law enforcement agents were extremely rare. Because the US government response to Kiki Camarena's murder was relatively strong and swift—the southwest border came to a virtual standstill for months while US Customs agents searched for Camarena's body—cartel leaders who didn't want to meet Félix Gallardo's fate backed off from taking similar actions for twenty-five years.

Then something changed. Cartels members started showing less and less concern for the fate of US agents who got in their way.

On February 15, 2011, US Immigration and Customs Enforcement (ICE) agents Jaime Zapata and Victor Ávila were on their way back to Mexico City after meeting with ICE staff in Monterrey, where they were picking up some "sensitive equipment" for transport. They were driving on busy Highway 57 in an armored Chevrolet Suburban with diplomatic license plates when two vehicles started driving very aggressively around them. Zapata and Ávila were eventually boxed in and forced off the road.

Hoping that their status as US law enforcement agents would prevent a violent confrontation, Zapata brought the vehicle to a stop. Unfortunately, when Zapata shifted the gear into park, the doors automatically unlocked. Gunmen forced the door open and tried to drag Zapata out of the SUV, but he managed to fight them off, get back inside, and lock the doors. He then cracked the window, the two men showed their identification, and repeated over and over that they were Americans and diplomats.[24] The attackers responded with "We don't give a [expletive],"[25] shoved an AK-47 through the window crack and started to fire. Both agents were hit; Zapata took six rounds and was fatally wounded. As he was dying, Zapata managed to put the car in gear and drive away before collapsing. He later died from his wounds, but Ávila recovered from his injuries.[26]

A week after the shooting, Mexican authorities arrested six members of Los Zetas in the San Luís Potosí area. Initial reports—partly derived from "confessions" obtained from detained cartel members—indicated the attack was a case of mistaken identity, and that the Zetas involved in the attack thought they were pulling over rival cartel members in their armored vehicle. However, later reports provided to members of Congress pointed to a deliberate ambush.[27] It's very hard to believe the tragic confrontation wasn't intended, given the vehicle's diplomatic plates, the identification presented by the agents, and the fact they were unarmed—an inconvenient legal requirement for US agents working in Mexico.

This attack was very much in the minds of drug war observers on the morning of August 24, 2012, when two CIA agents assigned to the US Embassy in Mexico City were shot while riding in an armored vehicle just north of Cuernavaca, about an hour's drive south of Mexico City. Jesse Garner and Stan Boss—likely cover names—were riding with a Mexican marine captain in an armored Toyota SUV with diplomatic license plates to a naval training base called El Capulín. In a nearby area called Tres Marías, individuals in another vehicle pulled up alongside the Toyota and displayed several weapons. The Toyota's driver tried to evade the vehicle, then got back on the highway. Four other vehicles joined the first chase car, and all their occupants opened fire on the Toyota, hitting the armored SUV at least thirty times.[28]

The captain was able to call the army base and ask for assistance. Several army and navy personnel arrived on scene, and so did officers from the federal police. The two American agents had non-fatal gunshot wounds and the Mexican officer had only minor injuries. Strangely enough, the attackers were easily identified—they were all federal police officers. They claimed they were in the area looking for a kidnapping suspect and happened to come across the Embassy's Toyota in yet another case of "mistaken identity." However, the attackers were all wearing civilian clothes and riding in different civilian unmarked vehicles. The shell casings found at the scene came from AK-47s, which are not standard issue weapons for *federales* (federal police).[29]

Former Mexican President Felipe Calderón suggested a few days after the attack that the officers might have had ties to criminal organizations, a conclusion everyone else had already reached. Mexican authorities believed leaders of the Beltrán Leyva Organization might have been living or operating nearby, and the corrupt police involved—sixteen total were arrested—were working on orders from the cartel.[30]

As brazen as they were, these three attacks on US officers happened in Mexico, where cartel members are used to getting away with pretty much anything. On the US side of the border, it's usually a different situation. If a crime is committed, the police can be relied on to respond in a reasonable amount of time and conduct a thorough investigation. Cartels are often hesitant to get involved in violent situations in the United States because it brings too much unwanted attention to their presence and operations, and this has a negative impact on their drug profits.

The presence of law enforcement agents along the border has increased over the last several years, making it more challenging for our cartel enemies to smuggle drugs and people into the United States. However, instead of backing off and taking their business elsewhere, smugglers have become more aggressive in order to keep their American customers happy. They're much more willing to take risks and aren't as concerned as they used to be about keeping a low profile. This puts our men and women involved in border security operations directly in harm's way on a daily basis.

On a mid-December evening in 2010, Border Patrol Agent Brian Terry and several fellow members of his Border Patrol Tactical Unit were patrolling in Peck Canyon, just north of Rio Rico, Arizona, and eleven miles from the Mexican border. The canyon lies in the middle of one of the busiest smuggling areas in Arizona, which starts just west of Nogales, heads east into Cobre Ridge, then up into the Atascosa Mountains. Then the Peck Canyon corridor, as it's called, descends into the canyon itself, which divides the Atascosa and Tumacácori Mountains. It's a rugged area and remote, which is why it's such an attractive trail for smugglers.

Terry's team had been in this area for a few days and was very tired after a long day of searching for smuggling activity. They were about to call it a night when they spotted movement at the canyon's entrance. One team member noted five "bodies," meaning people in Border Patrol–speak, and the agents readied their weapons. As the people got closer, the team realized they were a rip crew—a group of "border bandits" who rob smugglers of their drug loads at gunpoint in the US, thus saving themselves the trouble of actually having to get the loads across the border. One agent yelled *"Policia!"* and another yelled "Border Patrol! Don't move!"[31]

What happened next has been recounted in a few different ways. Some accounts say that an agent fired a weapon first, but that he fired a bean bag round—essentially a non-lethal projectile designed to get the target to comply before using lethal force. Unfortunately, someone from the rip crew fired back with real bullets, and a brief firefight ensued. Terry was hit just once, but the bullet caught him between panels of his protective ballistic gear. It entered Terry's lower back and traveled upward, severing his spinal cord and the main artery to his heart. Medevac helicopters were not dispatched to the team's location reportedly because the terrain was to rugged for a safe extraction, but other accounts indicated the Medevac unit made a command decision not to deploy the helicopter for fear of taking fire from the bandits.[32]

As a result, members of the team had to haul Terry for over a mile across that terrain to get him out of the canyon and to a location where the Medevac unit could pick him up. By then it was too late; Terry died from his wounds on the way to the hospital. He was forty years old and had been an agent for only four years. He had been looking forward to a trip home to Michigan for Christmas to see his family.

The five members of the rip crew were identified, but four fled and only one was arrested at the scene. In July 2012, the FBI offered a $1 million reward for information leading to the arrest of the four fugitives. In September 2012, the FBI announced a second rip crew member had been apprehended in

Mexico and was awaiting extradition to the United States. In October 2012, the lone rip crew member in US custody pled guilty to first-degree murder.

And this is just one example of a deadly confrontation between Mexican smugglers and border agents. In July 2009, three Mexican nationals—including one juvenile—crafted an ambush near Campo, California, intended for Border Patrol Agent Robert Rosas. They planned to rob him of his night vision goggles, which they could use in their human smuggling operations. Near the Shockey Truck Trail, they laid a set of footprints to make it look like a group of illegal immigrants had headed into some brush. Agent Rosas, upon discovering the footprints, followed them into the brush and was attacked by five men. Rosas was shot multiple times by at least two of his attackers and died as a result of his wounds, leaving behind a wife and two children. After the shooting, the men stole Rosas's night vision equipment, as well as his bag, firearm, handcuffs, and other items.[33] Shortly after the murder, the juvenile suspect was identified and apprehended in Tijuana, Mexico, after he was seen showing off Rosas's gun to friends.[34]

There are dozens of other incidents where smugglers have fired shots both across the border at agents, as well as on the US side of the border during pursuits and agent attempts to apprehend them. This is more disturbing than the usual cops-and-robbers activity that happens in countless US cities every night, simply because the attackers are often foreign nationals who have entered our country illegally. Certain Mexican cartels are also increasing their intentional attacks on innocent bystanders and showing more and more disregard for the consequences of murdering those who have historically been off-limits.

It's not often that teenagers living in the middle of Murder City can just kick back and relax without fearing or worrying about something. The sprawling Mexican metropolis of Ciudad Juárez—a literal stone's throw across the border from El Paso, Texas—earned the nickname for one year after another of record-setting homicide rates, all related to the battle over control of the border's most lucrative drug smuggling route. 2010 was a banner year for the city in the worst possible way, when it would chalk up over 3,100 murders mostly related (according to the Mexican government) to the drug trade.

Imagine trying to grow up as a good kid in a place like this. Juárez is home to hundreds of *maquiladoras,* or huge mass-production factories owned by foreign companies, so it draws a lot of people from elsewhere in Mexico who are looking for work. Historically it has been an industrial hub and has its working and middle class, but much of the city and its outskirts remain poor. Good schools are a rare commodity in many places, and because of the city's street design and public transportation system layout, parents who want their children to get an education sometimes have to subject them to hours-long bus rides in each direction.

Even if a teenager is able to get a good education and mostly stay out of trouble, he or she is constantly surrounded by reminders of the drug war—dealers on every corner; pimped-out SUVs cruising the streets; narcos with their fashionable clothing, jewelry, and bombshell girlfriends; and last but not least, the masked and armed Mexican soldiers and police constantly patrolling the city in armored vehicles. Teenagers and even adolescents are continually being harassed by gang members who want them to work as lookouts, drug mules, or even hit men. The lure of easy money and the glamorous narco lifestyle is extraordinarily difficult to shy away from for too long, especially when parents are divorcing frequently, single mothers are working two or three jobs to keep multiple children fed, and youths have fewer and fewer opportunities to escape their circumstances.

Given all this, coming across not just one but five dozen honest and hard-working Mexican teenagers—many of whom are outstanding students and athletes—is a wonderful thing that holds hope for so many in this ravaged country. In late January 2010, one such group was celebrating the simple fact that it was a Saturday night in the Villas de Salvárcar neighborhood of Ciudad Juárez. It's a working class neighborhood where everybody knows everyone and parents keep an eye on their kids, and on this night, these young high school and college students were enjoying a party without a care in the world.

At some point during the festivities and unbeknownst to the revelers, seven vehicles and roughly twenty armed men pulled onto the street where the party was being held. Before they approached the house, they barricaded the street so no one could get in or out. The men were not there to join the party; they were hit men for the Juárez cartel, and they were under strict orders to kill the members of the rival gang Artistas Asesinos, who they thought were inside the house.

Seconds later, the thugs stormed into the house and started firing indiscriminately on the partygoers with high-caliber rifles and handguns. The sounds inside the house were deafening from the gunfire and the screaming, and the smell of gunpowder and blood would soon permeate the air. The gunmen weren't there long, tearing out of the house as quickly as they came in, but not before leaving behind a macabre scene of bodies and bloodstained walls and floors. In all, fifteen people were killed—most of them teenagers—and over a dozen were injured, many critically.

Contrary to the beliefs of the hit men and initial police and media reports, the victims weren't gang members, but good kids with bright futures.

Five of the victims played American-style football for their high school teams. Two other victims were studying international relations at the Juárez campus of the Autonomous University of Chihuahua. Yet another wanted to be a doctor.[35]

In August 2011, Mexican authorities arrested high-level Juárez cartel member José Antonio "El Diego" Acosta Hernández, who had been linked to at least 1,500 murders in the northern Mexican state of Chihuahua. It was his job to eliminate rivals of his employer, the Sinaloa Federation, in Ciudad Juárez. Under the impression that the partygoers were members of the Federation-employed Asesinos, he gave the hit men the order to storm the house that night. He confessed to authorities that he had gotten bad information and acknowledged that most of the people at the party were innocent before saying he "felt bad" about the loss of life.[36]

There was no such remorse shown by five members of the Cartel de Jalisco Nueva Generación (CJNG)—a "mini cartel" that was aligned at one point with the Sinaloa Federation—after they committed possibly one of the worst atrocities in drug war history. In late January 2013, these five men kidnapped ten-year-old Irma Isaisa Jasmine Arroyo, a sweet little girl with long brown hair and big brown eyes, near Tecomán, Mexico. After they raped her, they executed her, partially incinerated her body, and dumped her in a lemon orchard. Irma wasn't even the right target; the CJNG thought they were kidnapping the daughter of a rival cartel member, and instead they grabbed an innocent little girl whose family had nothing to do with the drug trade.

Sometimes, cartels work hard to mask the innocence of their victims. The general assumption in Mexico that has been propagated by law enforcement and the government is that the vast majority of victims of extreme violence are involved in the drug trade. Cartels have been able to manipulate this mentality to their advantage. If a cartel leaves a note or sign with a pile of dead bodies, people are more likely than not to believe whatever the message says. They're also more likely than not to believe that the pile of bodies consists of a bunch of dead traffickers. But a bit of digging—a deadly prospect in Mexico—reveals that all is not necessarily what it seems when it comes to mass casualties.

In September 2011, the Gente Nueva, a secretive armed wing of the Sinaloa Federation, parked two trucks containing thirty-five dead bodies on a highway overpass in Boca del Río, a town on the outskirts of the coastal Mexican city of Veracruz. A few men unloaded the bodies onto a busy thoroughfare during rush hour under the eyes of horrified onlookers. At the time, no one knew it was the Gente Nueva that was responsible, but the Mexican government was quick to announce that the thirty-five semi-nude victims—most showing signs of torture—were associated with Federation rival Los Zetas. Veracruz state attorney general Reynaldo Escobar Pérez said at the time they had criminal records for kidnapping, extortion, murder, and drug dealing. A banner left at the scene was signed "G.N." and threatened Los Zetas, further solidifying the government's claims.[37]

But some things didn't add up so neatly. The narcomessage left with the bodies said that Luis Felipe "El Ferras" Ferra Gomez, a member of Los Zetas who had escaped from a local medium security prison the day before, was among the dead. In mid-December 2011—three months after the Boca del Río body dump—a very-much-alive Ferra Gómez was captured in a large military operation elsewhere in the state of Veracruz. The announcement of the victims' criminal history came only hours after the bodies were dumped—a miraculous achievement in background checking of thirty-five people by all global standards. In an interview with a Mexican journalist, José Cuitláhuac Salinas Martínez, the deputy regional director of the attorney general's office at the time, stated twice that the victims were not found to have cartel connections, and that only six of them had any type of criminal record. In truth: among the dead were housewives, high school students, and a highly decorated policeman.[38]

Other incidents followed where innocent Mexicans would be murdered and used as props by cartels. In May 2012, in Chapala, Jalisco, authorities found eighteen bodies of people who had been tortured, killed, and dismembered by the Milenio cartel, allies of Los Zetas. Reports came out soon after that the victims were innocent people, and that the body count was supposed to have been higher. Fifteen children had been kidnapped in the town of Tala and were supposed to be executed as well, but the executioner never showed and their guards got high and passed out, allowing all but two to escape. Tragically, those two boys were among the eighteen dead found in Chapala. A few days later, Juan Carlos Antonio "El Chato" Mercado, Tala plaza chief for Los Zetas and mastermind of the massacre, was captured. He said all the kids in the safe house were innocent. Mercado also explained how Los Zetas picked their victims: his boss would point to someone and say "that one," and Mercado would kidnap him.[39]

The same day El Chato was captured, a different cartel committed a different massacre hundreds of miles to the north. In this grisly scene, the perpetrators dumped forty-nine bodies on a highway leading out of Monterrey and near the town of Cadereyta. The bodies were mutilated like many others, but specific parts were notably missing: the heads, hands, and feet, meaning there were no teeth or fingerprints that could be used by police to identify many of the victims. Initially authorities and the media assumed Los Zetas were responsible for the massacre, based solely on a narcomessage left with the bodies and graffiti left at the entrance to the town. But several days later, the Mexican military arrested Daniel "El Loco" Elizondo and several others in connection with the killings—and they were members of the Gulf cartel, not Los Zetas, so there was the possibility that Los Zetas were being framed.[40] It also started to look more and more like the victims were innocent migrants from Central America who had been targeted out of sheer convenience.[41]

The reason for all this bloodshed boils down to one thing: money. More specifically, cartels slaughter each other, Mexican police, soldiers, and an increasing number of innocent people to make billions of dollars every year.[42] This is the enemy whose numbers within our own borders grow every year; the enemy who is more and more willing to violently confront our law enforcement officers every day; the enemy who operates under the radar and under our noses in every American community where there is a demand for illegal drugs.

Just the sheer fact that any Mexican criminal group would intentionally kidnap, rape, and execute a child—no matter what her family's cartel ties are—or murder dozens of innocent people to serve as a display of power should serve as a huge wake-up call. These actions are very clear indicators that the enemies our border agencies are facing now are no longer intimidated by an American lawman with a badge and a gun. Mexican cartels and the gang members and smugglers they employ are deadly, soulless killers who have only one goal: to get as much tonnage of illegal drugs across our southwest border as possible in order to maximize their organization's profits. They will do whatever it takes to accomplish this goal, including attacking—and killing, if necessary—US law enforcement officers on US soil. Our government needs to be prepared to do whatever it takes to stop these cartel enemies from invading our country even further than they already have.

CHAPTER 2

THE GUARDIANS

Our border patrol and immigration agents are doing a fine job, but we still have a problem. . . . Too many illegal immigrants are coming in, and we're capturing many more non-Mexican illegal immigrants than we can send home.[1]

—Former president George W. Bush,
The President's Radio Address, October 2005

A strategy that simply hires a lot of border patrol agents and puts them on the line is not an effective strategy.[2]

—Michael Chertoff, former DHS secretary, August 2005

It was 3:00 A.M. in California, and US Border Patrol Agent Kevin Simmons[*] was working the mid shift in the southern California foothills. He was out in the field with several other agents when something tripped a seismic sensor nearby. After dispatch notified Simmons and his fellow agents of the sensor hit, one agent set up an infrared scope to look for migrants or smugglers—"bodies" in Border Patrol parlance—in the dark. Pretty quickly, they detected a large group of people coming down into the area through a canyon.

To get to the group quickly, all the agents got into their trucks and started driving down an access road toward the opening of the canyon where it spills out onto the flatlands. Then Simmons and the others got out of their trucks and saw through the scope that the group was "laying up," or resting/hiding momentarily, on a nearby hillside, most likely because they saw the Border

---

* This is a pseudonym used to protect Agent "Simmons's" true identity for his safety.

Patrol vehicles approaching from the road below. The half-dozen or so agents then started to fan out, moving toward the group.

It wasn't long before they were apprehending one illegal immigrant after another—the group had approximately sixty people traveling together. After rounding up the majority of the migrants, the agents got to the point where they were using their infrared scope to pick out any stragglers who were attempting to get away. Agent Simmons was coming down the hill when he heard through his radio, *Hey, head back up the hill to just above where you were because I've got some bodies laid up there; looks like two or three.* So Simmons started heading back up the hill with his flashlight on to avoid any hazards. His radio sounded again: *Okay, you're getting close; it looks like they're in some rocks right up above you.*

Simmons decided to circle around to his left so he wasn't heading directly toward them, and formulated a plan to approach them from higher ground. *Perfect, they're right below you. Start coming down and you'll see 'em,* his radio squawked. Sure enough, Simmons soon saw them with his flashlight. He started telling them in Spanish, "Don't move!" and he noticed it was one male and two females who were hiding. Simmons had to jump down off a rock to get into the area where they had been laying up, and after getting his footing, he grabbed the male migrant in order to handcuff him. However, the man had other plans. He immediately grabbed Simmons right back, who thought, *Okay, the fight is on.*

Simmons and the man were grappling on a hillside strewn with rocks and boulders, and the migrant seemed intent on throwing Simmons around as best he could. The agent tried to gain solid footing and get the man off of him with short, rapid punches. However, Simmons fell backward right onto a rock, and although his body armor absorbed most of the impact, the fall still knocked the wind out of him. His assailant took advantage of Simmons's brief disorientation to jump on top of him while the two women he was with started grabbing at Simmons's shirt and hair. The women started throwing punches, and the man got in a particularly good swing at Simmons's face. *That felt awesome,* Simmons thought wryly. Simmons had trained extensively for what happened next but had prayed it would never happen: the man reached with his right hand across Simmons's body and went for his gun.

Simmons was put through these scenarios at the Border Patrol Academy, was trained in weapons retention, and told that in the event someone tried to disarm him, that would be a deadly force situation. An assailant wasn't going to take his gun and throw it in the bushes; he would take it and use it against him.

Things started moving in slow motion. Simmons slammed his own hand on top of the migrant's to prevent him from pulling the gun out of its holster, then started trying to strike his assailant with his left hand to try to get the man off of him. Unfortunately, while all of this was going on, the two female migrants were still trying to beat up on Simmons.

Simmons just said to himself, *You know what? I'm just going to have to take a couple of punches.* He stopped trying to block the man and put both hands over his holster to protect his gun. While this succeeded in forcing the migrant to remove his hand from Simmons's holster, it also freed up both of the man's hands, which promptly began pummeling Simmons in the face. Simmons comforted himself with the thought, *Oh well, at least you don't have my gun.* He rolled over onto his right side (where his gun happened to be strapped) and knew that from that position he could protect his firearm. The male migrant finally got off of Simmons, grabbed one of the female migrants and started running across the side of the hill. A few moments later, the second woman started running after them.

As soon as they started running, Simmons jumped up and started chasing them across the hill. He caught up to the second woman and was able to tackle her to the ground. However, because the hill was so steep, they started tumbling and Simmons ended up on top of her. The woman started fighting with all her strength, which Simmons found to be considerable and more than he expected; he was having a very hard time holding her down. He started yelling at her to stop fighting and be still while he tried to maneuver her into a handcuffing position. Then she lifted up her head and took a solid bite of the meat on Simmons's hand between his thumb and index finger.

Simmons was raised in a very traditional household where he was taught to always respect women; he loves his mother very much and values all the lessons she has taught him over the years, including showing restraint with his pesky sisters. The one thing he knew a man should *never, ever, ever* do is raise his hand to a woman under *any* circumstances. Except this one. He drew his hand back and socked his female assailant as hard as he could. To her credit, she could take a punch. Rather than going crazy on Simmons, she started screaming in Spanish, "Help me! Help me!" as loud as she possibly could. That was when Simmons heard a rustling in the bushes nearby.

Simmons thought, *S—t, here come these guys to help her.* Simmons scooted up on the female immigrant and held her down with his knee to keep her in place. He then unholstered his gun and drew down on whoever or whatever was in the bushes, trying to be ready for anything. He saw a person start to emerge and got ready to pull the trigger, thinking it was the man who assaulted him earlier. But Simmons looked harder and saw it was another female immigrant, and she wasn't one of the two beating on him earlier. He started yelling at her in Spanish to get down on the ground, and as soon as she saw the gun, her arms shot up in the air and she gave Simmons a look that said she wasn't interested in attending that party. She got down on the ground and started screaming in Spanish, "Don't kill me! Don't kill me!"

Agent Simmons holstered his gun and looked around to make sure no one else was approaching or trying to catch him off guard. He rolled the first female immigrant, whom he had been holding down, over so he could handcuff her. The fight had completely gone out of her once she realized no one was coming to help her. Simmons was finally able to get on the radio and ask for backup, wondering why the scope operator—who had sent him to that location in the first place—had not dispatched agents to help him. After what seemed like an eternity, fellow agent Tom Burke* finally arrived. Simmons explained to him what happened and the general direction that his male attacker and his female companion had gone. Burke immediately started checking the ground for footprints, or "sign" in Border Patrol-speak, to track their path. Within a short period of time, Burke and another agent were able to finally apprehend both individuals a short distance away.[3]

THIS WASN'T EXACTLY WHERE Kevin Simmons pictured himself just a few years earlier. Growing up on the East Coast, he spent a lot of time outdoors and was college educated, but was well into his twenties and still living at home with his family when he decided he needed to start exploring some career options. The Border Patrol was engaged in a huge recruitment drive in the mid-1990s, and it seemed like a viable option after years of odd jobs and stints in construction. Within a few months of applying and completing the interview process, the agency offered Simmons a position as an agent. He headed (about a year later due to a hiring freeze) to his basic training course, which at the time was conducted at the Federal Law Enforcement Training Center in Glynco, Georgia. A little over five months later, Simmons graduated and was on his way to his first station assignment.

Given that Simmons went through Border Patrol training almost twenty years ago in a different location than the current academy in Artesia, New Mexico—as well as through a program somewhat different than today's—I asked him in mid-2013 how his classmates compare to recent Border Patrol Academy graduates. "Back then, you couldn't help but have people who weren't good at what they did, but it seemed like everybody wanted to be

---

* This is a pseudonym used to protect Agent "Burke's" true identity for his safety.

good. Back then, the one thing you did *not* want was to be branded as a slug. Most guys I worked with back then really wanted to work, and the work was there. Aliens and dope, and in 1996 it was *everywhere*. We were super, super busy."

"If I had to compare that with today," he continued, "I would say that the whole generational-differences thing we've been getting really hammered into us for the past ten years is really accurate. You have so many people coming in now, these twenty-somethings, who just feel entitled to everything. They think they're the smartest guys in the room and they have nothing to learn from anyone else." Simmons did say it wasn't all of the newer agents, but the phenomenon seemed a lot more prevalent in recent years than it had in the years following his graduation.

Border Patrol Agent Daniel Blake* is one of those newer guys coming in now, and I wanted his perspective on the caliber of his peers. Blake is a former Marine, so he has high standards for himself, as well as high expectations for decorum among agents. "There isn't a lot of respect for the supervisors and their rank. People look at supervisors like any other agent and treat them more like a friend than a superior. Comparing that to the Marine Corps . . . when I was a corporal, if someone told me to do something, the immediate response was *Yes!* and it got done. With a lot of agents, a supervisor can say, *Hey, I need you to get this training done,* and the reaction will be, *Eh, that's stupid.*"

Oddly enough, changes to the organization that people might view as equitable could be making some Border Patrol sectors less effective. Blake explained, "There's a culture of fairness, at least at my station, where they try to rotate everyone through every assignment along the border as evenly as they can. We have a lot of rugged terrain in our sector, and we've had agents and aliens alike go down from dehydration because of conditions in the summer. Some of our agents are in their mid-fifties and can't hike well, some who are really overweight and can't hike well, and some who are just plain lazy and don't want to hike. But to meet that culture of fairness, they'll be assigned to those positions, even though you've got young guys who have a lot of energy and want to do everything they can. He's put on an 'X' where he can't move for the entire shift."[4]

All that being said, both Simmons and Blake love what they do, organizational and personnel shortfalls aside. They love hiking and being outdoors, and they both love the rush that comes with apprehending drug smugglers

---

* This is a pseudonym used to protect Agent "Blake's" true identity for his safety.

and stopping illegal border crossings. Both agents agreed that most Border Patrol agents work very hard and believe in the mission, although they feel stymied by an antiquated bureaucracy filled with red tape and frequent shows of favoritism.

Being on the front lines of our borders is not an easy job, regardless of whether you're a CBP agent or a sheriff's deputy. Not every agent or officer is a hero, and not every agency is perfect. But these men and women have taken on the herculean task of trying to stop potential terrorists, violent drug smugglers, and illegal immigrants from entering the United States at the direction of a government that can't even define what a secure border looks like.

DHS has doubled the ranks of the Border Patrol and increased funding for ports of entry over the last decade, but agents continue to struggle to catch just a small percentage of people and drugs coming across the border illegally. Local law enforcement agencies are fighting to keep their heads above water with community policing because now they have the added burden of a border security mission that belongs to the federal government. But despite these challenges, our guardians on the border are passionate about what they do. They are often maligned by the media, which also tends to overlook the thousands of lives they save every year, the billions of dollars in cross-border trade they facilitate, and the positive impact of their presence in the communities where they patrol. This is a brief look into the lives of some of these guardians.

THE US BORDER PATROL has come a long way since its mounted guards first started to prevent illegal border crossings back in 1904. They numbered only seventy-five agents back then, and patrolled out of El Paso as far west as California to keep Chinese immigrants—some of which were opium smugglers—from crossing into the state from Mexico. The mission of these border guards became more important after the Eighteenth Amendment—known as Prohibition to most—passed in 1920 and immigration acts limiting the flow of migrants into the United States were passed in 1921 and 1924. In May 1924, Congress passed the Labor Appropriation Act of 1924, officially establishing the US Border Patrol for the purpose of securing the borders between inspection stations.[5]

During the organization's early years, Border Patrol agents only made $1,680 per year, which is roughly equivalent to $20,000 today; they didn't have uniforms until 1928, and had to supply their own horse and saddle. Today, there are over 23,000 agents working across twenty-one geographic sectors. Over 18,500 of those agents are assigned to southwest border sectors alone, and the agency's annual budget has grown from $263 million in 1990 to $3.5 billion in 2012.[6] They use age-old tracking tactics like cutting for sign (looking for evidence of human passage) in conjunction with advanced technology to determine where border crossers have been and where they might have gone. They are apprehending hundreds of thousands of illegal immigrants and thousands of tons of illegal drugs every year from San Diego to Brownsville and from Miami to Detroit.[7]

While some sectors are locked down tight and see very little cross-border traffic, other sectors are hot spots for drug and human smugglers, with nonstop activity. The Rio Grande Valley sector in south Texas experienced one of these nonstop weeks in August 2013. Over the course of just a few days, Border Patrol agents discovered the corpses of eight illegal immigrants, chased a large SUV loaded with more than 1,600 pounds of marijuana, seized an additional 1,400 pounds of marijuana in another part of the sector, and took down three stash houses where human smugglers were harboring 115 illegal immigrants. Total drug seizures by Border Patrol agents for just that week amounted to over 13,000 pounds—about the weight of a full-grown elephant.[8] In places like south Texas, there's a high concentration of agents, but this isn't the case in more rural and sparsely populated sectors.

US CUSTOMS AND BORDER PROTECTION (CBP), the Border Patrol's parent agency, has also seen an infusion of personnel and funding for the ports of entry where agents inspect hundreds of thousands of vehicles every day. CBP's mission differs slightly from that of the Border Patrol in that, while they're still charged with stopping terrorists, criminals, and illegal immigrants from entering the United States, they're also responsible for facilitating cross-border trade by making the inspection process as efficient as possible. It's a high-pressure job that can be very difficult, but also extremely rewarding.

CBP inspectors work at every port of entry in the United States, meaning anywhere where people or products arrive into the United States from a foreign country. This includes land border crossings like highways and pedestrian bridges, seaports, and airports. At the busiest land border crossings, like San Ysidro in the extreme southwest corner of California, the traffic lanes can number ten or more, and the wait time to enter the United States from Mexico can exceed three hours. The people waiting in these lines can include day trippers, business people, shoppers, tourists, truckers, drug couriers, and human smugglers. The challenge for CBP agents is to thoroughly examine the documents of every individual who passes through their lanes. The whole time that they're keeping an eye out for contraband, they're also tasked with facilitating cross-border trade, and it's a fine line to walk between making sure bad things or people don't get through and making sure trade goods do get through as quickly as possible.

Agents have an arsenal of technology at their fingertips to go through the vehicle inspection process, from least intrusive—walking around it with a drug detection dog—to most intrusive, which usually involves screwdrivers, crowbars, and power saws. I had a chance to witness up close how those "least intrusive" furry inspectors learn how to do their jobs when I visited the CBP Canine Training Facility in El Paso, Texas. I was also able to see how these dedicated canines inspect vehicles at the Nogales, Arizona, port of entry and at a highway checkpoint just north of Nogales in the town of Tubac.

CBP uses mostly German shepherds for their canine units, but also employ Labrador retrievers and Belgian Malinois. A select group of vendors provides the dogs to DHS, starting when they're roughly two years old. They go through a detailed vetting process to ensure they're healthy and have the right temperament—two qualities just as important for their human handlers to have, who get paired up with them after the dogs have completed their training. Just like their counterparts at local law enforcement agencies, CBP and Border Patrol canines are equivalent to their human handlers in many respects. If a canine is responsible for the detection of a load of narcotics, it's the canine's name that goes on the CBP report. If a drug smuggler

CBP K-9 officer runs a car selected for secondary exam. Photo courtesy of CBP.

injures, shoots, or kills a CBP canine, that smuggler will be charged with assault or murder of a CBP agent.

The use of canines in Border Patrol work highlights the agency's search and rescue mission. All too often, the media paints the Border Patrol in a negative light, as villains rather than border defenders who are routinely in harm's way. This isn't to say all agents are perfect; they're not. But just one publicized incident where an agent and immigrant get into a physical confrontation—regardless of who was in the wrong—can obscure the reality of the hundreds, if not thousands, of lives that Border Patrol agents save every year with the help of their canines. On a blisteringly hot day in the Sonoran desert, having a Border Patrol canine unit on duty can mean the difference between life and death for migrants who are dehydrated, sick, or injured. The dogs are also trained to detect human remains—something that, while macabre, is incredibly important to the families of the migrant who has perished and who needs to be identified for return to his or her country.

According to CBP officials I spoke with, canine inspections are responsible for roughly 80 percent of drug seizures along our borders. Agents who train these canines and work with them every day lament the fact that there aren't more dogs assigned to ports of entry and Border Patrol stations. However, the DHS budget is limited. Agents in Nogales say they could use triple the dogs they have now, but canines and their handlers are routinely being decertified because of budget cuts. Despite the unmatched detection skills these dogs have and the force-multiplier effect they have on port operations, these units are often the first ones to get cut.

The canine program is one of the best examples I've ever seen of the way in which CBP and US Border Patrol have integrated in the past few years. The agents in dark blue and dark green train together and support each other. If CBP inspectors at a port of entry require canine assistance with vehicle inspection and don't have a CBP dog on duty, then one of the Border Patrol units from a station nearby will drive out to the port to help inspect. It is obvious to anyone who watches these CBP and Border Patrol handlers for even a few minutes that they absolutely love what they do. Both the handlers and their canine charges are highly motivated and perform an aspect of the border security mission that is too often unseen and not well understood.

When sequestration—the mandatory across-the-board budget cuts mandated by Congress—went into effect in April 2013, DHS had to find ways to reduce the budget of CBP and its Border Patrol component by about $500 million without compromising border security. Planned cuts included furloughs of up to fourteen days per month, the reduction of daily work hours from ten to eight, and significant cuts on overtime. Even though some of the cuts were delayed, agents in some of the busiest sectors were feeling the pinch. Supervisors could no longer take work vehicles home, agents had to work two to a vehicle instead of one, and fuel consumption was restricted. Some agents also had to limit their time in vehicles and patrol more on foot.[9]

Based on what Border Patrol agents have told me, the fuel rationing issue has become a total joke. The same number of agents are still reporting to work, but have half the presence because they have to double up in trucks. Some sectors are requiring that their agents turn off their truck engines while in stationary locations—regardless of whether it's 107 degrees in Arizona or ten below zero in Montana.[10] And while CBP and Border Patrol agents are being required to make do with less, some local law enforcement agencies are being forced to pick up their slack.

In late July 2013, I made arrangements to spend the day in southeastern Arizona with the Cochise County Sheriff's Department. I had met Sheriff Mark Dannels at a conference a few months earlier, and he was more than happy to help introduce me to the locals' point of view regarding border issues. Deputy Mike Magoffin would be my tour guide for the next few hours. Magoffin was as local as you could get, ready for patrol in jeans, boots, and a cowboy hat, which he doffed when we shook hands. His family owns the Magoffin Ranch not far from Douglas, Arizona, and he grew up in the local ranching community. He also spent time helping build sections of the border fence installed near his childhood home several years ago.

Shortly after we got into his patrol truck and left the station, we stopped for gas. The subject had come up of my previous military service and law enforcement work, and he asked me if I was familiar with the M-16 rifle. I thought he was just asking out of curiosity, so I replied that I was, along with other weapons I had used as a special agent in the Air Force. He then directed my attention to the M-16 and shotgun he had secured in his truck, as well as the ballistic vests tucked in between our seats. Magoffin specifically pointed them out "in case things get hairy," which told me our little tour had the potential to get very interesting very quickly.

We headed east toward the town of Douglas, made (in)famous in the border community after local rancher Robert Krentz was murdered in 2010 by either a drug smuggler or illegal immigrant. Douglas isn't a one-stoplight town by any means, but it's the kind of place where everyone knows everyone and it serves as a home to multiple generations of the same family. The demographic is largely Latino, which is typical for a border community, but also allows drug smugglers and cartel members to blend in easily—if not subtly. As we drove east, we passed by some gorgeous homes that could actually qualify as estates. Magoffin looked at me and said, "There aren't a lot of high-paying jobs in Douglas, so you have to ask yourself, *Who's living in these homes?"*

Magoffin led us into the southeastern reaches of Cochise County via a rough dirt road called Geronimo Trail. He explained that this area was one of the busiest corridors in the state for drug and human smuggling, and it was easy to see why. The nearby foothills were excellent places for spotters to set up shop with binoculars and radio to their coyotes when the coast was clear of any Border Patrol or other law enforcement vehicles. The bushes and scrub provided an infinite number of places where migrants or drug mules could hide or stash drug loads for later pickup. There were also plenty of trails and footpaths to allow for clear passage without having to cut back any vegetation. We did see several Border Patrol vehicles on Geronimo Trail, and there were underground sensors across the area and a tower equipped with infrared sensors. However, the border fence is just a vehicle barrier in this part of the county, and anyone on foot can easily hop over it.

While we didn't come across any border crossers that day, there was plenty of evidence, like empty water containers and scattered bits of clothing, along the roadside that indicated people had been this way. The landscape is

Normandy-style vehicle barrier along the southern edge of Cochise County, Arizona.

beautiful and greener than someone would expect for this part of the country, but it's deceptive. Southern Cochise County weather easily hits triple digits in the summer and drops down to the twenties in the winter. The ground is sandy and very uneven, making for an arduous hike that could easily result in a broken ankle—a death sentence if a coyote chooses to leave an injured migrant behind, exposed to the elements. Getting lost and disoriented, which is common during bouts of severe dehydration, is easy when the scenery more or less looks the same in every direction. There are no natural sources of water and food (by way of hunting/catching) is nearly impossible to come by. Magoffin, as he pointed out the various ranches along the way, said that local homes are frequently burglarized by illegal immigrants who are more often looking for food and water than valuables.

Sheriff Dannels is very frustrated by what he sees as a failure by the federal government to do the job of border enforcement. When DHS started building the border fence in earnest in 2006, the plan was to wall off urban areas to reduce trafficking and illegal immigration in those areas. The fence would then force border crossers to go somewhere else—typically more rural parts of the border—where they would pose less danger to US citizens, and where Border Patrol agents could more easily apprehend them in the open. This strategy was actually preceded by Operation Gatekeeper, a huge push during the 1990s by the US government to stop illegal immigration, and it's been a headache for local law enforcement ever since.

"If you take a look at our county, which is considered one of the non-populated areas of the southwest border, we're still seeing 50 percent of all smuggling activity. That operation [Gatekeeper] from the 1990s is working; we're getting flooded," said Dannels. "[DHS] has addressed some of the issues here. They put up a fence from just south of Bisbee to east of Douglas, but beyond that fence, it's wide open. They've also significantly increased the number of Border Patrol agents working here. This is not to knock the Border Patrol; they're doing a great job. But there are 1,500 federal agents here to secure our eighty-three miles of border, and it's still not secure."[11]

Like most border sheriffs in the southwest, Dannels routinely gets calls from ranchers in his county who complain that smugglers and migrants are trespassing on their land and cutting their fences. "[DHS] needs to finish Operation Gatekeeper and not just put a Band-aid on the situation. This needs to be a serious matter, not just a political posture by the people in Washington, DC. I know one rancher whose home has been burglarized four times. I had another case just a week ago where a resident was hit over the head with a two-by-four by someone who wanted to steal his water, and it's just tragic to hear these stories. Our border is not secure, no matter what the media is saying. Come and see it, is what I say to officials in Washington. Talk to the people who are really living on the border, and they'll give you a realistic picture of what's going on."[12]

One of Dannels' concerns is that he doesn't receive additional funding for a border security mission. "The things we do that go beyond our normal job of patrol, the domestics, the DUIs, the crashes . . . I have to take from those resources and do more with less. That border is a federal border, and my guys aren't sitting on it," said Dannels. "They're going to be working across the county to make a difference there, so I don't have the resources, and I have to be very careful and creative with how I put these response units together to make a difference. And it's tough. I have eighty-six sworn deputies in a county of 6,300 square miles, but we have to try to make a difference."

Not every border sheriff works in the same environment. El Paso County Sheriff Richard Wiles and his deputies operate in a unique part of the country that is home to one of our largest border cities, which is also ranked by Congressional Quarterly (CQ) Press as the safest city in the United States, and which happens to be located a stone's throw from one of the deadliest cities in the Western Hemisphere. There are also parts of his county that are more rural, and the challenges that come along with high levels of drug trafficking are present everywhere.

"El Paso has always had a really good reputation with regards to crime and safety. I think a lot of that has to do with the fact we have a law-abiding community with strong values and families," explained Wiles. "Coupled with that is a good relationship between the citizens and law enforcement. On top of that is, we have a lot of law enforcement here," he said with a chuckle. "We're a border community and we have several huge ports of entry, so we're home to many Customs agents and Border Patrol agents, ATF, FBI, DEA . . . and on and on it goes. We work really well together in letting each other know what's going on. We're a big city, so we definitely have some crime issues, but people feel safe here."[13]

Wiles offers a unique perspective on El Paso because he was the chief of police before he retired and was elected as the sheriff. "What has made El Paso such a great place has been the bi-national and bi-cultural experience, but the flow has changed. A lot of people on this side are afraid to go into Mexico now—including me, and we used to all the time." Wiles told me when he worked at the police department, he would meet with the Ciudad Juárez police chief in Mexico, and the chief would also come to El Paso for meetings. Officers from both departments would attend joint events like memorials and school visits, and they would share information like auto theft, gang member, and sex offender data to prevent certain individuals from crossing the border to commit crimes and evade law enforcement.

"You get that concern here of, *Who can you trust?* But at some point you have to trust that people in certain positions are going to do the right thing," Wiles said. "But I will say that when the violence started escalating, the [police department's] liaison unit stopped going over there, I stopped going over there, and now we go through the FBI to facilitate that information exchange."[14]

Even though crime rates are very low in El Paso, Wiles knows there are still bad people living in his county; after all, the Ciudad Juárez/El Paso smuggling corridor is one of the busiest and most lucrative along the entire southwest border. The city is merely a transit zone for many smugglers and illegal immigrants, but there are gang members and other criminals who cross back and forth, and Wiles needs the cooperation of his community to help keep crime at bay. "We've established relationships with neighborhood watch groups, local businesses, etc. It's been very successful, and there's an understanding in this community that we need them to be our eyes and ears because I've only got about ninety deputies who are out on patrol," said Wiles.[15]

Getting calls when crime happens from residents who are living in El Paso illegally requires Wiles to put forth a very specific message. "My thought has always been, both as the police chief and as the sheriff, that we do not get involved in immigration enforcement. That's not our jurisdiction; it's a federal issue, and it's also a basic financial issue. El Paso is a poor community. We're limited in the number of police officers and deputies we have, and as such, those officers who are being paid with local tax dollars should be in the neighborhoods patrolling and keeping the neighborhoods safe. It seems unfair to me that we should divert local resources to handle a federal immigration problem when that responsibility should be borne by the entire nation, not the local border communities."[16]

Every law enforcement agency that has a presence along our borders will have its own way of doing business, its own point of view. But one of the more unique perspectives of border patrol work comes not from agents, cops, or deputies, but from Hollywood.

It's a cool Thursday night in late February 2013, and I'm sitting in the lobby bar of Los Angeles's historic Culver Hotel, 1930s-era jazz playing in the background. After wrapping up two presentations about Mexico's drug war for a local organization, I'm meeting two good friends for dinner, drinks, and conversation about border security. That may sound odd, but my friends—Nick Stein and Natalia Baldwin-León—aren't average people in Tinseltown.

For three years and five television seasons, Nick was the series producer and Natalia a field producer for *Border Wars,* a show on the National Geographic Channel. I started watching the show when it premiered in January 2010, a time when my consulting business didn't even exist. I had been working on my drug war blog for almost two years, and Nick happened to come across it several times. Out of the blue, he sent me an email that essentially said, "We really ought to know each other." What followed was a great new friendship with Nick, a working relationship with National Geographic, and an inside look at the first documentary/reality television series that embedded cameras with Border Patrol agents in the field and CBP agents conducting inspections at the southwest border ports of entry.

This wasn't the first time a show had been dedicated to providing a behind-the-scenes look at DHS. Nick and Natalia actually met while working on the show *Homeland Security USA* in 2008. However, *Border Wars* was the first in-depth portrayal of the border guard experience; viewers watched agents crawl through a border tunnel barely wide enough for one person, dismantle a car to find hidden compartments filled with narcotics, and jump out of a helicopter with only one wheel touching the top of a mountain so they could apprehend a group of migrants.

If you haven't been to the southwest border, it can be a very inhospitable place, with over 100-degree temperatures during the day and freezing nights. To make the experience as real as possible, Nick, Natalia, and their film crew endured the same hardships that Border Patrol agents do on a daily basis. Nick explained, "We filmed from San Diego to Brownsville and back again, and the environments were incredibly varied. We were in coastal areas, swamp areas, incredibly hot and unforgiving areas. What you find when you embed the way we did is that whatever the environment is, that is an enormous part of the challenge for the men and women you're embedded with. In San Diego, smugglers were using the ocean and big mountains. They had marine layers of extremely dense fog coming in, and that was just in one sector. We shot through hurricanes, through floods and all sorts of things, and it's never a dull moment when the geography dictates the situation."

The changing border environment was actually fodder for some of Natalia's favorite stories. "It was things like being dropped on top of a mountain by helicopter and seeing the helicopter fly away, saying, *Bye! Hike yourself out!* I had to spend two weeks sleeping in between my cameraman and audio guy in a tent out in the middle of the desert." Nick and his crew knew these hardships were only temporary, and were worth the effort to get infrared shots of ultralight aircraft carrying marijuana across the border, or smugglers purposely driving their trucks at high speed into the Rio Grande and then swimming across the river to Mexico to avoid apprehension. For Border Patrol agents, this is a long-term lifestyle.

Along with the hardship comes danger, both from human and natural sources. "We were in a Huey helicopter working the scene between New Mexico and Arizona, and we were working a group [of migrants] all day long, with many agents and two helicopters. When we finally got our hands on this group, they escaped down the side of a canyon. We flew into the canyon, and when we got into position to get a camera shot, the Huey started spinning around and around. We didn't know at the time what in the hell was happening, and we found out later it was a freak gust of wind that caused the tail to temporarily lose effectiveness. The two pilots we were with had forty years of flying experience between them, and they told us it was the worst that had ever happened to either of them on the job. When you're in the canyon, you have no altitude, nowhere to go. It turned out the pilots had two seconds to get everything right and absolutely nothing wrong, and they got us out of there. But when they told us it was the worst thing they'd experienced, it sobered us up real fast! We were very close to crashing that helicopter."

When we spoke in Los Angeles, Natalia had just finished work on the first season of *Boston's Finest,* a reality show that follows officers in the Boston Police Department. Given that the majority of contact most Americans have with law enforcement officers happens at the municipal level, I asked her what some of the differences are between the police work being done in Boston versus the enforcement work going on along the border.

"One of the most fascinating things I'd see is the bulk cash going back to Mexico. You're seeing something like $800,000 going back to the cartels, and you're thinking, *Oh, this is big money, this is kingpin stuff with hundred-dollar bills everywhere!* At the border, we'd be sitting there and see $100,000 bundles in dollar bills. I'm thinking, *One dollar bills? Five dollar bills? This is so not glamorous.* Where do you think those dollar bills are coming from? It's the money from those little dime bags being sold on the street for $5, $10, or $20. People don't think that's affecting us, you know, *That little dime bag's not hurting anybody.* But I've seen that money go back to the border, and I've heard the grenades going off, and the .50-caliber guns firing right across the border. So you see the trail of money, and you see the trail of drugs, and it always goes back to the border."

Few people not working for CBP get to see the work ethic and desire for action most agents have. Nick said, "There's a certain irony about morale in the Border Patrol. Once they start achieving operational security in a sector, which they have along some parts of the border, morale becomes a problem." This caught me by surprise. Nick explained, "They're not as busy. There's a lot of time during which they're not detecting any crossings at all because they've locked that place up. We were always with agents who were pretty busy and they were happy. They're trained to chase. When they couldn't, you'd start seeing off-site discipline problems, domestic problems, drinking problems, and all kinds of things. A lot guys who were born to do this wanted to go to places like south Texas because they wanted the action.

"But despite that, from our perspective, it's incredible to see how they do keep their morale up. Their esprit de corps is amazing, even though they have this revolving door phenomenon where they'll see the same immigrants over and over, sometimes several times in a week. They never seem to let it get the better of them. They have a mission and they're going to fulfill it, and I was really amazed at how dedicated they were to their jobs."

Nick understands that in normal circumstances, people are on their best behavior when they're on camera. But in a high-stress environment where things can change quickly and agents have to make split-second decisions, the awareness of the cameras over the course of months of filming eventually subsides. "We were with them so much that I *know* they forgot about the cameras," said Nick. "We worked with literally thousands of agents, and we

The author with former Border Wars *producers Nick Stein and Natalia Baldwin-León.*

watched them in unbelievably stressful situations. I never saw a single incident of abuse of any migrant."

Natalia had plenty of opportunities to speak to several agents off-camera
(and thus off the record). "One thing that was eye-opening for me, these
guys really understand the plight of people coming here from Mexico. More
than half of them are Latino . . . I think it's something like 51 percent . . . and
that was something that shocked me. America thinks, oh, it's just a bunch of
white guys grabbing Mexicans. And to see how many are Latino, how many
of them have family on the other side of the border, how many have illegal
border crossings in their family history . . . they're much closer to that border
than you can possibly imagine. Many of them grew up on the border, and
grew up crossing into Mexico all the time to eat lunch, going swimming in
the Rio Grande. There's a cultural connection that allows these guys to relate
to those people."

Nick summed up his overall takeaway from his time working on the series. "If people have simple solutions to the situation on the border, it's not
a solution. In fact, it pushes back on any progress on border security, or immigration policy, or anything else. When I hear people ask, *Well, why can't
we just seal the border?* I realize they don't know *anything* about the border. It
is two thousand miles of some of the most inhospitable terrain on the planet,
you have a poor country butted up against one of the richest countries, you
have cartel violence on the Mexican side. It is impossible to 100 percent secure the border. It's not helpful when people keep harping on the idea that it
can be done."[17]

I NEVER GET TIRED of listening to Border Patrol war stories, and I asked Agent Blake
to tell me one involving a chase or tons of illegal drugs or guns being drawn.
He thought about that for a minute, then said, "You know, I'm actually going
to take you in a slightly different direction, and at the end of the story you'll
understand why."

A couple of years ago, Blake was on patrol in a more remote part of his
sector and was tracking a group of three illegal immigrants. It was light out,
and the agents on shift prior to Blake had actually handed them off to him
when their duty ended. He spent all of a very frustrating day trying to figure
out where they went because they were climbing over rocks (which leaves
little to no foot sign) and traveling in a very erratic manner without sticking
to the trails where footprints are more visible. Blake was stymied. He had
spent his entire shift out there looking for three people with no luck at all.
But just as his shift was ending, he noticed fresh footprints crossing a road
where there had been none half an hour earlier. The footprints led into a

large canyon where Blake did not plan to venture on his own while dusk was falling.

He came back to work the next day, was off for two days, then went back on patrol a full four days after having to abandon the chase at the canyon's entrance. As he was driving out to the field that morning, he planned to stop at one of the more common highway loading points in the sector, where trucks would pick up illegal immigrants who had been traveling on foot and take them to their final destination. As Blake approached, he saw a small group of migrants waiting for a pickup, so he stopped his truck some distance away and got out. They were sitting on the ground a distance from the road and didn't hear Blake approach because the highway noise masked his steps. He looked at the three individuals, assessed they were illegal immigrants and started talking to them.

But before he loaded them into his truck, he had a hunch. Blake asked the migrants to show them the bottom of their shoes. He was only mildly surprised when he saw that the tread of their shoes exactly matched the footprints of the three illegal immigrants he had started tracking four days earlier. While there was no surging adrenaline or heart-pumping action involved in this particular day on patrol for Agent Blake, he could barely describe the sense of catharsis and closure he derived from finally apprehending these three migrants. It was one of the best moments he's had in his tenure as a Border Patrol agent. It was also proof that sometimes an enormous sense of satisfaction for agents like Blake comes not from chases and confrontation, but from just accomplishing the mission.

All law enforcement agencies with a border security mission have challenges to deal with, including bureaucratic red tape, lack of funding, increasing rates of corruption, low morale, and personnel and management problems. But the core agents and officers strongly believe in the mission and feed off of their victories enough to get them through to the next day. Many of them—particularly in CBP and Border Patrol—are regularly dealing with conflicting or nonsensical information from DHS regarding policies and procedures, but they soldier on because they believe in the mission, an honest hard day's work, and protecting the homeland from terrorists and drug smugglers while apprehending illegal immigrants in compliance with federal law.

CHAPTER 3

THE BORDER FENCE

It's going to be 20 feet high. It's going to have barbed wire on the top. It's going to be electrified. And there's going to be a sign on the other side saying, "It will kill you—Warning."[1]

> —Herman Cain, former presidential candidate, October 2012

I question whether spending billions more on a fence between the United States and Mexico is really the best use of taxpayer dollars.

> —Sen. Patrick Leahy (D-Vermont), April 2013

The fence that runs along parts of our southern border with Mexico is the most tangible evidence of our government's failure to establish a solid and consistent border security strategy, even when presented with a barrier concept that is proven to work in the right circumstances. It's also the epitome of government waste and financial mismanagement, even after almost a decade of mistakes from which to learn.

I often wonder how people envision the border fence. Seeing it in a photo doesn't convey nearly the same amount of information as actually standing next to it—particularly in the places where two kinds of fence meet or one kind abruptly ends without explanation.

In July 2011, I got a chance to do a ride-along with the Border Patrol in its San Diego sector. Americans who aren't familiar with southern California geography sometimes think that San Diego is directly across the border from Tijuana, Mexico, but in reality it's over a dozen miles away. The border fence starts just west of San Ysidro, home of the world's busiest land border crossing, and runs east through its sister port of entry in Otay Mesa. In this area, it's actually a double fence, with the original (and old) rusted-out corrugated steel plate version running parallel to the newer, shinier, and much taller metal mesh fence just a few dozen yards to the north.

The newer setup was completed in January 2010, and Border Patrol agents in the sector are thrilled to have it. At the time, my public affairs escort explained to me that the newly paved road that runs between the two fences reduced the response time for agents down to around two minutes. That strip of land is also equipped with stadium lighting and state-of-the-art cameras and motion sensors. The mesh barrier is topped with concertina wire and rises eighteen feet straight up. It seemed highly unlikely that anything or anyone was going to cross that zone without being detected and interdicted.

Then I saw the patched-up holes. I pointed them out to my escort, who smiled and sort of shrugged in silent acknowledgement that even such an impressive piece of barrier engineering wouldn't stop everyone. But this was nothing compared to the condition of the older "primary fence" yards to the south. Holes and gaps make it easy for people on the Mexican side to look through it or pass something to the other side. It isn't that tall, so climbing over it doesn't pose much of a challenge to the just slightly determined. During our familiarization ride, we even got a glimpse of a burning car pressed right up against the primary fence (and next to a big hole in it), flames shooting up into the sky and no one really paying any attention.

But even the new fence isn't enough along this part of the border. There is a dangerous area of Tijuana that sits on a hill, conveniently rising above both fences and providing any opportunists on the Mexican side with the higher ground advantage. American engineers worked for years to raise a berm high enough to reduce this advantage, but based on limited resources and topography, the berm could only go so high, limiting that advantage.

Three months later, I found myself at the opposite end of the border on another Border Patrol ride-along in the McAllen sector of south Texas. This section of the fence comes in a completely different configuration, due mostly to the area's defining feature—the Rio Grande. The river that separates Texas from Mexico is a brown winding snake that, in an overhead satellite image, looks like the ejected contents of a Silly String can. The challenges of erecting a fence here are immediate and obvious.

I knew before seeing the fence in person that it had been erected in most places as close to the river as possible, and sometimes in a zigzag fashion. I also knew this had created a kind of no-man's land in the strip of US territory between the riverbank and the border fence. In my mind, I thought that strip of land could be no more than a few dozen yards wide. Imagine my shock when I saw that *entire farms* and enormous tracts of land—containing homes and vehicles and families—lay exposed to smuggler traffic. In some places,

Tijuana residents overlook Border Patrol operations along the fence in San Diego sector.

the fence is a mile away from the US-Mexico border because engineers had to avoid building on the flood plain.

The fence in this sector is built in a completely different fashion than in San Diego. It's a "bollard-style" fence, meaning it consists of very tall poles that are bent at the top (toward Mexico) and very narrowly spaced apart. In many places, the fence sits on top of a sheer concrete wall that varies in height, but has no easily identifiable way of being scaled. When I viewed it in October 2011, construction crews were working to get remote-controlled gates installed where the fence sat on top of the levee. They were also working to repair a part of the fence where a few of those bollards had been bent and displaced by a driver who felt his pickup truck was up to the task of going through it. As of October 2013, many of these gates have not been installed due to funding problems, essentially rendering the entire section of fence useless as an effective barrier.

I understood the gate system, remembering that San Diego sector had something similar to allow agents in vehicles to quickly cross the barrier. However, there aren't any people living between the primary and secondary fence in San Diego. I asked my Border Patrol escort in McAllen how the gates worked for residents living south of the fence, and he explained they would have remote control devices that would open the gates with a code. This system would probably work just fine if this was a gated community in Houston, but residents here have many concerns they don't think the Border Patrol can adequately address.

I reached out to a contact of mine in Texas state government to ask whom I should speak with to get different perspectives about the border fence. He said, "Basically, there are three groups of people in Texas when it comes to the fence. You have officials and people in urban areas who think the fence works. It protects their cities, their businesses, and makes them feel safe. Then you have people who live in rural parts of the state, but don't need access to the river. They're not ranchers, so they don't need the water for their cattle, or farmers who need it for their crops. They're pretty happy with the fence, too. Finally, you have people in the [Rio Grande] Valley who don't want it at all. It's just impossible to build a fence right along the river, so they have to be cut off."[2]

Pamela Taylor is one of those residents who feels cut off. She lives on the "Mexican side" of the border fence in Brownsville, on a strip of land about one quarter-mile wide between the fence and the Rio Grande. Although she has warning signs on her property that inform trespassers they're being observed by surveillance cameras, that hasn't stopped them from breaking into her house. She once found an unidentified man in her house who "had used [her] bathroom, he had shaved and cleaned himself off and he was watching the border patrol go by, sitting in [a] rocking chair." Years later, she found a forty-kilogram bundle of marijuana hidden in her flowerbed. Taylor has had groups of immigrants pounding on her door in the middle of the night, and although the Border Patrol responded and arrested them, she still sleeps with a gun and a Taser in her house.[3] "My son-in-law tells people we live in a gated community," she joked to *The Los Angeles Times* in 2011. But she also lamented, "We feel abandoned here."[4]

The exact origins of the first fence along the US-Mexico border are somewhat hard to pinpoint. We know some sort of barrier dates back at least to 1971, when then-first lady Pat Nixon inaugurated Border Field State Park in Imperial Beach, California. After giving a speech and shaking hands with several Mexicans on the other side of the border, a member of her security detail cut a portion of a barbed-wire fence in place at the time, and she reportedly told the *Los Angeles Times,* "I hate to see a fence anywhere."[5]

Prior to that, any sections of fence were sparse and located in mostly urban areas. Border enforcement started to ratchet up after the Bracero Program was repealed in 1964 and the flow of migrants illegally entering the United States from Mexico started to increase. In the late 1970s, officials in

Gap in the border fence near McAllen, Texas. Residents on
the "Mexican side" are still waiting for gates to be installed.

California were most concerned about this cross-border traffic, so the federal government installed a ten-foot-high chain-link fence along the seven westernmost miles of the state's border with Mexico, augmented by floodlights and increased helicopter patrols. This fence—which ultimately was more symbolic than effective—was the predecessor of the rusted-out landing mat barrier that exists now as the primary fence in the Border Patrol's San Diego sector. That was completed in 1993, covering the first fourteen miles of the border from the Pacific Ocean.[6]

Then 9/11 changed everything. US government officials and politicians started looking to Mexico and Canada as potential sources of transiting terrorists attempting to enter the United States by land. This concern manifested itself in the Secure Border Initiative (SBI), which was announced in November 2005. That month, then-DHS Secretary Michael Chertoff explained that the "SBI addresses the challenges we face with an integrated mix of increased staffing, a greater investment in detection technology and infrastructure, and enhanced coordination with our partners at the federal, state, local, and international levels."[7]

SBI was an ambitious project, to say the least. The two main aspects of the initiative were border control and immigration control beyond the border, and its main goal was to have operational control of the northern and southern borders within five years, or roughly by the beginning of 2011. Essentially, DHS wanted to revamp the way it had been thinking about border security by integrating fences and barriers, agents, and technology, and working more efficiently with law enforcement and intelligence partners.[8]

The original SBI announcement and program guide didn't go into any detail about plans for expanded fencing, but implementation was close behind. Less than a year later, former president George W. Bush signed the Secure Fence Act of 2006—the first piece of legislation to outline exactly how much border fence should be built in particular locations. Specifically, it says: "the Secretary of Homeland Security shall provide for at least 2 layers of reinforced fencing, the installation of additional physical barriers, roads, lighting, cameras, and sensors" along roughly 850 miles of border. It also highlighted the Laredo, Texas, port of entry as a "priority area," and allowed for the use of alternate barriers in areas where the land elevation grade exceeded 10 percent.[9] Prior to the signing of this act, there were only seventy-eight miles of pedestrian fencing in place and fifty-seven miles of low vehicle barriers.[10]

While construction on these sections of fence continued, Congress passed the Consolidated Appropriations Act of 2008. Buried deep within the Act's six hundred-plus pages were more detailed demands concerning fence construction. It required the fence to be reinforced and run a length of seven hundred miles. The sites for the fence would be selected based on how practical and effective it would be, and the sections had to be flexible enough to allow for the installation of additional barriers and sensors. Under the Act, 370 miles of fencing had to be completed by December 2008.[11] The race was on. But as most Congressionally dictated timelines go, this one came and went without the goal being met.

In late January 2009, CBP announced that 601 of the 700 miles of fencing required under the Secure Fence Act had been completed, and 69 miles still needed to be built. Between the signing of the Act and that announcement, Congress appropriated $2.7 billion for the fence's construction. However, there was never any fixed estimate for how much the required fencing would ultimately cost to complete, let alone maintain.[12]

How did Congress arrive at the figure of "no less than 700 miles"? More specifically, why didn't it mandate the walling-off of the entire two thousand-mile length of the US-Mexico border?

There was actually a legislative predecessor to the Secure Fence Act, called The Border Protection, Antiterrorism, and Illegal Immigration Control Act of 2005. The US House of Representatives passed it by a vote of 239–182, but it died in the Senate. Despite this, the so-called Sensenbrenner Bill—named for sponsor US Representative Jim Sensenbrenner (R-Wisconsin)—kicked off a flurry of debates and subsequent legislation related to the border and illegal immigration. Notably, this bill contained the original language calling for the seven hundred miles of reinforced fencing, which would be located "in

This setup of bollard-style fence, a few feet in front of a crumbling post-and-wire fence, meets the "double reinforced" standard.

sectors that have the highest number of immigrant deaths, instances of drug smuggling and illegal border crossings."[13]

So is the border fence doing its job? Before that question can even be addressed, it's important to understand that the fence was never designed to truly *stop* anyone. My Border Patrol escort in San Diego was very clear about this: "The border fence *is*, however, designed to slow people down long enough so we can respond." While it was good to know agents aren't naïve enough to think anyone will believe the fence is impenetrable, they don't really go out of their way to explain that response time to an attempted breach can vary from two minutes in San Diego sector to never in other places with bad weather, washed-out roads, or insufficient agents near the breach site.

Back in the early 1990s, the primary fence "by itself, did not have a discernible impact on the influx of unauthorized aliens coming across the border in San Diego," according to a Congressional Research Service analysis. As a result, the US government launched Operation Gatekeeper, which sent a massive amount of agents and equipment to the border in a herculean effort to slow down the flow of illegal immigrants in that sector. Gatekeeper and other initiatives from the 1990s worked temporarily, but they were prohibitively expensive and forced agencies to conclude a more fixed barrier system would be necessary.[14]

After the secondary fence was completed in San Diego sector, apprehensions of illegal immigrants by agents from just the Imperial Beach station dramatically plummeted from approximately 187,000 in 1994 to about sixteen thousand in 1998. They dropped even further, to roughly 9,100, in 2004. The Chula Vista station experienced a similar decline, with apprehensions dropping from about 141,000 in 1995 to just over three thousand in 2002.[15]

While these decreases are stunning, it's important to remember that other parts of San Diego sector weren't fully fenced at this time, and more significant to note that those non-fenced areas also experienced a large decline in apprehensions during the same time period—just not nearly as dramatic. Immigrant apprehensions spiked in the rest of the sector in 1996, implying that the newly completed fence simply pushed immigrants east to non-fenced parts of the California-Mexico border. But over the next few years, they steadily dropped as well. Even more curious is the fact that overall southwest border apprehensions peaked in 1992 at 1.2 million, and then peaked again at the same number in 2004, despite the initial deployment of reinforced fences to parts of the border prior to the Secure Fence Act.[16]

One thing that could help explain this dip—in addition to (or in spite of) the construction of the secondary fence—was a complete shift in Border Patrol tactics at the time. Instead of agents actively pursuing immigrants and smugglers along the border, they engaged in a strategy of deterrence that involved a huge show of force. Agency leadership felt at the time that would-be crossers would see an overwhelming army of agents, decide not to risk apprehension, and head back to Mexico.[17]

The problem with this strategy was that agents weren't allowed to leave their vehicles and pursue border crossers, who soon figured out what was going on. They either went around the phalanx of agents, or found a convenient spot to cross between the "Xs" on which agents were required to sit. It logically follows that due to the inability of Border Patrol agents to give chase under this policy—which coincidentally began around 1993—less apprehensions would be made, artificially driving down statistics and making it even harder to determine a correlation between migrant and smuggling activity and fence construction.[18]

Today's fence and Border Patrol tactics, however, paint a completely different picture. Since construction began in earnest on the remaining mandated seven hundred miles of border fence in 2006, overall southwest border apprehension rates have dropped every year, starting with almost 1.1 million in fiscal year 2006 and dropping to just over 340,000 in fiscal year 2011. After the secondary fence, paved road, stadium lighting, and cameras were completely installed in San Diego sector in 2009, apprehensions there decreased from almost 119,000 in 2006 to about 42,000 in 2011.[19] There's a strong likelihood that the fence had a lot to do with that, but arguments for building even more fence cannot rest solely on apprehension statistics.

A report by the Congressional Research Service explains that apprehension data can be misleading because it "focuses on events rather than people," and can't be compared to how many people got away. In other words, it's relatively meaningless to know that half a million illegal immigrants were apprehended in a particular year without knowing if half a million and one or ten million people tried to cross in that same year. It's impossible for Border Patrol to say with any degree of accuracy that they caught 10 percent or 90 percent of people attempting to cross each year because right now, they have absolutely no way of knowing. Even though the report warns policy makers against drawing conclusions based on these statistics, it acknowledged that "they remain the most reliable way to codify trends in illegal migration along the border."[20]

Analysts have attributed several factors to the drop in illegal border crossings in the past few years, with increased border enforcement being only a small part. Others include the declining US economy (which means fewer jobs), increased violence against migrants in Mexico, and new policies and state laws cracking down on illegal immigration. But even while acknowledging that cross-border migration is too complex to fully encapsulate with numbers, it appears at least at first glance that the fence—in conjunction with effective and efficient agent response—is having some positive impact on the flow of migrants across parts of our southwest border.

But is it slowing down the bigger threat, that is, drug smugglers?

The Buenos Aires National Wildlife Refuge is a beautiful span of over 117,000 acres along the Arizona-Mexico border. The Refuge was established in 1985 and purchased under the Endangered Species Act. Since that time, visitors have enjoyed hunting, fishing, and hiking amongst 200-million-year-old volcanic rocks in Brown Canyon. But since October 2006, visitors have been refused access to 3,500 of those pristine acres that run along roughly four miles of the refuge's border with Mexico due to "human safety concerns." Here is a portion of the notice the US Fish and Wildlife Service published at that time:

> The situation in this zone has reached a point where continued public use of the area is not prudent . . . Violence on the Refuge associated with smugglers and border bandits has been well documented. Many of these

activities are concentrated at, or near, the border. The concentration of illegal activity, surveillance and law enforcement interdictions make these
zones dangerous. Closure is in effect until further notice.[21]

Oddly enough, no one really noticed or cared until FOX News published
a story that scared the pants off of some Americans and downright angered
many others. The story erroneously claimed that the closure area stretched
along eighty miles of the border (it was actually closer to four). The online
report also contained a three-minute video showing border crossers climbing
a very high border fence with ease while Pinal County (Arizona) Sheriff Paul
Babeu speaks in the background. No one points out that the video wasn't
taken at the border with the refuge.[22]

This report and several others annoyed the Fish and Wildlife Service
enough that four days after the FOX News story came out, they issued a media advisory to clear up some misinformation. The advisory pointed out that
the closed-off section of the park comprised only 3 percent of the entire refuge. It did say that there were no immediate plans to reopen that portion of
the park, but "since 2006 the Refuge has experienced a significant decline in
violent activity in the area thanks to ongoing cooperation between the US
Fish and Wildlife Service and US Customs and Border Protection."[23] This
was when fence construction began in that border stretch.

Refuge Manager Sally Gall explained that since the barrier was completed in 2008, smuggler and immigrant traffic in the park has dropped. Before that, Gall said, they were seeing around a thousand immigrants a day
coming up through the Altar Valley and into the refuge area. "To say that's
totally [a result of] the fence would be difficult because, of course, the economy changed quite a bit at that time and surely other factors have played into
it." She also noted complications with the fence, stating, "For a wildlife refuge
with a pedestrian fence, you have an impact on wildlife and their ability to
cross the border, so I'm sure there are environmental effects there we don't
like to see."

But from her perspective as refuge manager, Gall sounded like there was
more good than bad to come from the fence. "That said, there are some positive effects of having that barrier. The vehicle traffic that we once saw from
the south has declined significantly. I think at one point we had nearly a hundred vehicles abandoned on the Refuge, but since then it's only been one here
and one there. And those aren't vehicles coming from the south, but more
likely vehicles coming from the north to pick up drugs, then breaking down
after they turn around. [The fence] has really helped because those vehicles
that once crossed the border and came on the Refuge were really degrading

the land in many areas. It's also helped diminish the number of cattle from Mexico trespassing on the Refuge. The vegetation has been restored in many areas because of the fence. We're still seeing [smuggler and immigrant] traffic, but most of that is to the west of us."[24]

On its own, this is a "good news" story for DHS and fence supporters. However, this seems to be the exception to the rule—not just along unfenced or "lightly" fenced areas, but in spots where the border is heavily fortified.

Hypothetically assume for a minute that a full two thousand mile-long border fence is practical, affordable, and achievable. Then imagine a vast expanse of arid desert with sand dunes and naturally formed berms as far as the eye can see. Picture a dark brown seam cutting a straight line across that stretch, stitched together with fourteen-foot-high steel poles spaced a few inches apart, and propped up on both sides by more steel poles. The mere sight of such a structure in a forbidding place like the Sonoran desert might be enough of a deterrent for some, but not for the most determined.

In November 2012, some enterprising drug smugglers tried to get creative. They propped two metal ramps—each a bit wider than a truck tire—up against the border fence on both the Mexican side and the US side near Yuma, Arizona. Then they drove a white Jeep Cherokee, which was probably loaded with illegal drugs, up the Mexican side. Once the Jeep hit the top of the fence, the smugglers realized they'd miscalculated the ease with which the Jeep would actually pivot over the pointed tops of the bollard poles. Needless to say, they were stuck. They managed to escape back to Mexico, but not before emptying the Jeep's contents and leaving it teetering fourteen feet above the Arizona desert.[25]

Other smugglers in Arizona have gone back in time for a more tried and true method—the catapult. In January 2011, National Guard troops working along the border near the Naco Border Patrol Station in Arizona filmed drug smugglers using an old-fashioned catapult to attempt to launch roughly forty-five pounds of marijuana over the border fence. They would likely have launched more if the guard and Mexican authorities hadn't disrupted their efforts.[26] Smugglers who aren't thinking in terms of bulk and just need to pass small packages across don't even worry about going over the fence; they just go through it. Several kinds of illegal drugs can be compressed and are now being shaped into tubes or wide and extremely thin packages that can be slipped either through holes or in between the fence bollards.

Making ramps and dragging car carriers into the desert and shaping custom-made drug bundles isn't always cheap, and can be a lot of work. A quick search on YouTube will yield dozens of videos of people working hard (and sometimes getting hurt) climbing over several varieties of border fence, using

wire cutters to get through vehicle barriers, or using blow torches to open up
a hole in the decades-old rusted-out primary fence. But why go through all
this trouble when you can just walk across with little to no impediment?

The town of Rio Rico, Arizona, sits about eleven miles north of
Nogales—a city that shares its name with its "twin" just across the border in
Mexico. Rio Rico sits right next to Peck Canyon, which is where Border Patrol
Agent Brian Terry was shot and killed by Mexican border bandits in December 2010. David Lowell is in his mid-eighties and owns the Atascosa Ranch in
the midst of these Arizona canyons. His ranch also sits in the busiest—and
deadliest—corridor along the southwest border for both illegal immigrants
and drug smugglers. In the last few years, Lowell has seen both types of people, plus drug users, dead bodies, parts of dead bodies, and rape trees* either
on his property or adjacent to it in Peck Canyon. Drug mules have trespassed
through his back yard, looked through his windows, and even attempted to
break into his home.[27]

After reading about Lowell and similar situations occurring on ranches
neighboring his, I thought that surely there must be a huge gap in the border
fence just south of him that would allow all this traffic to pass through his
land. Well . . . yes and no. The city of Nogales has had a border fence in place
for over a decade, but it was rusting out and essentially falling apart. In 2011,
DHS tore out much of the old landing-mat fence and replaced it with a new
one, averaging eighteen feet in height and reaching thirty feet in some spots.
The problem is that the new fence separating Nogales, US, from Nogales,
Mexico, is only 2.8 miles wide.[28] On either side of the city limits, the old
pedestrian fence abruptly stops and converts to a Normandy-style vehicle
barrier—big and strong enough to prevent a pickup truck from passing
through, but anyone on foot can just crawl under or over it.

Then there are just odd gaps only a few yards wide between fortified sections of the fence that defy any sort of logic. DHS said in October 2012 that
it planned to close a strangely placed half-mile gap in the fence just west of
downtown El Paso, but a local Border Patrol spokesman said the exact date
when construction would start was uncertain. The delay seemed to stem from
right-of-entry issues and disputes with property owners over the construction that needed to occur on their land to close that gap.[29] Arizona passed a
state law in 2011 authorizing the state to close its border fence gaps without

---

* A rape tree is a spot where paid human smugglers, or coyotes, rape the women in
their group and hang their undergarments from the branches to demonstrate their
conquests. Many of these trees dot the landscape throughout Arizona, and are sometimes located on private property belonging to ranchers like Lowell.

federal assistance, but getting that effort jumpstarted has been difficult—again, due to lack of funding, and despite the fact that some contractors and manufacturers have offered to donate materials for new fence construction.[30]

The US Border Patrol has often said that some of these gaps are intentional, and quite useful. The fence funnels smugglers and migrants toward these gaps, where agents can stage and prepare to apprehend them. But some of the gaps—like the ones in south Texas intended for gates that haven't been installed yet—are not intentional, and agents can't always be at the end of every section of fence all day and all night. Coyotes and drug smugglers know this; so they wait, knowing that their opportunity to breach the billion-dollar pieces of fortress will come soon enough.

Knowing how vulnerable our border is with these gaps in the fence, why *wouldn't* we build the other 1,300 miles of fence to completely wall off the border? There certainly has been no shortage of calls to do so from prominent politicians, particularly during the run-up to the 2012 presidential election. The most obvious obstacle to building a concrete-and-steel fence that spans the entire southwest border is funding. For fiscal years 2006 through 2009, the SBI program received about $3.6 billion in appropriated funds, of which about $2.4 billion was allocated to complete approximately 670 miles of primary vehicle and pedestrian fencing. The average cost per mile of fencing varied from $1 million to $5.1 million, a variance which a Government Accountability Office (GAO) report attributes to a variety of factors: the difference between building on private or public land, vehicle fence costs versus pedestrian fencing costs, differences in terrain, and the use of private contractors versus government employees.[31]

By the end of fiscal year 2008, CBP was able to build thirty-two miles of secondary fence at an average cost of $2 million per mile. However, a mere 3.5 miles of secondary fence to be built in San Diego came at a planned cost of $16 million per mile due to the rough terrain there. On top of that, CBP officials said, "SBI would need to undertake significant earth and drainage work, construct all-weather access roads, and deploy additional lighting."[32] Taking all of these different average costs into account and using 2009 rates, CBP conservatively projected at the time that it would cost $22.4 billion to build a *single* fence across the 1,400 non-fenced remaining miles (in 2009) of border. That projection did not include the cost of future land acquisition or maintenance, which CBP estimated in March 2009 to be $6.5 billion over the course of the next twenty years.[33] By August 2012, the US government published a maintenance estimate for the existing 690-plus miles of fence—$20 million *per mile* to keep it at its current integrity level for a twenty-year life span before it would need to start making major replacements.[34]

Another practical reason for not building another 1,300 miles of fence is the often-unforgiving terrain. Many parts of the border are nowhere near flat or straight, and the cost of trying to build some sort of fixed barrier would be astronomical. Some spots are also just too inhospitable for even the most daring of border crossers, which means that would-be terrorists, drug smugglers, and illegal immigrants aren't clamoring to enter the United States along every inch of the line. In California, there are two major breaks in the fence-barrier system, and a handful of small ones in the almost solid line running along the Arizona border with Mexico. Some of these breaks are at altitudes over 3,500 feet, or rocky outcroppings that are nearly impossible to climb. In Texas, there are barriers or sections of fence that run southeast from El Paso about forty miles before they end in a river valley surrounded by more than 4,000-foot-high mountains with no water source or populated areas in sight.

This being said, DHS seems to have reserved the right to change its mind, as well as to go against all common sense. The Otay Mountain Wilderness Area in southern California encompasses almost seventeen thousand acres in the San Ysidro Mountains. It's about twelve miles east of the city of Otay Mesa and just north of the Mexican border. Some parts of the wilderness area rise up quickly from sea level, reaching a peak of just over 3,500 feet at the summit of Otay Mountain. After the passage of the Secure Fence Act, CBP had to make a decision about the path of the fence in San Diego sector knowing it would have to pass through these mountains. In 2006, Richard Kite, the US Border Patrol spokesman at the time, told *The Arizona Daily Star*, "You simply don't need a fence [on Otay Mountain]. It's such harsh terrain, it's difficult to walk, let alone drive. There's no reason to disrupt the land when the land itself is a physical barrier."[35]

But in 2009, then-spokesman for Border Patrol Daryl Reed explained that border security plans change based on shifting migrant and smuggler flows. He told the *Los Angeles Times*, "We're always going to adapt and change." DHS proceeded to spend almost $58 million to "cut roads, remove boulders, bulldoze hillsides and remove about 530,000 cubic yards of rock" in order to install just 3.6 additional miles of fence and a five-mile long access road. Because overall migrant apprehensions have declined since the Otay Mountain fence addition, and not just apprehensions in that specific area, it's very difficult to say if this barrier project has been worth the time and money.[36]

Another consideration in fencing the entire border is the potential harm it could cause in several environmentally sensitive areas. Numerous environmental groups have been protesting for years about the fence's impact on water flow, animal migration patterns, and detritus buildup along the fence base. DHS has publicly expressed concern for and sensitivity to its ecological footprint, but its actions in this regard have been contradictory at best.

There are at least three dozen environmental laws that protect parts of the border, including more well-known laws like the Clean Water Act and the Endangered Species Act. Nature preserves and wildlife refuges are also protected by laws that prohibit certain activities within their confines and encroaching actions by government agencies. However, the REAL ID Act of 2005 changed all of that with regards to actions taken by DHS.

To the vast majority of Americans, the REAL ID Act is all about creating standardized drivers' licenses and identification cards. What many don't know is that the REAL ID portion was just "Division B" of Public Law 109–13, which granted sweeping powers to DHS that a lot of voters were probably never aware of. Section 201 allows the DHS secretary to waive any legal requirements that he or she feels would stand in the way of "expeditious construction of the barriers and roads under this section."[37] Congress was kind enough to allow a provision by which people could file a claim against the US government through the district courts in case they felt DHS was abusing this authority. Not surprisingly, there has been no shortage of these claims.

Since 2008, DHS has approached hundreds of landowners with offers to purchase their property to make way for border fence construction. Some of them thought they were getting a fair deal, until they started talking to their neighbors. Then they realized they were getting paid only a tiny fraction of the sums the federal government was shelling out for similar land only yards away. Many of these border residents who felt short-changed never hired attorneys, unlike their now-richer neighbors who had the advantage of legal support to guide them through a seemingly arbitrary process.[38]

Eloisa Támez ended up getting an attorney, but not because she was seeking fair compensation; DHS sued her to get access to her ancestral land, which inconveniently stood in the path of planned border fence construction.

Támez has an impressive family history, as she is of Lipan Apache and Latino descent, and her family is one of the last Spanish land grant heirs in Cameron County, Texas. They received over 12,700 acres in 1767, which was affirmed by the Government of Mexico in 1833. In the 1930s, however, the US government took roughly half of her family's land to build flood levees without paying any compensation.[39] She was raised in a traditional indigenous community with a large family, and later excelled in the nursing field, even serving in and retiring from the US Army's Nursing Corps. Today, she holds a Ph.D. and is a professor at the University of Texas in Brownsville. Támez is also the cofounder of the indigenous rights advocacy group Lipan Apache

Women Defense. To say she feels strongly about her history, her people, and the three acres of precious land still in her name is an understatement.

When DHS came to Támez in 2007 seeking permission to survey her land for the construction of a new border fence, it seems they weren't prepared for the fight she was going to put up. In June 2008, Támez's daughter Margo penned an "Open Letter to the Cameron County Commission," in which she wrote that her mother started getting repeated phone calls in July 2007 from DHS officials who were pressing her to waive her land rights for fence construction. Margo said the calls came at home, at work, in the evenings, and on weekends, and the pressure increased through August 2007. At that time, Támez summoned representatives from various DHS agencies and, in their presence, officially refused to sign a waiver.[40] In February 2008, she filed a class-action lawsuit against then-DHS Secretary Michael Chertoff and a high-ranking CBP official for trying to confiscate her land. Also that month, the US Army Corps of Engineers sued Támez for refusing Border Patrol access to her land for surveying purposes.[41]

In April 2009, after a year of being in and out of court with DHS, Támez received word that a federal judge ruled DHS had the right to seize one-quarter acre of her property for fence construction.[42] Her only small consolation was that the same judge ruled in a hearing a month earlier that DHS had not properly consulted with Támez before condemning her land.[43] So the fence went up in tiny Calaboz, Texas, cutting Támez's property in two. The only way she can access the south end of her property is through a gap in the fence 1,200 feet away, and she has to trespass on her neighbor's property to get there.[44] But that wasn't the end of it. Based on a review of court records, she discovered DHS seized one-tenth of an acre more than they said they would, so she took them to court once more. Támez told the media in April 2013 that DHS wanted even more of her land; specifically, a tract south of the border fence.[45]

She finally reached a settlement with DHS in late July 2013, but as this book goes to press, she has no idea how much money the US government is going to give her. She insisted the entire ordeal for her was never about the money, but the meaning of that parcel of land to her and her family. "I feel like people like myself who were losing land were ignored and taken advantage of because we don't have the means to fight the government in court," Támez told me. "From the beginning, when I started to raise my voice about this, I didn't want just a letter from the government saying they needed my land to build a border wall. I wanted to know *why*. All the communications they had with me were over the phone, which shows the lack of respect they have for me when they want me to sign all these papers and give up my land on just a phone conversation."[46]

Támez became a spokeswoman of sorts for many of her neighbors who didn't speak English and couldn't interpret the documents DHS was asking them to sign. "These people had no idea what was going on. I was scared. I didn't know what I was going to do or how I was going to do it," she said. But Támez soon learned that her voice was her biggest asset. The more she spoke out about the plans DHS had for the fence and her property, the more media attention she started receiving. Unfortunately, Támez said she also started getting more attention from Border Patrol agents in her neighborhood. Her property is already divided by a levee, and now again by the border fence. Whenever she would drive onto the levee to reach the other side of her land, she said it would only be a matter of minutes before several Border Patrol agents would approach her wanting to know her business.

"I felt like I was being punished by my own country," said Támez. "Who do they think we are? We've been living here for generations. It's not like we just crossed the river today. When they approach me, I challenge them. I say, *I am Dr. Eloisa G. Támez, I own this property, and I'm going to be here as long as I want to.* They've never touched me and they back away, but the intimidation was there."[47]

After DHS tried to seize part of Támez's land a second time, the media came calling again. "This is what I told them," she said. "I am by myself. I am taking care of my issues. I'm looking for equal protection, and I'm not getting it from my own government. I don't have a weapon, I don't own any weapons. But I do have one thing that I'm going to continue to use—my voice. They can take my land, they can build a wall across it, but they can never take my voice." During the last meeting between Támez and the government attorneys, she requested direct access to the rear of her property; her request was denied.[48]

While the bulk of fence construction mandated by legislation has been completed, there are still small gaps scattered along the southwest border that need to be closed, and those closures require this process of eminent domain, lawsuits, and lowball land offers to continue. It's often the same people who demand stronger border security measures and more fencing who also demand that the rights of private property owners be respected. Many Americans who live north of the border don't understand how incredibly complicated it is to build additional sections of fencing.

That being said, it's still frustrating that Congress has mandated a fixed length of border fencing and barriers to confront a problem that is anything but fixed. There are some parts of the border that don't need fencing right now because migration and smuggling patterns have shifted elsewhere. In that vein, "elsewhere" is probably not fenced at the moment, or perhaps only has post-and-wire or Normandy-style vehicle barriers that won't stop the more determined. It's not financially or logistically feasible to build a pedestrian concrete-and-steel wall along the entire two thousand mile–long border, nor prudent to tear down the entire fence and call it an abomination. So should we give up on the fence and call it a day, or add more miles regardless of need or impact in the name of national security?

Before the US government can even consider adding more length to the fence, it needs to evaluate the strength and effectiveness of the existing fence and barriers. For instance, the double fence in the San Diego sector is probably as good as things are going to get. It has proven itself effective in deterring cross-border traffic and there are few improvements that could or need to be made. However, there are other stretches in other sectors where the fence consists of a simple post-and-rail setup or Normandy-style vehicle barriers. These will stop cars and trucks and ATVs, which is a good thing because they can tear up environmentally sensitive areas and be used to transport large amounts of illegal drugs through remote and sparsely patrolled areas. However, the fences can easily be traversed by anyone on foot.

Todd Staples has been the Commissioner of the Texas Department of Agriculture since 2006. The department's interests in Texas go beyond consumer protection, the marketing and safety of food and livestock, and pesticide regulation. Commissioner Staples has become one of the most vocal advocates of improved border security measures on behalf of Texas farmers and ranchers. The Lone Star State's border with Mexico spans 1,241 miles, and most of it consists of private property—land owned by longtime Texas residents who are tired of the incursions onto their farms and cattle ranches, and tired of feeling like their concerns and frustrations are falling on deaf ears in Washington, DC.

"I kept hearing reports, with unconfirmed data, from landowners who were suffering at the hands of drug cartel members—and keep in mind, with two-thirds of the border, Texas has often had crossover issues," Staples told me when I asked what prompted his increased interest in border security. "They would complain about petty theft to shootings to kidnappings. So with this increased level of activity and reports, I started realizing that it's not just isolated incidents; more and more landowners were coming forth with horror stories. Then there were some very vivid descriptions of what was occurring [on the border] from our Farm Bureau members, our Texas and Southwestern Cattle Raiser members, and we investigated and recognized that it was a very chronic issue."[49]

With regards to the benefit of the fence, he tries to be practical. "A farmer called me the day fence construction crews left his property, and he said he went out and looked at it and found a camouflaged ladder in the brush nearby. So fences alone will not solve the problem. Fences do infringe upon the rights of private property owners when it divides their land and causes them difficulties. Strategic fencing, in cooperation with landowners and communities, can have an effective role in securing our border. But it's unrealistic to think that fencing alone will solve all of our problems."[50]

That's ultimately what the conundrum of the border fence boils down to: having just the right amount of fence in just the right places, but also having a sound strategy in place for managing the border locations where the fence has been deemed unnecessary or impractical. One way DHS has attempted to effectively monitor these spaces is through the use of technology. However, as you'll discover in the next chapter, technology by itself won't solve all our border problems.

CHAPTER 4

TECHNOLOGY ON THE BORDER

We want to stay cutting-edge, we want to pull in the private sector who has the technology and the resources to assist us with . . . state-of-the-art equipment we will need to secure the border.[1]

—Jarrod Agen, former DHS spokesman, April 2006

When DHS hands over Mexican border security to the private sector . . . national security becomes another sorry example of commodification. It becomes another product, bringing into play the same economic dynamics as the buying and selling of the most mundane of services.

—Robert Lee Maril, *The Fence*

To the untrained eye, one of the Department of Homeland Security's integrated fixed towers (IFTs) in southern Arizona looks like a typical radio tower, or maybe a cellular signal repeater. Only upon closer inspection you can tell that it's mounted with a variety of devices, including cameras, radio, radar, and other sensors. Other than that, it's pretty unremarkable to the average US citizen. However, to coyotes leading groups of illegal immigrants or drug smugglers looking to cross the border into the United States, this silent metal tower is to be avoided at all costs—assuming it's actually working properly.

This is only one of twenty-three IFTs just like it in a fifty-three-mile area of the Arizona-Mexico border designated Ajo-1 and Tucson-1. The towers were part of a now-defunct program that intended to line the entire border with these technologically superior eyes and ears, augmenting the reach and effectiveness of Border Patrol agents. Only the program was a complete failure that was scrapped after five years of effort and a billion dollars in funding. These twenty-three IFTs are still working and do provide many benefits to the agents in the Tucson sector who use them, but they also serve as a stark reminder that technology is not the be-all and end-all solution to border security. In fact, DHS may be relying so much on border technology to close the gaps in the border fence that it's turning a blind eye to system defects, as well as to flesh-and-blood solutions that are far superior than any man-made machine.

That being said, DHS is using a great deal of impressive technology along the border and across the United States in pursuit of securing our homeland. DHS has also wasted a lot of money on substandard—and sometimes completely useless—technology solutions, and in other cases has not even begun to exploit the full potential of resources it already has. While there isn't nearly enough space here to cover every single gadget in the DHS arsenal, there are definitely some worth highlighting—the good, bad, ugly, and worse. But clearly in many situations along the border, a flesh-and-blood solution is better than any machine in existence today.

The majority of reliable and useful technology currently employed along our land borders, with a few exceptions, seems to be located at the ports of entry where it's all about scanning—seeing into cars, trucks, and trains, and sometimes into people. Tens of thousands of cars line up every single day so their occupants can cross our borders into places like Detroit, Buffalo, San Diego, and El Paso for work, shopping, vacation, or a friendly visit. Sometimes those border crossings have sinister purposes, like transporting illegal drugs, people, cash, or firearms. CBP inspectors can't possibly hope to personally inspect more than a small percentage of these cars and trucks, so they have increasingly relied on a variety of scanning devices.

Over a decade ago, DHS deployed dozens of Vehicle and Cargo Inspection Systems (VACIS), which use gamma rays (as opposed to X-rays) to help CBP inspectors look for hidden compartments in vehicles and trains. Used at various ports of entry, the systems can be taken apart and put back together in a day, making them portable. When a vehicle or train is scanned, the image is sent to a terminal where a CBP inspector can look for dense areas that might contain illegal drugs or other contraband. If the agent sees something suspicious, then he or she can take the next step of calling for a canine unit or detailed manual inspection. The mobile version of VACIS can scan at seven feet per second, and speed and accuracy are crucial at ports of entry where trains don't fully stop unless CBP agents have good reason to believe contraband is on board.[2]

Mobile scanning technology is a critical CBP tool, and they expanded their arsenal through the introduction of Z Backscatter Vans in 2007. These vans scan using X-rays; the rays scatter after they interact with various

organic and inorganic materials. The signals are particularly strong whenever the incident X-rays interact with explosives, plastics, and other biologi-
cal items. Of particular benefit to CBP is the fact that the vans can scan and
move at the same time, which means the time to scan multiple tractor trailers
or cargo containers at a seaport can be significantly reduced.[3]

If a drug or human smuggler manages to make it through this technological gauntlet at a port of entry, he's not necessarily home free. Another successful scanning system is currently in use along the southwest border, but
this one is much less obvious to the casual observer—and perhaps equally as
controversial as ones you'll find at the airport. Anyone who has ever received
a speeding ticket in the mail without having been physically pulled over by
a police officer knows they surreptitiously got nailed by some sort of traffic
camera.

Known most commonly by the acronym ALPR for Automatic License
Plate Reader/Recognition, the units have been in use across the United States
for some time. They're used to fine drivers who blow through toll booths
without paying, find kidnappers in "Amber Alert" situations, and track
down stolen vehicles. They can also be used to find drivers with suspended
licenses, no insurance, or multiple unpaid parking tickets. In some places,
like New York, the volume of traffic is so high that the readers don't check
every plate against a full database in real-time. Instead, the readers match
scans up against a "hot list" of plates belonging to people who have committed a crime or violation. The hot list can contain any set of plate data, from
terrorist watch lists, to stolen vehicles, to parking scofflaws.[4]

In addition to this scanning on the ground, there's also some scanning
coming from the sky near our borders. Most of us who have ever driven
along a main thoroughfare lined with car dealerships have seen some sort of
airborne advertisement, often in the shape of a blimp or other eye-catching
form, so the sight of a relatively large blimp in south Texas or parts of Arizona should do anything but surprise residents. In fact, these plain-white
blimps—varying in length from thirty feet to over two hundred feet—are
anything but everyday, and not nearly as innocuous as they look. Formally
called aerostats, they're high-tech surveillance systems that have been used
by the US military in Iraq and Afghanistan for missions such as finding terrorists and monitoring elections. In recent years, CBP has been using them to
help detect, identify, and track individuals suspected of illegal activity along
the southwest border.

The aerostats are made by Aerostar International, Inc., which is a wholly
owned subsidiary of Raven Industries. Part of an entire surveillance platform called TARS (Tethered Aerostat Radar System), these systems have also

The TARS seen here is operated by CBP's Office of Air and Marine to assist in alleviating drug trafficking on the Southwest Border. Photo by James Mills, courtesy of CBP.

been used in the Florida Straits and parts of the Caribbean to assist with US Northern Command's counterdrug program. The Aerostar carries a sensor made by L-3 Communications that operates similar to a camera, and has a very sophisticated surveillance capability that has proven effective in the deployed environment of the Middle East.

In August 2012, CBP issued a press release announcing it would start testing the aerostat systems in the Rio Grande Valley of south Texas. The evaluation was part of a broader effort to test various surplus pieces of military equipment no longer needed by the US Department of Defense (DoD) that might be successfully used for border security operations. In fact, the use of aerostats along the southwest border was nothing new. CBP—which was the US Customs Service at the time—actually began to build up a network of aerostat sites on the Mexican border in 1984 to detect illegal drug trafficking. A total of eleven sites were operated at one time, but as of 2003 only eight were still operational.[5]

Aerostats have been used on and off for several years along the northern border with Canada and also in Arizona, where the aerostat's reputation is mixed because one crashed in the town of Sierra Vista in May 2011. Pieces of the blimp scattered into a populated neighborhood, and strong winds sent the balloon into power lines just south of the Fort Huachuca US Army base. It should be noted that on the day the aerostat crashed, the local weather services had issued a wind advisory for gusts up to fifty miles per hour,[6] so the incident was more a result of operator error in allowing the blimp to go up than of the blimp itself. But this wasn't the only adverse incident involving the blimps. Small plane pilots have snagged their tether lines, the blimps have been separated from their tethers, crashed several times in high winds, and one was even snagged by a lobster boat that was subsequently sent airborne.[7] In late March 2012, Aerostar seemed to have redeemed itself, helping US border agents make almost one hundred arrests in Arizona.[8]

Despite successful demonstrations and a decently long history of use in counterdrug and counterterrorism applications, the US Air Force—which actually paid for the aerostats—took steps in early 2013 to terminate the program. On January 17, ITT Exelis management (which managed the TARS sites) sent out an email to employees stating they had received a government request to shut down the program by the end of the fiscal year because the government did not intend to extend the contract. The email also indicated that after ceasing operations in mid-March, the rest of the fiscal year would be used to "deflate aerostats, disposition equipment, and prepare sites for permanent closure."[9] The government did not provide an explanation for why they decided not to extend the contract. The company tried to work with DHS to negotiate a transfer of funding and management from the Air Force, but those initial negotiations failed.[10]

Fortunately they picked up again, and in March 2013, DoD and DHS finalized the details of an agreement to transfer control of the aerostat program from the former to the latter so it could be continued. As of October 2013, the blimps were still operational.

This is a good-news story because the blimps serve a dual purpose along our land borders—surveillance and deterrence. They can pick up movement very well, so smugglers and migrants will avoid them once they see them; after all, they're not exactly the least obtrusive objects in the sky. This falls in line with the strategy of the border fence, which is to corral border crossers away from populated areas toward places where Border Patrol agents can apprehend them more easily. They also come at a lower financial, environmental, and civic cost than building more border fence. However, not every piece of equipment tested and ultimately purchased with tax dollars by DHS has met with the same success.

On October 2, 2012, Border Patrol Agent Nicholas Ivie was killed in a friendly-fire incident in Tucson sector. He was responding to a tripped ground sensor in the middle of the night at the same time as two fellow agents who were traveling together. As the agents approached the sensor from two different locations, they had no idea what had set the sensor off, and a combination of low light, bad radio communication, and mistaken identity led to Ivie's death. Tragically, there was a strong possibility that the sensor trip that brought the agents out there in the first place was a false alarm.[11]

The sensor the three agents were responding to is one of almost thirteen thousand unattended ground sensors (UGS) scattered across our southwest border. Many of them are at least thirty years old and have been rendered useless by animals or the environment. As a result, they have an atrocious track record for accuracy. In 2005, the DHS Inspector General released a report that said, "only 4 percent of the ground sensor alarms signaled confirmed cases of smugglers or others trying to cross the border. Another 34 percent were false alarms, and the final 62 percent could not be determined."[12]

Since that report came out, DHS has made plans a few times to replace them—first under the Secure Border Initiative that rolled out in 2006, and then the Arizona Border Surveillance Technology Plan in 2011. The former was cancelled in 2010 after spending $1.1 billion with little to show for it. The latter has allocated $1.5 billion over ten years partly to update a number of surveillance gadgets along the border—including the sensors—but the money is being spent at a snail's pace due to being hung up at the understaffed CBP acquisitions office.[13]

The odds are high that Border Patrol Agent Nicholas Ivie and the other two agents involved in the friendly fire incident responded to a false sensor trip. Because of the sensor's location, there were no camera towers nearby to indicate what might have triggered it. There are also indications that the three agents lost radio contact in a "dead spot" right before the shooting started. These spots are common in more remote and mountainous parts of the sector. Border Patrol agent Art Del Cueto told *The Arizona Republic* a few weeks after the shooting that "agents have difficulty communicating in valleys and ravines because there are not enough repeater towers to adequately boost radio signals." Despite radio upgrades, communication between agents relies on line-of-sight with a repeater tower. Building a new site for a new repeater can cost anywhere from $100,000 to millions of dollars, and some sites are so remote they can only be accessed by helicopter.[14]

While the three agents were in radio contact prior to Ivie firing his weapon, there is still no indication as to whether or not they were in radio contact after the bullets started flying. In a high-stress situation at 1:30 A.M. in remote desert terrain, they had to rely on their training and what their eyes and ears were telling them, probably without the knowledge of each other's exact positions. It's impossible to know if more repeaters and better radio communication would have helped. However, had that sensor and thousands of others like it been replaced long ago with available technology that can easily differentiate between foot, animal, and vehicle traffic, this tragedy might have been prevented.

It isn't just unmanned ground sensors that aren't meeting the demands placed on them by the dynamic environment along the US-Mexico border. Finding any one of the myriad of drug smuggling tunnels used by Mexican cartels can be like finding a needle in a haystack. One way DHS has tried to improve their agencies' odds of finding them is by implementing a number of different detection devices in areas where tunnel construction has been more prevalent, like Otay Mesa, California, and Nogales, Arizona. But despite the existence and use of tunnel detectors that use state-of-the-art seismic technology to discover anomalies in rock and soil, finding these clandestine routes from Mexico into the United States hasn't gotten that much easier.

In December 2012, Sandia National Laboratories issued a news release about a two-year tunnel detection study they had undertaken using seismic devices. During the study, Nedra Bonal of Sandia's geophysics and atmospheric sciences organization said she was surprised when standard refraction and reflection processing techniques Sandia used could not successfully pinpoint some tunnels. Part of the problem was that earlier studies didn't focus on the areas where the tunnels met the earth, which is an important aspect of seismic tunnel detection. Other problems arose from rain, geology, and soil variations, and where the tunnels sat relative to the water table. Bonal said that despite evolving tunnel detection technology, most border tunnels are found by tips from people.[15] More than seven hundred drug tunnels have been discovered along our southwest border in the last eight years, all of which were discovered through conventional law enforcement practices—the use of informants, accidental discovery, or through a standard investigation.[16]

There's no doubt that finding smugglers underground is a difficult prospect, so DHS has focused considerably on airborne technology to detect smugglers and illegal immigrants above ground. Without making a sound, invisible sets of eyes patrol our southwest border with Mexico, four miles above the ground. Virtually undetectable by the naked eye, unmanned aerial vehicles—better known as UAVs or drones—silently patrol the border, looking for potential terrorists, drug smugglers, and illegal immigrants. One model, the Predator B, easily outlasts its human counterparts, with up to twenty hours of continuous flight time and with visual sensors superior to

A CBP unmanned aerial vehicle, or UAV, stands by ready for patrol along the southern border of the United States. Photo by Gerald L. Nino, courtesy of CBP.

those of any living creature. The aircraft is piloted by human beings from several dozens of miles away.

The CBP's Office of Air and Marine (OAM) first began using the Predator B for border enforcement operations in the southwest in 2005, and along our northern border with Canada in 2009. In 2008, the OAM and the US Coast Guard began working together to develop a maritime variant of the Predator B, now known as the Guardian. The Guardian was modified from a standard Predator B with structural changes, avionics, communications enhancements, and the addition of a marine search radar and an infrared sensor that is optimized for nighttime maritime operations.[17]

As drug trafficking routes have started expanding from Mexico back into the Caribbean after a twenty-year hiatus, the need for a bigger law enforcement presence has increased. As a result, DHS decided in July 2012 to expand the use of Guardian UAV systems into the Caribbean basin. Lothar Eckardt, executive director of CBP national air security operations, told the media, "The goal is to be [in place] long enough to detect and track targets making their way through the transit zone and bring in units for the intercept [that] can track a variety of smuggling vessels, including semi-submersibles and go-fast vessels."[18] While UAV technical capabilities sound impressive, many question the system's usefulness as an aid to US law enforcement agencies, as well as its expense compared to the benefits it provides.

Through early 2011, CBP had three Predator Bs in Arizona, two in North Dakota, and one Guardian each in Florida and south Texas. In mid-June 2011, the DHS Inspector General released a report indicating CBP had nine drones in operation, with a tenth drone on the way. However, the report scolded DHS for not having enough ground support to make full use of UAV flights, and for having no system in place to prioritize missions. It also said given the number of aircraft, CBP should have been able to fly more than ten thousand hours of missions per year. In the year under review, the agency flew less than four thousand hours.[19]

Each Predator B drone system costs about $18 million, and DHS has spent a total of almost $241 million on the UAV program. Yet, UAV effectiveness in both border and maritime regions has been questionable. The unmanned craft have had only a minor impact on border security, contributing to the capture of less than 2 percent of illegal border crossers apprehended on the US southwestern border in the 2011 fiscal year.[20] Two unnamed homeland security officials told *The Los Angeles Times* that test flights for the Guardian showed disappointing results in the Bahamas. During more than 1,260 hours in the air off the southeastern coast of Florida, the Guardian assisted in only a handful of large-scale busts, they said.[21]

The UAVs have also raised some safety concerns. Incidents have included a crash due to a remote pilot inadvertently cutting off fuel supply, and a communications failure between the aircraft and controllers that resulted in the fleet being grounded for six days in June 2010. Accident rates of UAVs are several times higher than those of manned aircraft, and there are fewer backup systems built into the unmanned units. Weather conditions in the desert southwest can also adversely affect certain UAV platforms, depending on what sensor packages they contain, and can render them virtually useless in rain, high humidity, or heavy cloud cover—situations that can be exploited by border crossers who know of these vulnerabilities.[22]

Unmanned aircraft used by DHS are guided by GPS. In June 2012, DHS invited researchers at the University of Texas to demonstrate whether or not UAVs could be vulnerable to a type of GPS hacking known as "spoofing." The demonstration was a complete success—if you were on Team Longhorn—or failure—if you were on Team DHS. From a kilometer away, the researchers were able to repeatedly take over navigational signals being sent to the UAV and input a new flight path. The flight path in this case was one that took the test UAV straight into the ground—until it was "rescued" at the last minute by a safety pilot.[23]

To top off all of these flaws, the Inspector General's office published another report about the UAV program in May 2012. It stated: "CBP has not ensured that adequate resources are available to effectively operate its unmanned aircraft," and "CBP has not adequately planned to fund unmanned aircraft-related equipment." A full year after the June 2011 report, the same deficiencies persisted, and they were listed yet again in the current 2012 report—namely, UAVs were still not achieving desired flight hours or provided with enough support for the missions.[24] When the UAVs actually made it into the sky and missions were conducted for various agencies, CBP had no system in place for prioritizing one mission over another, and agencies had no clue how to actually request a priority status.[25]

The fiscal and overall mission mismanagement involved in the UAV program is ridiculous enough without even really digging into the Inspector General reports. But at least the UAVs are capable of flying and accomplishing something useful. The capabilities and potential benefits of the UAV program are huge, but are largely limited by human mismanagement. However, the program's flaws and failures, as dismal as they seem here, are dwarfed by the ultimate DHS boondoggle known as the virtual border fence.

Since the beginning of our government's efforts to make our southwest border less permeable, there has never been any intention to completely fence the entire two thousand–mile length of it—at least, not with a physical fence. After all, the Secure Fence Act and subsequent legislation only called for seven hundred miles of it in the most highly trafficked areas. But DHS felt it was important to have some sort of surveillance coverage along the unfenced areas. It needed to find a way to achieve this that was cost effective and quick. However, the agency was also painfully aware that it did not possess the in-house expertise to accomplish this, so the outsourcing of our physical border security began.

With the announcement of the SBI strategy in 2006 came the introduction of SBI*net*—a program that, in theory, would bring together the brightest minds and best border technology available to create a network of surveillance platforms along the unfenced parts of the border. The program was soon commonly known as the virtual fence, and was doomed to become the most colossal failure in the history of US border security efforts. Even more damning: such a project had been tried twice before, with very discouraging results.

An earlier attempt at mixing technology with traditional fencing came in 1998, when the former Immigration and Naturalization Service announced a system—the Integrated Surveillance Intelligence System (ISIS)—that would connect new ground sensors, towers with cameras, and computers to identify and interdict illegal border crossers. The initial contract was for the modest sum of $2 million and was awarded without the usual competitive bidding process to International Microwave Corporation. Walt Drabik, the ISIS project director, claimed in 2000 that the thirteen thousand old unattended ground sensors would be replaced with ones that were more sensitive and less likely to result in false alarms. They would then be connected to seventy-three high-resolution and infrared cameras in twenty-one Border Patrol sectors.[26]

In fact, this sensor integration should have happened a decade earlier but never materialized. That 1989 project was called the Intelligent Computer-Aided Detection system, or ICAD. Information gleaned from the integrated sensors was supposed to be analyzed by law enforcement communications assistants, who would then filter the most important information to Border Patrol agents who could respond to a sensor alarm. ICAD went through a series of modifications, or "improvements," in 1994 and sometime later entered its third iteration. ISIS would come to incorporate the data gathered through this system.[27]

The biggest problem with ICAD and ISIS was that the data they were basing their systems on—coming from thousands of bad sensors—was fundamentally flawed. Over the course of eleven years, no one seemed to have caught the fact that everything they were collecting and ultimately producing was garbage because it was based on false alarms or unknown causes of sensor trips. However, that didn't stop ISIS from soldiering on; in 2000, Congress allocated $200 million to keep developing. Two years later, after audits, it became apparent that the $239 million appropriated for the virtual security project known as ISIS had been completely spent by contractors on a system that was "functionally inoperable."[28]

It isn't clear why DHS chose to pursue the construction of another technological border barrier so soon after the ISIS debacle, or what members of Congress who approved funding for SBI*net* were thinking when they decided to slap down $1 billion for its construction. Regardless, Boeing was awarded the contract to build the new virtual fence after claiming it could complete the first twenty-eight miles of it—later called Project 28 in Arizona—in just eight months, and completely wire the southwest border in three years. Boeing also claimed that its system would be able to identify and initiate apprehension of approximately 95 percent of all border crossers.[29] Needless to say, things didn't exactly work out as planned.

Instead of creating a customized system of sensors and cameras that were optimized for operation in the various southwest border environments, Boeing just grabbed whatever gadgets it happened to already have from other projects (called COTS for "commercial off-the-shelf") and tried to tweak them for this purpose.[30] The upside of this tactic is that the systems were familiar and had been tested for functionality. The downside of this is that Boeing could charge whatever DHS was willing to pay them without having to invest that money in research and development or any other overhead costs associated with creating a custom-built system. Never mind the fact that no one bothered to ask Border Patrol agents what they wanted or needed from the virtual fence, leading Boeing to integrate components that agents later found cumbersome at best and useless at worst.

From the start of SBI*net*, some members of Congress expressed concern about the amount of money involved in the project, as well as the lack of a concrete plan for moving forward with construction. In early 2006, before the virtual fence contract was awarded to Boeing, Homeland Security Appropriations Subcommittee Chairman Harold Rogers (R-Kentucky) told Homeland Security officials during a hearing, "We've been at this juncture before. We have been presented with expensive proposals for elaborate border technology that have eventually proven to be ineffective and wasteful systems, such as the Integrated Surveillance Intelligence System and America's Shield Initiative . . . When presented with questions like this, we apply a simple formula: no plan equals no money."[31] During the same hearing, Homeland Security Appropriations Subcommittee ranking member Martin Olav Sabo (D-Minnesota) added, "I'm worried that DHS thinks that the solution is to hire a private technology company to run the SBI, and then sit back and watch."[32]

And that's exactly what happened. But DHS didn't dive into the virtual fence head first; it decided to get its feet wet with Project 28, which was plagued from the start with cost overruns, delays, and not enough CBP employees to run the system. The CBP employees DHS did have on hand to run Project 28 had little to no project management experience, resulting in fiscal mismanagement and an inability to hold Boeing accountable for any contract missteps. Still, Project 28 continued with the goal of erecting nine towers upon which state-of-the-art surveillance systems would be mounted. Because the systems were "off-the-shelf," many at both Boeing and DHS thought the cameras and sensors would just snap into place and start working with little fuss; this accounts for the quick turnaround time projected by Boeing management.[33]

Then the setbacks began. Boeing engineers couldn't work out bugs in the system. Rain and blowing sand rendered the surface radar—technology that's been in use for more than half a century—on the towers useless. The type of radar integrated into the towers was designed to detect large military vehicles, and was less than stellar at identifying smaller objects like people. The computer system also couldn't be integrated properly. DHS didn't have enough people with the skills or training to use the finished product.[34]

In 2008, then-DHS Secretary Michael Chertoff announced the completion date of the virtual fence would be pushed back *three years* to 2011. The SBI*net* budget by mid-2009 had reached $770 million, and a new government stimulus package provided an additional $200 million in funding. At around this time, both CBP and Boeing management acknowledged Project 28 was a mess. Engineers admitted they cobbled together components, some of which weren't even theirs and were purchased from Radio Shack and other retailers. All this came out *after* CBP accepted Project 28 as functional in 2008. And despite this, plans continued to roll out the next iteration of Project 28, known as Tucson-1 and Ajo-1 and hailed as the "real" SBI*net*.[35]

The new project turned out to be as much of a dud as its predecessor. Tucson-1 and Ajo-1 comprised fifty-three miles of southwest border in Arizona, and to this day is the only section of the US-Mexico border to be touched by the virtual fence. This is because in January 2010, former DHS Secretary Janet Napolitano called for a systemic review of SBI*net*. Specifically, she wanted to know if the virtual fence was viable, if it could meet the original goals (which were never clear in the first place), and whether it would be cost effective in the long run.

In October 2010, the GAO issued a report titled, "Secure Border Initiative: DHS Needs to Strengthen Management and Oversight of Its Prime Contractor." Yes, that really was the title of the report.[36] In January 2011, after spending $1 billion of taxpayer dollars on only fifty-three miles of virtual fence that mostly didn't work, Napolitano announced that SBI*net* systems "were not appropriate for the entire southwest border and did not meet current standards for viability and cost effectiveness."[37] The initial cost estimate that Boeing provided in 2006 for the virtual fence, which would consist of 1,800 towers once completed, was $2 billion. That estimate was later raised to $8 billion, and the Inspector General suggested the true cost down the road would be closer to $30 billion. The original completion date for the full virtual fence was 2009, and that was ultimately pushed back to 2013.[38]

Still, DHS continues its trial-and-error strategy for finding a technological solution to securing our borders. Again, Arizona will be the test bed for the technology acquisitions plan, dubbed Alternative (Southwest) Border Technology. It calls for combining the existing virtual fence infrastructure with integrated fixed-tower systems (IFTs), remote video and mobile surveillance systems, unidentified handheld equipment, and unattended ground sensors (no indication if they mean existing sensors or new ones that actually work). The projected life cycle cost for CBP's plan is $1.5 billion.[39]

This sounds like a bad idea, and the GAO can easily confirm any doubts. In November 2011, one of its reports stated, "CBP does not have the information needed to fully support and implement its Plan in accordance with DHS and [Office of Management and Budget] guidance . . . CBP's newly proposed approach is at an increased risk of not accomplishing its goal in support of Arizona border security."[40] DHS must have accepted this as a challenge, since it solicited only one month later for contractors willing to put together "commercially available, non-developmental systems" that would meet the needs of this new plan to virtually secure Arizona's border with Mexico.

In October 2012, CBP said an announcement of the contract award could come as soon as a few months' time. In early May 2013, DHS announced that it had finally narrowed down the list of potential contract winners, and anonymous sources said the final four bidders were General Dynamics, Raytheon, Lockheed Martin, and the American arm of the Israeli company Elbit.[41] As this book goes to press, that award still has not been made, almost two years after the original solicitation was issued. Due to sequestration-related budget cuts, the progress of IFT program, while not likely to get cut, is being delayed for an unknown period of time.

In 2006, Michael P. Jackson, then-deputy director of DHS, told the various firms competing for the virtual fence contract that he wanted them "to come back and tell us how to do our business." Deborah W. Meyers, then senior policy analyst at the Migration Policy Institute, told the *Washington Post,* "It's a little bit scary when the government throws up its hands and says, *We have no idea how to do this. Please tell us.* It just seems like the government is putting policy in the hands of the contractors."[42]

The biting—but not entirely unreasonable—truth is that our government does not have the in-house ability to think up, develop, test, evaluate, and deploy many of the complex technological devices we rely on for homeland security purposes. Our military is the same way, and relying on private companies to do government-directed work isn't always a bad thing. When done properly, government agencies can use competitive market forces to improve product quality and reduce costs. However, when the project gets bigger than the agency controlling it, human error and sheer incompetence can also end up costing taxpayers billions of dollars while leaving an agency with hunks of metal and wiring that work best as huge paperweights.

Another uncomfortable truth for those who believe technology is the answer to everything border security–related is that human (and sometimes canine) skill, experience, and intuition often trump the utility of any mechanical device humans can create. The CBP canine handlers from the Nogales, Arizona, port of entry explained to me that a dog's nose is five to ten thousand times more sensitive than a human's nose. It is so sensitive that it can detect a scent in the quantity of five hundred parts per *trillion*—the equivalent of detecting one red blood cell floating in a swimming pool. There is nothing in the entire technological arsenal of planet Earth with a sensory capability superior to Fido's nose. Despite this astonishing fact, DHS insists on spending our tax dollars on more machines—and paying more than they're actually worth—instead of investing in more shepherds, labs, and human handlers.

CBP inspectors working at a land border crossing have to know a lot about not just vehicles and their hiding places, but about people and how they react under stress. When a driver from Mexico or Canada approaches a CBP agent and provides his or her passport and any other required documents, the CBP agent soaks in dozens of data points in a very short period of time that will guide his or her line of questioning.

In between the ports of entry, Border Patrol agents have been engaging in a hunting practice that has been around for thousands of years. It's called cutting for sign, and was perfected in North America by Native Americans tracking both men and animals. Sign cutting is much more complex than simply following footprints in the dirt. According to ITS Tactical, a joint venture started in 2009 by military veterans and individuals in the Special Operations community, a trained tracker "looks for kicked-over rocks, soil depressions, clothing fibers, changes in vegetation, changes in the environment, ambient noise or lack thereof, etc. Basically, the tracker looks for the disturbance—the sign—left behind by the person or persons being tracked."[43]

Experienced Border Patrol agents can look at a footprint and determine if it was made by a man, woman, or child, and if that person was carrying something heavy. Often, migrants will strap pieces of burlap over their shoes to disguise their footprints, but agents recognize this, too. They can tell the direction the person was heading, if he intentionally backtracked to try and throw agents off his trail, or if he was walking or running. Trackers will look at the dew on soil and vegetation first thing in the morning to see if it has been disturbed and look for fabric fibers in bushes where a migrant or smuggler's shirt got snagged in haste. The "freshness" of the print can tell agents approximately how much time has passed since the prints were made.[44] No machine on earth can do all of this with any degree of accuracy.

Despite the stumbles and falls DHS has made over the years, there is still hope they can create a more successful border technology solution. I've been to enough border security conferences and walked down the aisles of enough expo halls to see the possibilities. Some ports of entry in late 2012 were the test sites for an ATM-sized machine that can analyze a person's physical movements and speech to determine if they're nervous or under stress—for example, a potential terrorist or drug smuggler.[45] In August 2012, DHS awarded a $100 million contract to SRCTec in New York to build nine ultralight aircraft detection systems.[46] It's incredibly difficult for standard radar to detect small and low-flying craft, so a fully operational system could be a huge help to the CBP Air and Marine folks.

I have no doubt that once systems are fully functional and reliable, Border Patrol agents in the field and CBP inspectors at the ports of entry will wonder how they ever did their jobs without them. But I would happily take the billion dollars spent on the failed virtual fence and use it to hire dozens more agents or assign a drug dog and canine handler to every vehicle lane in ports like San Ysidro, Nuevo Laredo, Nogales, and Detroit. Yes, machines like radar towers, infrared cameras, and UAVs augment the limited abilities of human agents' eyes and ears, but what good are they if skilled agents aren't available to respond to what they see, or more importantly, make apprehensions of illegal immigrants or drug smugglers?

The truth is we've spent billions of taxpayer dollars on border technology without a truly significant degree of improvement in security along our borders. Maybe the incompetence of DHS over the years has prevented them from finding the right technology solutions, but I don't really think that's the main problem. There are people in the DHS Science and Technology division who are really good at what they do. Unfortunately, bureaucracy almost always gets in the way, and too many people in Washington, DC, are looking for the holy grail of border security in a machine when they should be investing more in flesh-and-blood solutions.

CHAPTER 5

BORDER VIOLENCE SPILLOVER

The spillover violence in Texas is real and it is escalating.[1]

—Sen. John Cornyn, US congressman (R-Texas), March 2010

We haven't seen what I would define as spillover violence.[2]

—Janet Napolitano, secretary, US Department
of Homeland Security, December 2009

Martin Cota-Monroy was about to have a really bad day. It's doubtful he would have seen it coming, considering he had just returned from a killer weekend in Las Vegas with his buddies from California and some new friends from Mexico. They had rounded up some more people they knew in the Phoenix area before heading to "Sin City" Friday night, and they went straight to the MGM Grand and Palms casinos for a night of gambling and debauchery. But the fun eventually had to come to an end, and the group arrived back at their hotel in Phoenix around 6:00 P.M. Saturday night.

Not wanting to wrap up the weekend so early, part of the group started to get ready at the hotel for a local night out, and Martin took a few of the guys back to his apartment in the suburb of Chandler so they could get cleaned up there. Later that night, Martin and his friends Alberto, Manuel, and Juan met up with Daniel, Jorge, Adolfo, "Joto," and "El Muñeco" at one of their favorite watering holes, the Coyote Bar. The night did not disappoint; they got drunk, closed the bar down, and Juan even got temporarily kicked out after getting into a fight with someone over some cocaine.

Hungry after a wild night, half the group went to the Filiberto's drive-through for some food, and the other half—including Martin, Manuel, David, Juan, and "El Muñeco"—went back to Martin's apartment. Martin and his friends arrived at the drive-through a bit later, brought out more alcohol, and Manuel invited his friend Edna to come by. She was nice enough to bring a friend, and the group just hung out in the parking lot for a while, drinking and talking. Manuel left briefly around 3:30 A.M. to take Edna's friend home.

When he got back to Martin's apartment, Manuel realized he needed to charge his cell phone. He went inside the apartment, where Martin, David, Juan, "Joto," and "El Muñeco" were all still talking. At this point, their conversation about mysticism and death—and the looks in the eyes of the five men—was getting crazy enough for Manuel that he only charged his phone for five minutes and got the hell out of the apartment at around 5:00 A.M. Edna went with him to get a ride home.

Shortly after getting into the car with Edna, he saw David, Juan, and "Joto" leave the apartment, get into the red SUV they were driving, and pull out of the complex. Thinking something might be wrong, Manuel warned Edna to stay put in the car while he went back to the apartment. As he was walking into the living room, Daniel was coming out of one of the bedrooms. They both looked down and saw Martin's lifeless body, blood pouring out of a stab wound, and his severed head lying two feet away.

Later in a conversation with a Chandler police officer, Manuel would try to put the pieces of the puzzle together. He didn't know Martin very well, and "Joto" was a relatively new face for him, too. David and Juan, however, were Manuel's childhood friends. David and Juan had introduced Manuel to "Joto," and the four of them had been living in Manuel's apartment for the last few weeks. They even took road trips together to Perris, California, on a regular basis, although Manuel didn't really know why at first. Then, it started to sink in: the frequent stops at Western Union locations, David and Juan's use of several different cars . . . there was a good chance his childhood buddies were in the drug business. Manuel never asked questions and had no interest in getting involved, but he was getting worried that his two friends might have had something to do with Martin's murder. When asked, he truthfully told the police officer he didn't know where they were.

Shortly after they finished their interview with Manuel, police officers picked up one of the suspects, Crisantos Moroyoqui (a.k.a. "El Muñeco"); his shoes and pants were stained with Martin's blood. He agreed to talk to the police, but said he couldn't remember any details from the night before because he was too drunk. But then the Chandler Police Department caught a break. They got a call from Jorge and Daniel, who knew that David, Juan, and "Joto" were currently in the Úrsulo Galván neighborhood of Valle Empalme in Sonora, Mexico. Following up on this lead, detectives met with members of the US Border Patrol's Intelligence Unit in Tucson, Arizona, to see if they could uncover some of the mystery surrounding Martin's grisly demise.

They learned that Martin, known as "Jando" in his hometown of Nogales in Sonora, had stolen four hundred pounds of marijuana from the Sinaloa Federation, which was collaborating with the Sonora state police investigative unit (PEI for Policia Estatal Investigadora). Martin had also been "pinching" small amounts of methamphetamine from the cop-backed cartel. His most egregious misstep was telling his narco bosses not that he had lost the marijuana load, but rather that the US Border Patrol had seized it. It's bad enough in the eyes of the cartel to lose a drug load in the process of evading authorities, but this is sometimes forgiven as a cost of doing business. However, it's a death sentence to steal from them, then lie about it to try and cover it up. The cartel saw through the lie, and hired an enforcer crew called Los Relámpagos (The Lightning) to kidnap Martin in Nogales.

Martin was initially able to talk his way out of getting killed. He said he would put up the home he said he owned as collateral, and swore to pay all the money back for the drug load he stole. But after they let him go, Martin continued to make bad decisions. He fled to Phoenix and went into hiding, fearing for his life because he didn't actually own the home he put up as collateral. He knew the cartel would eventually figure this out and would come looking for him. They did; a subsidiary of the Federation known as "El Gio" sent David, Juan, and "Joto" to befriend Martin in Phoenix and keep an eye on him until the order to kill him came down.

But even Martin's murder didn't settle the score. Martin was apparently a mid-level member of the Beltrán Leyva Organization (BLO), a smaller family-run cartel that had once been part of the Federation and split off in 2008. David, Juan, and "Joto" had been seen out and about in Valle Empalme, and the Border Patrol agents told the Chandler detectives the word on the street was the BLO had put hits out on the three men in retaliation for Martin's murder.[3] The cycle of "narco justice" had been happening on the Mexican side of the border for decades, but this was the first drug-related beheading ever known to have occurred in the United States.

In the days after Cota-Monroy's beheading, news of the incident could only be found in local media outlets. About three weeks later, only two conservative national outlets—FOX news and the *Washington Times*—were reporting on the killing, and using the term "spillover violence" in their stories. Only when the Chandler Police Department's report was released in early March 2011, making a definitive connection between the murder and a Mexican cartel, did more national news outlets come on board to report the story. But by then, the decapitation was old news.

There have been many attempts to define border violence spillover. This is the currently accepted federal interagency definition used by DHS and DOJ components since at least 2009:

> Spillover violence entails deliberate, planned attacks by the cartels on US assets, including civilian, military, or law enforcement officials, innocent US citizens, or physical institutions such as government buildings, consulates, or businesses. This definition does not include trafficker on trafficker violence, whether perpetrated in Mexico or the US.[4]

There are several things wrong with this definition, including the fact that it sounds more like a definition of a terrorist attack. Most glaring is that it doesn't take into account trafficker-on-trafficker violence. As you read in Chapter 1, the fundamental nature of drug-related violence happening in Mexico is trafficker-on-trafficker, as well as trafficker-on-law enforcement. Excluding that kind of violence from a definition of spillover is a convenient way to allow the federal government to say spillover isn't happening. The definition is irresponsible and misleading, painting a false rosy picture of some communities along the southwest border where Mexican cartel associates and hired gang members routinely kill or kidnap each other on US soil.

Some state and local agencies along the southwest border have made their own attempts at creating more fitting definitions. In May 2011, US representative Michael McCaul (R-Texas) testified before Congress that "the Texas Department of Public Safety's definition of spillover violence includes aggravated assault, extortion, kidnapping, torture, rape and murder. The Director of Texas DPS, Colonel Steven McCraw, says there is 'no question spillover violence is growing in Texas.'"[5] In March 2010, Texas governor Rick Perry even launched the state's own "Texas Spillover Violence Contingency Plan."

The range of public differences of opinion about spillover violence can be mind-boggling. Former DHS Secretary Napolitano said in early 2011, "It is inaccurate to state, as too many have, that the United States side of the border is overrun with violence or out of control." In June 2011, the US Border Patrol sector chief for the Rio Grande Valley said, "We're not seeing cartel-on-cartel violence here in the US that I'm aware of." After a 2009 cross-border kidnapping and murder that El Paso Mayor John Cook acknowledged was spillover, he said, "This drug war now has lasted for three years, and you have one case of spillover violence that we can clearly identify in a city of 800,000 people," as a way to indicate the rarity of such incidents. Sheriff Lupe Treviño in Hidalgo County, Texas, told NPR in a June 2011 interview, "We have always had drug violence anywhere in the United States because that is the nature of the business . . . You know why it's spillover now? Because that is the flavor of the month."[6]

Treviño changed his tune four months later when one of his deputies was shot in a botched kidnapping attempt. The individuals involved were members of a local gang, acting on orders from the Gulf cartel. Treviño told the media, "I have to say that with this particular incident, the way the witnesses and the information that we have gotten particularly in the federal system, this is the first recorded spillover violence event that we have experienced and unfortunately got one of our deputies shot."[7] In March 2012, the late Sheriff Larry Dever of Cochise County, Arizona told NBC News, "I'd say the border is more dangerous than it's ever been . . . We're getting overrun from the south, because the federal government isn't doing its job." Steve McCraw also told NBC News, "The border's not secure, clearly. I think by any indication it's not secure."

There are generally two approaches being used by various agencies to attempt to prove or disprove the existence of spillover violence—statistics and stories. Statistics can be aggregated and segregated and charted, and for the most part they're easy to understand if presented properly. However, statistics can also turn into smoke and mirrors for an agency with an agenda.

Stories can also be a double-edged sword. They breathe life into faceless statistics, and serve as hard-hitting reality when presented in full-color on television or a news website. Listening to an angry rancher explaining his frustrations about smugglers continuously trespassing on his land, or a hysterical woman holding a crying baby after their home was accidentally burglarized by drug dealers has a much bigger impact than reading numbers on paper. But stories like these, when amassed, often don't seem as significant in number compared to crime statistics. Also, many anecdotes are hard to verify because the incidents are never reported to police (and thus not captured in police reports or databases), and unless the stories are heard first hand, the game of "telephone" takes over and the story gets completely distorted by the third telling.

I hope to present here something closer to a universal definition of spillover violence, one that helps to reconcile the discrepancies between the portrayals of statistical data and personal experiences.

In an oft-cited speech at the University of Texas at El Paso in January 2011, former DHS Secretary Napolitano announced that FBI crime statistics showed violent crime rates in southwest border counties were down 30 percent over the previous two decades, and were "among the lowest in the nation."[8] In May 2012, CBP Laredo field office director Gene Garza testified before Congress that areas on the US side of the southwest US-Mexican border are "some of the safest communities in America," and added:

> Violent crime in border communities has remained flat or fallen in the past decade, according to the Federal Bureau of Investigation's (FBI) Uniform Crime Report, and some of the safest communities in America are at the border. In fact, violent crimes in Southwest border counties overall have dropped by more than 40 percent and are currently among the lowest in the Nation per capita, even as drug-related violence has significantly increased in Mexico.[9]

Napolitano and Garza aren't the only two government officials who have publicly cited the FBI's Uniform Crime Report (UCR) statistics to support their assessments, and it's a reasonable thing to do. The FBI was charged with managing this crime statistic aggregation database back in 1930 by the International Association of Chiefs of Police, and the UCR contains data provided by almost seventeen thousand law enforcement agencies across the country.

There are thousands of ways to pull data from the UCR database because it classifies the information by city and county and region, by population, by type of crime, etc. Thus, it's relatively easy to pull statistics in a way that supports almost anyone's theory about the rise or decline of criminal activity in certain areas. However, for the purpose of this debate, three particular data pulls are very helpful: violent crime (murder, rape, robbery, and aggravated assault) in US border cities with a population above one hundred thousand people, violent crime in border counties, and property crime (burglary, larceny, motor vehicle theft, and arson) in border counties. When statistics are analyzed for all three data sets between 2007 and 2011, they show an average decline in all three cases. In those five years, violent crime in larger border cities declined by 14 percent, in border counties it declined by 15 percent, and property crimes declined by 11 percent.[10] But do these statistics paint a full and accurate picture?

One thing that isn't publicly mentioned about UCR data is the fact that the information is voluntarily provided by those seventeen thousand agencies. There is no federal mandate to provide crime data to the FBI or any other federal agency for inclusion in the UCR or any other database, and there are agencies that choose not to do so. The database can also only include crimes that have been reported and documented. It's difficult for anyone to speculate how many crimes might qualify as border violence spillover but have just never been reported. Because the victims of these crimes are often illegal immigrants and other criminals—two groups that have a strong disincentive to call the police—it's hard to say what the real crime picture along the border looks like. The fact that kidnapping and trespassing aren't included in the database is also problematic, since those are crimes very commonly associated with drug trafficking and human smuggling activity in the southwest border states.

There's much more to the story than just numbers. Imagine for a moment you're the mayor of a small border city with a population of around 150,000 people. You have some concerns that are common to mayors of all American cities: job growth, small business opportunities, crime reduction, tourism, etc. But as a border mayor, you're more sensitive to how safe your city's residents feel in their homes and communities. Just as an example, assume there were one hundred incidents of violent crime in your city in 2011. Then in 2012, due in part to expanded policing and community safety measures, that statistic dropped to sixty incidents of violent crime. Any mayor would be thrilled beyond belief to experience a 40 percent drop in violent crime from one year to the next.

But take this curve ball into account. What if, in 2011, only 10 percent of those one hundred violent crime incidents could be directly attributed to cartel- or drug-related activity, and in 2012, 30 percent of the year's sixty incidents were cartel- or drug-related? You have a significant drop in overall violent crime, but the nature of those crimes has taken a decidedly unsavory and potentially dangerous turn. Which is more important to you as mayor—the fluctuations of violent crime in your border city, or the fundamental nature of those crimes? There is no right or wrong answer to that question, and each and every small town or big city mayor along our southwest border has to find his or her own answer. But the question highlights one of the fundamental problems with trying to determine whether or not spillover is happening at the statistical level: it's almost impossible to capture the nature of a crime with a number or standardized data entry field.

For years I have been providing training on Mexico's drug war to law enforcement officers in the southwest border states, and in the classes where I cover spillover violence, I always ask the same question: *Is there anywhere in your standard police reports or databases where an officer can code or otherwise identify a crime as cartel related?* I have yet to receive a positive answer to that question. That being said, a good number of border- or drug- or cartel-related crimes that happen in the United States involve gang members, and police reports often contain a fair amount of gang-related data, like tattoos and other markings, clothing labels and logos, etc. But if a suspect mentions anything during an interrogation about working for a Mexican cartel, the only place to capture that information is in the narrative portion of a police report—*if* the investigating officer knows what questions to ask to obtain that kind of information. It is not input into any sort of nationally tracked or searchable database where an analyst can search for them, like the FBI's UCR database.

This creates two problems. First, if an agency like DHS or a research outfit like the Congressional Research Service tries to pull crime data from sheriffs' offices and police departments along the southwest border, it will be impossible for them to determine exactly what proportion of violent crime committed in those cities and counties are directly related to cartel activity in the United States. Second, even if some statistical capture mechanism existed that was standardized and searchable, each and every department can classify incidents however they want. One sheriff's office could have fifty cartel-related incidents in a span of a year because that sheriff identifies direct links between suspects and Mexican cartels and categorizes them as spillover. Meanwhile, the sheriff in the county next door believes that all drug-related crimes, cartel-related or not, are just "the drug business as usual," and records them as simple homicides, aggravated assaults, etc.—meaning that county will have zero spillover incidents as long as that sheriff remains in office.

The federal government has acknowledged this absence of data. In May 2011, Grayling Williams, director of the Office of Counternarcotics Enforcement, testified before Congress, "I don't have exact stats or information on, you know, the violence that we're seeing between actual, identified cartel members versus other cartel members."[11] In a 2011 Congressional Research Service report on spillover violence, DHS acknowledged, "[we] don't have exact stats on violence between cartel members [in the US]."[12] If law enforcement officers in the field don't keep track of statistics with possible spillover characteristics, and the federal government doesn't keep track of them, either, then no one can say with any certainty that spillover is or isn't happening by using statistics as evidence.

Going back to the hypothetical mayor scenario, some people might think these kinds of statistical details don't matter as long as overall violent crime levels are declining and Americans living along the border feel safe. But what happens when many of them don't feel safe, and tell harrowing stories of home invasions, kidnappings, armed trespassers, and parking lot shootings—all with likely cartel connections and happening on US soil?

Logic dictates that "border violence spillover" should refer to those instances where Mexican cartel-related violence occurs on US soil. Therefore, the official and standardized definition of border violence spillover should look like this:

Border violence spillover includes any violent act related to drug trafficking activity and committed by an identified member or associate of a Mexican cartel against another cartel member or associate, US law enforcement officer, immigrant, government official, or innocent bystander in the United States.

This definition succinctly encapsulates the fundamental nature of cartel-related violence in Mexico, and therefore what spillover would look like if it happened on US soil. *When it happens on US soil* might be better wording, as there are dozens, if not hundreds, of examples in the last several years.

In late September 2011, Jorge Zavala and an unidentified 22-year-old man were hanging out at the Tex-Mex Lounge strip club in Edinburg, Texas. Around 2:00 A.M., the two of them started to head home in Zavala's SUV. Heading west on an expressway, they suddenly took fire from a Chevrolet Tahoe that had pulled up alongside them. The gunfire caused Zavala to lose control of his SUV and crash. He died at the scene from multiple gunshot wounds, and his companion was taken to a local hospital for serious injuries. The shooters were never caught, but there were several indicators pointing to a likely motive. Zavala had been a close associate of Gulf cartel plaza boss Gregorio "El Goyo" (or "El Metro 2") Sauceda Gamboa, who was arrested by Mexican Federal Police in April 2009. This association linked him to "los Metros," a faction within a divided Gulf cartel that was in the midst of battle with the "Rojos" faction. Sources familiar with Zavala believed the hit was directly tied to the feud between the two camps.[13]

This was certainly not the first time a cartel hit had been carried out in south Texas. In early October 2010, Omar "El Omarcillo" Castillo Flores and Jose Guadalupe López Pérez were riding in a gray Dodge Ram pickup on FM (for farm-to-market road) 511 in the northwest outskirts of Browns-ville, Texas, when they started taking gunfire from behind their truck. They stopped on the median, and their unidentified attackers approached the truck and killed both Castillo and López. The next morning, local police found the shooters' abandoned Chevrolet Silverado pickup with Tamaulipas, Mexico, license plates. Brownsville Police confirmed Mexican law enforcement reports that Castillo and López were members of Los Zetas, and that Castillo was the younger brother of former Gulf cartel member Alberto "Beto Fabe" Castillo Flores. Omar was the younger brother of Oscar "El Apache" Castillo Flores, the head of a Zeta cell operating in Matamoros, Mexico—directly across the border from Brownsville. Oscar and his group belonged to a cell of the Gulf cartel and switched sides to Los Zetas after Gulf cartel leaders had Alberto killed.[14]

While south Texas is arguably one of the hottest spots for this kind of cartel-on-cartel violence in the United States, it's not the only one. In September 2012, Carlos Noe Flores and an unidentified man had planned to sell twenty pounds of marijuana in Phoenix, Arizona. However, the deal went bad when Flores and his associate were robbed of the marijuana at gunpoint. Two days later, they went looking for the dope thieves. But, it seems, Flores started having some suspicions about his associate. According to a police report, while they were driving, Flores told the man he was going to take him to the river and kill him. The man jumped out of the car, and as he did, Flores shot him in the side. After being captured and charged with first-degree murder, Flores admitted to shooting the man with the intent to kill him. He said his boss, who is a member of a Mexican cartel, told him to kill the man or be killed himself.[15]

In another incident, Manuel and his family were just going about their business when they exited a Phoenix Radio Shack one afternoon in February 2009. Then a Latino man approached Manuel, held a gun to his head, and forced him to get into a Ford Expedition parked close by. Manuel's wife noticed another man in a Chrysler sedan with some kind of rifle pointed in their direction. Witnesses said shots were fired at some point during the abduction, but no one was hit and the vehicles took off with Manuel inside. The kidnappers contacted Manuel's wife, told her he owed them a drug debt, and demanded $1 million and his Cadillac Escalade as ransom. Two men, both illegal immigrants from Mexico, later tried to retrieve the Escalade and were apprehended. They told Phoenix police they'd been paid by a man with high-level drug connections to drive the vehicle to Tucson, Arizona. Lt. Lauri Burgett of the department's home invasion and kidnapping squad told *Newsweek*, "[Manuel was] a drug dealer, and he lost a load. He was probably brought to Mexico to answer for that."[16] While Manuel's ultimate fate is unknown, he was never seen in Phoenix again.

These incidents—just a miniscule sample of the kind occurring regularly along parts of the border—all have a clear connection to Mexican cartels and drug trafficking activity, which makes them easy to classify as likely episodes of spillover. But the local newspapers along the border are filled with incidents that reek of cartel activity, but are never publicly and explicitly connected to cartels. For example, in October 2012, a family of three in an SUV, including an eleven-year-old boy, stopped at an intersection in San Juan, Texas, just before 5:00 A.M. Before they could continue, three men approached them from the east and crossed in front of their vehicle. One of the men pulled out a gun and fired a round into the car. The bullet penetrated the passenger's side window, hit the driver's arm, and exited out the driver's side window. The driver was able to pull away and drive to the closest police station, and the family was taken to the hospital for treatment.[17]

So many questions arise from this brief news story: Who were the three men, and why did they shoot at that vehicle at that location at that time of day? Were they gang members? Was it a cartel hit? Who was the driver, and did he have any connections to the drug trade? Was it just a random act of violence by some men who wanted to carjack a nice SUV? San Juan is a small town of only thirty-three thousand people with a population that's 95 percent Latino. As an analyst, I look at this incident and think, *That* had *to be an intentional hit,* based on the time, location, and methodology atypical of a standard carjacking. Any number of conclusions can be drawn from the circumstances, but none of them can be proven solely by the information made available to the public.

In another unproven example, in late December 2012, a group of men stormed into a party in a Mission, Texas, home in the middle of the night with loaded rifles. The men kidnapped the homeowner and forced him into a car. Before fleeing the scene, they killed one of the other men there. Police later found the homeowner, alive and in one piece, in the trunk of the captors' abandoned car, and the three attackers were identified and charged with capital murder. However, they remain at large, and their motive remains unclear.[18] Again, the questions pop up: Who were the attackers and the men at the party? What were the criminal affiliations, if any, of the kidnap and murder victims? What did the attackers want, and did they work for a gang or Mexican cartel? This is another incident that was duly recorded in statistics as a kidnapping and a homicide, and is likely reflected in the UCR database.

In a perfect example of anecdotal evidence of spillover violence, Texas Agriculture Commissioner Todd Staples debuted a sixteen-video series in August 2012 consisting of interviews with Texas ranchers, residents, and law enforcement officials. Each video addresses the incursions and threats—real or perceived—posed by illegal immigrants and armed drug traffickers trespassing on ranchlands and causing damage all along the way. The roughly two-minute videos, called The Texas Traffic Series, are compelling. In the first video, Othal Brand from the Hidaldo County Water Improvement District 3 recounts an incident in July 2011 when two of his employees working on a pump station were nearly shot by men firing at them from across the Rio Grande in Mexico. They called Border Patrol, who responded but has no record of the incident. Border Patrol officers did tell the workers, however, that they were free to carry firearms on the job to protect themselves.[19]

The main impact of the videos, however, isn't necessarily the information being relayed by the interviewees. There is no doubt the ranchers are angry and the officials are frustrated. The videos lend a key visual aspect to their claims, showing the exact places on the ranches and along the border where these trespassing and shooting incidents occurred. The videos enable non-locals to visualize just how close to the border these things are happening, and how emotional and incredibly upset their fellow citizens have become over this situation.

This being said, there a few downsides to the presentation of anecdotal evidence of spillover violence, particularly in the media. The vast majority of incidents that could be classified as spillover never make it out of local media outlets, which tend to avoid sensationalizing border violence. When an incident does make it into the national news cycle, it can sometimes be made out to sound like armies of drug traffickers are barreling across millions of acres of US territory on a daily basis. Seeing the number of burglaries or aggravated assaults connected to the drug trade that occur in south Texas in a month on a piece of paper may be mildly discouraging to some. But seeing each and every incident reported at the national level on a regular basis by some outlets might be enough to have people calling for the US Army to be sent down to the border.

Another downside is the "telephone effect." Many of the stories told by ranchers and residents aren't of events they've actually witnessed or of crimes that have been committed against them. In July 2011, a Texas rancher told NPR, "What I heard is that they had killed a lady on the Old Mines Road, going towards Laredo, over like, a retaliation. They beheaded her, I mean, they cut her head off." No such incident has been publicly recorded. Other stories deemed false by local law enforcement include one of an American oilfield worker attacked and decapitated by immigrants who wanted his pickup, and another of a ranch outside of Laredo, Texas, taken over by members of Los Zetas.[20] These types of stories continue to circulate and augment the sense of tension and fear in some border communities.

Sheriff Mark Dannels in Cochise County, Arizona, told me anyone would be foolish to believe spillover isn't happening. "The people in Washington DC aren't living the problem," he said. "I can't say that enough."[21] Sheriff Richard Wiles in El Paso County, Texas, confirmed, "There's definitely spillover . . . You have drugs that come this way, and you have to deal with those issues. Luckily for us, a lot of those drugs don't stay here, but spillover violence definitely does happen, and much of it we don't even know about."[22]

How can the opposing sides of the debate over border violence spillover ever hope to come together? Actually, that's a huge part of the problem; the people who comprise the two sides aren't really trying to find common ground. Secretary Napolitano and various high-ranking DHS officials make occasional visits to the southwest border, the sheriffs and ranchers in the region have their own associations, and other law enforcement agencies have task forces and working groups. But there has yet to be a national-level summit or conference where representatives from all of these stakeholder groups are in the same place at the same time to hash out their different perspectives.

Does Janet Napolitano really know what it's like to live and work on a Texas cattle ranch only yards from the border with Mexico, and subsequently have to deal with broken fences, stolen trucks, dead cattle, and burglarized homes as a result of immigrant and drug trafficker activity? Do "border hawk" sheriffs know about the long days and nights DHS officials and staff members have to slug through just to squeeze a few thousand dollars out of Congress for a handful of night vision goggles for one or two Border Patrol sectors? Do border residents know about cartel hits happening in their communities, or what their local law enforcement agencies are doing to prevent innocent people from getting hurt in such situations?

In many cases, the answer is probably "no." No one can even begin to approach the challenge of defining spillover violence without hearing—and sufficiently acknowledging—all the different points of view that so many different border security players can bring to the table in such a forum. Once this is accomplished, maybe our officials and officers can start working together, instead of against each other in the media spotlight, to acknowledge that the truth about spillover lies somewhere in the middle of "it's a war zone" and "to my knowledge, it's not happening."

Anyone in this process with a public voice also needs to take more responsibility for the messages they send to border residents and the American people. The border is huge, and it is ignorant and irresponsible to try to categorize the security situation along the border as one homogenous problem. There's nothing wrong with saying El Paso and San Diego are very safe cities to live in and visit; they are. But there also needs to be nothing wrong with acknowledging that south Texas and parts of Arizona are hot spots for smuggling and violent cartel activity that needs to be dealt with because that activity could pose a danger to innocent Americans.

From the federal end, DHS needs to say, "Okay, cities A, B, and C are good to go. What do we need to do to help reduce cartel-related violence in towns X, Y, and Z?" From the local end, mayors and sheriffs who are not seeing spillover issues in their cities and counties need to reach out to areas that are seeing those problems to offer suggestions for success or lessons learned. More oversight and proper allocation of resources needs to occur with regards to these grants so that areas with higher rates of cartel-related violence receive the funds they need. All of this, of course, is predicated on the notion that these stakeholders can all play off the same sheet of music when it comes to defining and identifying border violence spillover.

CHAPTER 6

THE EVOLUTION OF CROSS-BORDER MIGRATION

Illegal immigration is bankrupting states along the border, but this is about more than economics—we're placing our national security at risk.[1]

—Jim Gilchrist, founder of the Minuteman Project, February 2006

If you think drug dealers and terrorists are much more dangerous than maids and gardeners, then we should get as many visas as possible to those people, so we can focus on the real threat.[2]

—David Shirk, director, Trans-Border Institute at the University of San Diego, December 2011

Few Americans have ever lived the experience of traveling from their home country to a foreign land in the back of a truck over the course of several days, and sometimes weeks, confined like sardines with dozens of other migrants. Fewer still have ever strapped themselves to the side of a freight train to keep from falling off and getting sliced up on the tracks as they nodded off for a few minutes of sleep. Yet, these are typical journeys for millions of migrants trying to come to the United States from Central and South America every year.

In August 2010, seventy-three such migrants were traveling north through Mexico in the back of two freight trucks. Some had paid up to $10,000 for safe passage to Texas through eastern Mexico, believing their coyotes, or paid human smugglers, knew this to be the safest route. Unfortunately, this route would take them through Tamaulipas state, the bloody battlefield of the rival Gulf and Los Zetas cartels. By the time they arrived in the town of San Fernando, roughly ninety miles from the US border, they knew they were getting close. But they didn't know about men like El Kilo.

When Los Zetas took over control of San Fernando, the cartel's leadership put Salvador Alfonso "La Ardilla" Martínez Escobedo in charge of the town. Martínez, in turn, put two cartel lieutenants in charge of overseeing day-to-day operations. One of these lieutenants was Martin Omar "El Kilo" Estrada Luna. Estrada had been a member of the Norteños gang in California and served time for breaking and entering, as well as for weapons charges. He was described by the police as "a narcissist and extremely violent." After being deported to Mexico, he went to work for the Zetas as a drug mule, and worked his way up the ladder to eventually oversee the drug distribution network in Reynosa in northeastern Tamaulipas.[3]

Then Los Zetas sent Estrada to San Fernando to ensure members of the Gulf cartel didn't take control of the area. In order to do this, Estrada enacted several harsh security measures: he implemented a curfew, hired young lookouts, and placed most of the police force on the Zetas payroll. But the harshest of these measures was the scrutiny of bus and commercial vehicle passengers on their way through town. El Kilo believed that all young men on their way to the border were either working for the Gulf cartel already or potential recruits for the Zetas's rivals. Estrada's people would routinely pull passengers off buses, interrogate them, and scroll through their cell phone messages. Anyone who didn't pass muster and left some suspicion in El Kilo's mind would be executed on the spot. It was into this environment that these seventy-three migrants entered on a fateful August day.[4]

At some point in the afternoon, the trucks were about nine miles north of San Fernando on Highway 101 when they came across a roadblock. Armed men wearing facemasks emerged from three vehicles parked across the road and identified themselves as members of Los Zetas. The men ordered all the migrants out of the freight trucks, put them into several pickup trucks, and took them to a warehouse on an abandoned ranch nearby. In all, fifty-eight men and fourteen women were lined up against a wall in the warehouse and interrogated about where they came from, where they were going, what they did for a living, and if they worked for the Gulf cartel. All of them denied having any links to trafficking organizations.[5]

Not completely satisfied with their answers, El Kilo's men offered the migrants one last chance—they could work for Los Zetas as forced labor. All of them refused. In reply to their refusal, the captors ordered the migrants to lie face down on the ground, then executed them with several rounds from assault rifles. To ensure everyone was dead, the men delivered a final shot into the head of every migrant. However, one of those coup de grâce shots went astray and caught eighteen-year-old Ecuadorean migrant Luis Fredy Lala Pomavilla in the neck instead of in the head. Despite being in a massive amount of pain from the bullet, which exited through his jaw, he played dead until his captors left the ranch.[6]

What happened next has been debated for more than two years, because Luis's account of events that day differed in many ways from the Mexican government's story—or cover-up.[7] It also took almost that long for the fearful residents of San Fernando to start sharing their recollections with the intrepid journalists who finally felt it was safe enough to travel to this trafficker-infested town. But despite the debate, this is the most likely account of what happened to the lone survivor of the San Fernando massacre.

After the Zetas left the ranch, the Ecuadorean teenager ran. He first followed a gravel road for several miles, then headed north when he saw a light on a utility pole across from a sorghum warehouse and cattle inspection station. The watchman on duty that night told Luis he couldn't help him, but directed him toward a Mexican marine checkpoint on Federal Highway 101; he just had to keep going south. Luis managed to run or walk over twelve miles from the abandoned farm shed to the checkpoint, after his stopover at the warehouse.[8]

After Luis told the marines what happened, they dispatched several helicopters to the ranch to investigate. The helicopters took fire from members of Los Zetas on the ground, and one marine and three cartel gunmen died in the exchange. Because night was falling, the marines withdrew to Matamoros, regrouped, and headed back out to the ranch with reinforcements the next day. Once the marines made it to the site of the massacre, they discovered the seventy-two bodies exactly as Luis had described. They also seized twenty-one firearms and detained a minor, most likely associated with the cartel.[9] Estrada and his people avoided the marine raid, and hid out in nearby Ciudad Victoria for several months. However, he and eleven of his accomplices were arrested in April 2011, although his boss, Salvador "La Ardilla" Martínez, remained at large.[10]

This wasn't the first time migrants had been targeted by cartels in Mexico. Shortly after the discovery of the bodies, the Mexican government confirmed at least seven cases of cartels kidnapping groups of migrants. Based on data collected between September 2008 and February 2009, the National Human Rights Commission claimed roughly 1,600 migrants are being kidnapped in Mexico every month. In a 2011 study, the Commission estimated that 11,333 migrants were kidnapped between April 2010 and September 2010 in 214 different events. These statistics shouldn't be accepted as gospel, considering they're based on Commission visits to shelters, churches, and other community centers, and some of the incidents are likely duplicates. However, they're the only remotely reliable statistics currently available, and serve to give a decent ballpark figure.[11]

The interference from drug cartels in long-established patterns of northbound migration has completely changed the environment in which people in Latin America migrate north to the US border. Cross-border migration has become a very dangerous business controlled by cartels in Mexico, and our border agencies are now dealing with the gray area where drug smuggling and human smuggling overlap. Further complicating the issue, border security policies and immigration laws have not kept up with this evolution. Illegal immigration can no longer be viewed as an economic symptom or inconvenience, and migrants coming to the United States to flee drug war violence or just to find work can definitely not be viewed as threats to our national security. The inability to successfully manage illegal immigration at the policy level instead of through law enforcement is putting more migrants in harm's way and compromising the effectiveness of our agents and officers to stop truly bad people.

The history of cross-border migration from Mexico and beyond goes back over a century and a half. Between 1850 and 1880, roughly fifty-five thousand Mexicans migrated to the United States for various reasons, including to mine during the Gold Rush and work on farms and railroads. By the late 1800s, roughly 60 percent of railway working crews were Mexican. This trend continued into the early 1900s, particularly after the end of the Mexican Revolution in 1910 and the beginning of World War I, when much of American labor was overseas fighting a war and people were needed at home to do their jobs. Cross-border migration had grown enough by that point that a US Border Patrol was created in 1924, and the term "illegal immigrant" was first coined.[12]

The same wartime labor shortage occurred in the United States during World War II, and once again Mexican immigrants crossed our southwest border in droves to fill those gaps. This time, the immigration flow was regulated through the Bracero Program, through which around four million Mexican workers were provided with contracts to legally work on US farms and ranches. After the war ended, however, Americans returned from serving overseas and wanted their old jobs back. Slowly the *braceros* became displaced from legal jobs, and over the years the number of Mexican workers coming to the United States to work illegally grew significantly. The distaste for illegal immigration also grew, and that, combined with a civil rights movement that viewed the program as exploitative and the increased use of mechanized harvesting, reduced the interest in keeping the program going. As a result, the Bracero Program officially ended in 1964.[13]

Illegal immigration continued after 1964, despite a growing presence of US law enforcement along the border and new legislation that tightened up immigration controls. The flow of migrants across international borders is often driven by economic circumstances, and historically that has been the major force behind the ebb and flow across our own southwest border. The passage of the North American Free Trade Agreement (NAFTA) in 1994 and the collapse of the housing bubble and banking industry are two examples of major shifts in the American economy that had a direct impact on the availability of jobs attractive to illegal immigrants.

In the 1990s, three operations helped reduce illegal border crossings: Operation Hold the Line in El Paso in 1992, Operation Gatekeeper in San Diego in 1994, and Operation Rio Grande in 1997 in the McAllen sector in South Texas. All three operations significantly increased Border Patrol agent presence in these areas and called for some sort of physical barrier placement or reinforcement, like lighting and cameras. Veteran Border Patrol official J. William Carter confirmed that "due to efforts in the nineties, entries into the United States decreased . . . [and] at those fortified borders where additional agents were placed, such as San Diego, CA and El Paso TX, apprehensions decreased significantly."[14]

Then two major events transpired after the new millennium that would completely alter how the US government viewed cross-border migration, as well as how Mexican and other Latin American immigrants would experience it: 9/11 and the start of Mexico's drug war.

The extraordinary push for border security and counterterrorism support from Mexico and Canada after the 9/11 attacks was felt most strongly by immigrants themselves, mostly in the form of an increased presence of Border Patrol agents and the National Guard troops assisting them. The creation of DHS in 2003 threw everyone for a loop as members of more than a dozen now-unified US agencies tried to figure out where they fit, and potential immigrants tried to figure out what their options were for entering the United States, both legally and illegally.

Everyone in America was suddenly terrified that our porous southwest border could be used to smuggle a dirty bomb or al-Qa'ida operatives who wanted to conduct another terrorist attack on US soil. Reports started emerging about the possibility of Middle Eastern men who could pass as Latino studying Spanish in South America and using fake identity documents to enter the United States. A new category of illegal immigrants was created, called

"Special Interest Aliens" (SIAs), to identify individuals from almost three dozen countries who either supported or had ties to terrorist activity. More attention was paid to migrants with nationalities "Other Than Mexican" (OTM), and there were unexplained increases in apprehensions of people from places like Albania or Bangladesh.

While DHS tried to figure out the best way to increase scrutiny of immigrants at both our northern and southern borders and still facilitate cross-border trade, something very menacing was growing in Mexico. Mexican and US law enforcement were all of a sudden challenging drug cartels that had operated with little government interference for decades. Some cartels, in order to hedge against any loss of profit stemming from drug seizures, decided to get more involved in the human smuggling business. This made sense in many ways, as human smuggling organizations often use the same northbound routes as cartels and have to pay some sort of tax or toll (known as *piso*) to the managing cartel to ensure their safe passage to the border. The primary negative consequence of the human smuggling business becoming more organized and directed from the top down by greedy drug traffickers was that migrants now had to pay coyotes exorbitant fees to get smuggled across the border. What once used to cost only a few hundred dollars now costs between a few thousand to tens of thousands of dollars, depending on where a migrant is coming from and how he or she plans to get across.

But the financial costs are no longer the only concern for ambitious would-be border crossers. Now cartels like Los Zetas, the CDG, the Sinaloa Federation, and other criminal groups in Mexico are actively preying upon hapless migrants who have little money and no way to physically defend themselves. The San Fernando massacre was just one example of migrants being forced into debt or servitude on penalty of death; many more abound, although admittedly some of the only evidence of these incidents is anecdotal. Even though the reporting of murders, kidnappings, rapes, and abuse of migrants in Mexico by gangs and cartel members has increased, relatively little is known about how organized crime groups manage human smuggling operations or the exact extent of the violence inflicted upon their charges. Much of the time, we have to rely on stories being told by people like Luis Fredy Lala Pomavilla. However, we do know that human smuggling is a $6 billion a year business in Latin America alone, although that figure still pales in comparison to the roughly $15-$25 billion cartels are bringing in annually from drug trafficking.[15]

And this is just the organized side of what human smuggling has become in Mexico; there is additional money to be made by cartel and gang members who hold migrants hostage for ransom, or extort those not using a coyote for obscenely high safe-passage fees. There is also a huge advantage for cartels that force migrants to work as slave labor during border crossings. In exchange for passage into the United States, migrants can be forced to carry drugs on their backs, to become mules for the cartels.

Elizabeth Rogers, a federal public defender in West Texas, has said most of her recent "backpacker" cases claim coercion. "About a year and a half ago, ourselves as well as our investigators started seeing these clients that would say, *I don't care how long I'm going to get [in jail time], I can't go home—they'll kill me*," she told NPR in 2011. "[We] have grown men, rawboned cowboy guys from Chihuahua, begging for protection from deportation." Raúl Miranda, a criminal defense attorney in Tucson, Arizona, has said about one-third of his clients have claimed they were unwilling drug mules. "They're told by the people—who obviously work for the cartels—that they have to carry the bundle, and they'll reduce the fee that they're going to have to pay, or they'll forgive the fee. But the people who are telling them this are armed, and the people feel threatened if they say no."[16]

This trend of coerced smuggling is indicative of a larger development in Mexico's drug war. "I think the US government has made it harder for smugglers from Mexico to use some of the traditional [drug trafficking] means and methods such as loaded cars, crossing on foot through the desert, etc.," explained Dr. Howard Campbell, professor of Anthropology at the University of Texas at El Paso. "Consequently, smugglers are increasingly relying on new forms of deception and subterfuge such as the coerced migrant smugglers." Campbell also added that this kind of forced labor lowers the overhead costs for cartels, since migrants likely won't be paid as much (if at all), and are completely expendable if they're apprehended by law enforcement.[17]

This shift in the nature of northbound migration and the way that cartels smuggle illegal drugs into the United States poses a big challenge to the Border Patrol and other law enforcement officers who encounter these migrants. How do they know if these migrants are telling the truth? Were they really forced at gunpoint or under the threat of harm to their families to smuggle drugs? Or did they voluntarily accept the grueling job for a handsome payout on the other side of the border? In 2011, Border Patrol Agent David Jimarez said of the shift in tactics, "There's less traffic, but traffic that's there is more threatening." The late Sheriff Larry Dever of Cochise County in Arizona added, "The guys smuggling people and narcotics now are more sinister."[18]

The threats posed to migrants by cartels and criminal gangs don't stop at coerced drug smuggling. Central and South American migrants headed north must cross the dangerous border between Guatemala and Mexico, and many congregate in the southern Mexican city of Tapachula in Chiapas state to hop on a freight train. These trains are collectively known as *La Bestia*, or "The Beast," for their size and the dangers associated with using them as free transportation to northern Mexico. In addition to the risk of death from falling off the train, migrants are routinely robbed, assaulted, extorted, and raped by roving gangs and cartel members looking to make a quick buck.

The danger continues even after these migrants cross the border. Routes in southern Arizona and south Texas are every bit as unforgiving as those in Mexico, and the rising annual death toll of illegal immigrants is a testament to that fact. In 2012 in the Rio Grande Valley of Texas alone, US authorities made 310 rescues and found 150 bodies, which was nearly double the numbers from 2011.[19] Temperatures along the border in the summer can reach 110 degrees and drop down to the thirties in the winter, and there is very little clean water available.

In the human smuggling "home base" of Altar, Mexico, female migrants stock up on birth control because they know the odds are good they'll be raped at least once during their journey. This is evident by the rape trees that dot the southern Arizona landscape, where coyotes assault their female charges and hang their undergarments like trophies. Those about to embark on the deadly journey can also find backpacks, water jugs, clothing, and almost any other item to try to make the trip north a bit easier at open air markets in the town square.

Few Americans even remotely understand what the process of crossing the US-Mexico border is like, with or without a guide. For that matter, many Mexican and Central and South American migrants are misled by their coyotes into believing the journey will be much shorter and much easier than it actually turns out to be. Acclaimed journalist and television producer Christof Putzel decided he wanted to follow in the footsteps of these migrants to see for himself what it was like to make this arduous trip.

In November 2010, the now-defunct cable channel Current TV aired an episode of its Vanguard documentary series titled "Life and Death on the Border," where Putzel and Mexican-American filmmaker Juan Carlos Frey recorded their attempt to smuggle themselves across the southwest border in a manner as close as possible to that of hundreds of thousands of migrants every year. Putzel and Frey decided to head to Altar so they could stock up on supplies and find a coyote willing to take them to the predetermined destination of Tucson, Arizona. A man selling border crossing supplies at a booth in the town square gave Putzel several suggestions for what to take with him, as well as a sobering warning: watch out for snakes, scorpions, and bandits who would be more than happy to rob you, beat you, or even kill you. Buying supplies and getting free advice was easy; finding a willing coyote was not.

"What was nuts is that, when we initially planned to shoot this, we thought we would just get some 'mom and pop' coyote operation, and those things don't exist anymore. The cartels run the show," Putzel told me about his experience. "So we needed to get permission from the cartels to do this [show]. Part of the deal was, they would be okay with us doing it as long as we only talked about migrants and didn't mention anything about drug trafficking. They really didn't want us reporting on that at all."[20] He enlisted a local priest to help him and Frey find a coyote willing to guide them.

Despite the fact that the priest arranged for them to meet with several coyotes, none they met with at first were interested in smuggling them north, and even more refused to meet with them at all because they were worried Putzel and Frey might be police officers. When they did find a smuggler interested in taking the job, the guide was still apprehensive, worrying that Border Patrol agents might be able to spot their camera. His pre-departure "briefing" didn't exactly reassure Putzel; the planned route he described was taken by some and not by others, meaning it was likely a risky one. The terrain was mostly through canyons, and the hike would take roughly three days in triple-digit heat with no natural water sources on the way.

Before actually heading out on foot, the journalists had to take a seventy-five-mile ride to the border in a van with broken windows, no seats, no shocks, and no air conditioning—the same van ride tens of thousands of northbound migrants take every year at a cost of $140. They had hoped to make the three-day trip with a large group of people to document a more "real" experience, but they found themselves almost alone in a van that could pack up to thirty people on the metal I-beam benches. Their only company was one other migrant and his coyote.

During the drive, Frey gave Putzel a heads-up that they were approaching a cartel checkpoint where they might see people with guns. Frey had to turn off the camera as they passed through the checkpoint, where they saw five men wearing black facemasks and carrying AK-47s. After getting cleared, they continued to their drop-off point. Five hours after departing Altar and under cover of night, Putzel, Frey, and their coyote, named José, were now about a quarter of a mile south of the border. They stopped in a cow pasture with nearby small buildings that served as a holding point for border crossers—a last-ditch place to rest and buy supplies. Eight hours later, at 4:00 A.M., José told them to grab their stuff because it was time to start the crossing. "We were carrying the same thing the migrants carry: a few pairs of socks, one change of clothes, and two gallons of water," Putzel narrated. "It isn't enough for three days in the desert, but it was all we could carry."[21]

The coyote set the pace of "walk hard for an hour, then rest." It got tiring soon after starting, partly due to the weight of the pack and water and partly due to the unstable sandy terrain. During the brief pit stop, José told Putzel they only had about ninety minutes left of walking before crossing the border and starting the two-day trek to Tucson, or so they thought; the march stretched out into hours. As the sun rose higher in the sky, Putzel and Frey started to crave water. They had been hiking for half a day and gingerly crossing through barbed wire fences as the temperature started to climb to one hundred and ten degrees. Putzel didn't know if they had actually crossed into Arizona or just someone's ranch on the Mexican side. He was having a hard time keeping up with his guide.

Putzel finally saw the border fence in the distance, but José started taking them west instead of north. He kept saying they would just walk past the border cameras and then cross, but that wasn't happening. Frey couldn't understand why they would rest during the coolest parts of the day and hike during the hottest times. The small group finally laid up in a shady spot were other migrants had clearly done the same, based on the trash they left behind. They had been walking for sixteen hours and half their water was gone. Then the situation started to deteriorate rapidly.

"[Frey] actually got dehydration sickness and went a little batty," Putzel said. "That was rough. We had this idea that we'd need a certain amount of water for a certain amount of days, it was already going to be really tough, and I was trying to calculate everything. But we were walking right along the borderline for quite a long time before crossing the border in the freakin' desert. That place is huge! That's when we started to realize this is going to be tougher than we thought." Frey, in his dehydration-induced paranoia and frustration, wanted to ditch their guide and head out on their own. Putzel said, "I was thinking, *Dude, that's how people die!* Unfortunately, our guide was the only person we could rely on. [Frey] wanted to make a run for it, and I thought, *Run where?!* He just kept acting kooky and had run out of water, and that's when things got really bad, really fast."[22]

As the sun started to set, José finally decided they would make their move and cross. They easily ducked under the metal poles of the vehicle barrier and crossed (without inspection, for the record) into Arizona. "We're in the US; we're in Arizona," Putzel tells the camera. "It feels like a minor victory. It feels good. But the truth is, we're nowhere close to where we need to go." They spent their second night of the journey in the Arizona desert, sleeping on trash bags they had lined with garlic to keep away scorpions and snakes. The next morning, José told Putzel and Frey he could go no farther. The cartel had allowed José to guide them across the border, but didn't want them seeing their operations north of the border. The guide did point them in the direction of a road he said would take them where they needed to go, but the journalists were now on their own for the rest of the hike to Tucson.

At that point, Putzel and Frey were crossing through a part of Arizona where over one thousand migrants had perished in the previous decade. They started to feel like they knew exactly how that could happen; they began feeling an intense need to just sit down and not move and tried desperately to focus on just putting one foot in front of the other. They had also both run out of water. In searching for the road, they got turned around. There were no major landmarks and everything on the desert landscape looked the same. After finally finding the road, they knew they wouldn't survive if they tried walking any farther, but they also worried their producer wouldn't be able to find them to pick them up. All they knew was that they were on an abandoned ranch somewhere on the Tohono O'odham Nation's reservation.

"Unlike real migrants, we had the luxury of being rescued by our production team," Putzel narrated. As their team's SUV approached them, the looks of relief on their faces at seeing their producer were evident. After reassuring him that they were okay, Putzel and Frey immediately asked for something to drink. Having forgotten that you should sip liquids when suffering from severe dehydration, all the Gatorade they chugged came up just as quickly as it went down. The two journalists then called their wives to tell them they were okay, and those conversations were emotional to say the least. At the time of their rescue, Putzel and Frey were well over sixty miles away from their planned destination of Tucson, Arizona. Had the journalists not been picked up by their producer—that is, had they been actual migrants—they likely would have perished, and their bodies perhaps never found.

Why do so many migrants make this journey knowing the perils that await them? For some, it still is the prospect of a job that will earn them enough money to sustain their family members back home. "It's amazing what people will go through for a *job*, just to try to get work. [Doing this show] is my job, we had the benefit of prepping, and while it wouldn't have been good [if we had gotten caught], we wouldn't have been sent back to Mexico," said Putzel. "Mexicans are very aware that if they do this, they could die, and they see this as their only hope. When you're in a country with so little opportunity and so much violence, they are so desperate. You can only imagine the level of desperation where they're willing to put themselves through this just for the chance to pick strawberries or wash somebody's dishes or clean somebody's house. That's insane, if you really think about it."

But for many others, it's a means to just stay alive. "They are expelled from their countries by fear," said Father Flor Maria Rigoni, an Italian priest who directs the Casa del Migrante shelter in Tapachula, a city in Mexico's southernmost Chiapas state. "They are seeking the possibility to survive. The violence there drives them. The migrants don't talk about the economic situation of the US—they just bet on the future."[23] Even if they successfully navigate the migration gauntlet between their homes and the US-Mexico border, they can still be discovered and deported. In some cases, this is the equivalent of a death sentence.

In the summer of 2009, Laura S. was just another Mexican immigrant living illegally in south Texas. She had three children with Sergio H. (names are shortened for anonymity), who had begun showing some serious violent tendencies. In March 2008, Sergio threatened Laura with a knife, and that was the last straw for her. She subsequently obtained a protective order against him from the McAllen, Texas, municipal court in April 2008. Angered by this, Sergio returned to Reynosa, Mexico—directly across the border from McAllen—and reportedly started working with a drug cartel.[24] Now a different nightmare was about to begin for Laura.

In June 2009, Laura was out with her cousin and two friends around midnight in Pharr, Texas, when an officer from the Texas Department of Public Safety pulled them over for a minor driving infraction. The officer demanded to see all the vehicle occupants' immigration documents, which Laura could not produce. She began to weep and begged the officer to let her go. She was afraid that Sergio would try to kill her if she got deported to Mexico, and she had three small children to care for—one of whom was scheduled for upcoming surgery. Laura also informed the officer about the protective order in place against Sergio. At that point, the officer turned over Laura and the other undocumented women in the car to an unidentified ICE agent, who drove them to a processing center in nearby Harlingen, Texas. She repeated the information about Sergio and her children to the ICE agent transporting them.[25]

At the processing center, several ICE and/or CBP agents processed paperwork on Laura and fingerprinted her. Once more, she repeated her story to all the agents present. According to what Laura told her family members, none of the agents questioned her or performed a credible fear interview. These are routine interviews conducted by agents when an immigrant is afraid of returning to his or her home country for fear of being harmed in some way. Also, none of the agents reportedly explained to Laura that she had the right to an attorney and a hearing before an immigration judge to inform her of her options for relief from removal, like asylum, withholding, or deferral. Instead, after the agents finished processing her and the other two women detained with her, they drove the three of them in the CBP van they arrived in to the Hidalgo/Reynosa international bridge. Laura begged and pleaded the entire way to the bridge, wailing that Sergio would kill her if the agent made her cross the bridge.[26]

The agent forced her to cross the bridge in the early morning hours of June 9, 2009 without placing her into formal removal proceedings, since Laura—unaware of her options for relief—had signed a voluntary departure form. Within a few days, Sergio learned Laura was back in Mexico. Upon finding her, he assaulted her by beating her and biting her ear until it bled profusely. On June 14, Sergio abducted Laura and took her to a Reynosa hotel, where he murdered her and left her body in a burning car. Laura's mother provided her testimony about the incident to police in Mexico, and Sergio was subsequently imprisoned—although available documentation doesn't clearly explain if he was imprisoned for Laura's murder, drug charges, or something else entirely. Regardless, Sergio escaped prison and remains at large today.[27] As a result of these events, Texas Rio Grande Legal Aid and the South Texas Civil Rights Project filed a lawsuit in June 2013 on behalf of the family of "Laura S." against the six unidentified CBP and/or ICE agents who processed her.[28]

The case of Laura S. is just one of hundreds brought before US immigration courts every year where Mexican nationals facing deportation to Mexico are also likely facing a death sentence soon upon arrival. I've worked as an expert witness in dozens of these cases in the last several years, and while the circumstances vary, there are two main categories these immigrants fall into: informants who provided information about cartel activity to US authorities in exchange for a reduced prison sentence (or a promised, but never provided, US visa), or honest people who witnessed illegal cartel activities, refused to work for cartels, or refused to give in to their demands. If they're able to find some legal help, they often apply for asylum. As the violence in Mexico has increased, so has the number of asylum applications filed each year. In 2005, there were 2,670 filed, and that number rose to 2,818 in 2006. By 2010, applications had increased to 3,231, and nearly doubled to 6,133 in fiscal year 2012. However, only 2 percent of requests from Mexico between 2007 and 2011 were granted, compared to 38 percent of requests from Chinese nationals and 89 percent from Armenian applicants.[29]

Unfortunately, while the nature of cross-border migration has changed significantly in the last decade, immigration laws and the guidelines for granting asylum have not. Asylum has historically been associated with the Cold War and communism, and refugees fleeing the political and social oppression imposed on them by tyrants. In decades past, we would hear about "defectors" from places like the Soviet Union, Cuba, and North Korea. Today, China and Cuba are still popular countries for citizens with asylum requests, but US courts are host to more and more applicants from countries like Afghanistan, Iraq, Iran, Somalia, and Pakistan—nations categorized as failed or failing states with governments that can't protect their citizens, and in some cases, are actively oppressing their freedoms and rights.

But it's not enough under US asylum laws to just be an individual suffering at the hands of a government. Applicants have to clearly show they are being persecuted on at least one of five protected grounds: race, religion, nationality, social group, or political opinion. Suffice it to say that some asylum requests are more cut-and-dried than others. Chinese and Cuban nationals, for example, fall under certain laws and provisions that make their admission through asylum cases a bit simpler.

Requesting asylum hasn't really been a popular or necessary option for Mexican immigrants until drug-related violence started spreading in earnest and the ties between government officials, law enforcement officers, and the cartels became stronger and more blatant. In some cases, it's very clear that the Mexican government is unable to provide adequate protection to an asylum applicant, the police are directly involved in the harm being caused, and the local government is obviously looking the other way while it happens. But in other cases, requesting asylum becomes a last-ditch effort by illegal immigrants to avoid deportation when they never would have considered applying if they hadn't gotten caught. This only delays the inevitable and clogs up the already backed-up immigration court system. The appeals process can also cost the family of the applicant a considerable amount of money in legal fees.

Matthew Green is a practicing attorney in Tucson, Arizona, with whom I've worked on a few immigration cases as an expert witness. Unfortunately, he doesn't see any changes on the horizon with regards to asylum law. "I don't see a political fix by the legislative or executive branch, really. What I see is that there might be a decision by one of the circuit courts that would make a change in the case law," he explained. "That's typically how the US government deals with asylum-based relief, unless there is some really acute change in the conditions of a certain country. Under *those* circumstances, the way DHS deals with it is by offering Temporary Protected Status to citizens of that country. And that's exactly what it is; it's temporary. Because they're not making a change in the asylum law forever, that's typically how they'll handle that."[30]

Because immigration law hasn't been modernized to take into account the changed political and security climate in many countries, Mexican asylum case resolution rests completely with immigration judges. In my experience, every immigration judge's views on Mexican immigrants requesting relief from removal are completely unique. Some know a decent amount about what's happening in Mexico and some have no idea. It's very frustrating to try to explain to a judge how corrupt the Mexican government and police are, along with the impact that would have on an applicant's safety, when he doesn't believe the security situation in Mexico is all that bad. The asylum denial rates for judges within the same court can vary wildly, so judicial outcomes can depend completely on the luck of the draw. For example, asylum denials between fiscal years 2007 and 2012 in the Cleveland immigration court ranged from 24.5 percent for Judge John Bryant to 81.9 percent for Judge Thomas Janas.[31]

The obvious solution to this inconsistency is to revamp asylum provisions to take into account the changing security situation in Mexico while preventing as many applicants as possible from taking advantage of the system. However, granting more latitude in how Mexican asylum cases are reviewed could open the floodgates to thousands more illegal border crossers and asylum applications, which would overwhelm a system that's been underwater for decades. In 2009 alone, 237 immigration judges decided more than 390,000 removal cases.[32] "The courts that make the law—the Board of Immigration Appeals and the Circuit Courts of Appeal—have made it very difficult for Mexican immigrants who are claiming asylum to win their cases," Green told me, with no small amount of frustration. "Essentially, unless a Mexican man can show that he is homosexual, transgender, or a snitch, that person can't even pass the threshold or even get in a position to encourage a judge to consider whether or not there will be an asylum-based grant. That's how hard it is."[33]

Officially granting asylum to more immigrants would also be a political hot potato, since it would strongly imply that the Mexican government is at least partly responsible for the harm befalling its citizens at the hands of cartels. Regardless of whether or not that's true, for the US State Department, any legal change that makes Mexico look like the bad guy would be a big diplomatic no-no.

As comprehensive immigration reform plans progress through US political channels, it's important to keep an eye on these little-known asylum provisions and how they might change. There are many Mexican citizens living illegally in the United States who would no doubt be murdered or kidnapped or harmed in some way at the hands of a drug cartel if deported to Mexico. Some of these people are innocents who were in the wrong place at the wrong time, denied the cartels, or had something the cartels wanted. Others are convicted felons who served time in US prisons. But it's just not as simple as many Americans believe to send illegal immigrants back to their home country when they'll probably turn up dead a few days or weeks after their arrival, and often at the hands of that country's police. Dana Leigh Marks, president of the National Association of Immigration Judges, said that now more than ever, "Immigration judges are doing death penalty cases in traffic court settings."[34]

As the drug war continues in Mexico, we can expect to see more migrants crossing the border illegally due to fear rather than the search for economic opportunities. As one asylum applicant stated after her application was denied, "I will not hesitate to stay here illegally. I would rather do that than ever go to Mexico again, even if it means illegal re-entry. It's not that I want to live in the US. I never did. But I cannot go back. I do not want to die."[35]

Somehow, in a clear example of how a lack of legal progress is going to come back to bite the US government, word about the option of requesting asylum managed to spread to immigrants from several countries living or temporarily staying in at least one part of Mexico. In August 2013, two hundred immigrants from Mexico and places like Haiti, Guatemala, Romania, and Iraq showed up at the Otay Mesa, California, port of entry, made claims of "credible fear" and requested asylum.[36] Any time that an immigrant does this, whether it's at a port of entry with a CBP agent or in the middle of the Arizona desert with a Border Patrol agent, everything has to come to a halt. By law, CBP and Border Patrol have to conduct a "credible fear" interview of the immigrant, meaning they have to determine exactly why they're afraid to return to their home country. This process also ensures that, if the immigrant's story meets the credible fear threshold, he or she will have his or her day in court before an immigration judge.

For logistical purposes, it doesn't matter if the claim is real or bogus; the immigrant making the claim has to be processed. So to say that agents at Otay Mesa were unprepared for the onslaught that day is an understatement. Migrants at the processing facility there and at nearby San Ysidro were sleeping on the floor because there wasn't enough room for everyone. ICE management started asking agents to work overtime and volunteer for weekend shifts in order to process everyone. ICE also reserved dozens of hotel rooms in San Diego for the asylum seekers so they would have a place to sleep. Other migrants were released and ordered to show up in court for their immigration hearings, which is a common practice for migrants with no criminal history. According to ICE, between 600,000 and 800,000 illegal immigrants fail to show up for their hearings every year.[37]

On one hand, I completely disagree with the tactics used by the two hundred border crossers at Otay Mesa because many of them—if not all—were exploiting a rule designed for immigrants who are truly being persecuted in their home countries and run the risk of being hurt or killed if returned. This is a process that is already difficult enough for Mexican nationals running to the United States for their lives, and now they run the risk of being discredited because of immigration activists trying to make a political point. On the other hand, DHS and the State Department deserve to have the flaws of our current immigration system put on display. While it was two hundred people in this particular incident, maybe it will be five hundred the next time, or one thousand the time after that. Our federal, state, and local law enforcement agents cannot continue to bear the burden placed on them by having to enforce outdated laws that need to take into account present-day reality.

I come from a family of Cuban immigrants, and I know from listening to their experiences in the 1960s—along with those of Cubans who have taken more dangerous measures to come here—what fear and desperation will drive people to do. I acknowledge that my family was in a different situation; they were able to come here legally under asylum provisions because of Fidel Castro's communist revolution. Despite that, immigration is still extremely dangerous for some Cuban migrants who to try to reach US shores by traveling across the shark-infested Florida Straits on makeshift rafts with little food and water. There are untold Cuban immigrants who have drowned trying to make the ninety-mile journey from Havana to Key West, just as there are untold numbers of Mexican and Central American migrants who have perished in the sand and scrub south of Arizona and Texas.

Whether it's Mexicans, or Cubans, or the Chinese, or Iraqis, foreigners will always want to come to the United States. Most of them will not be able to enter or stay here legally. Because the security situation in Mexico and Central America has deteriorated so badly over the last decade, citizens of those countries are more motivated than ever to run the risks of the northbound journey. And it doesn't matter to them how many Border Patrol agents get assigned to the border, or how many miles of fence we build. This is a concept that is extremely difficult for politicians and individuals in the anti–illegal immigration camp to understand. When a person's livelihood, his safety, and the safety of his children are at risk because of dangerous drug cartels, or when he is unable to feed his family, that individual will do whatever it takes—and as many times as necessary—to survive. Out of 364,768 illegal immigrants apprehended by US Border Patrol in 2012, 100,735 had been previously apprehended at least twice, and 21,684 had been caught at least six times. One hundred and forty-five Mexican citizens had been apprehended by agents at least thirty-five times that year while trying to cross the border illegally.[38]

Maybe twenty years ago it was easier to detect illegal immigrants along our borders, process them, and send them back to their home countries. But now our cross-border traffic has become a blur—a gray area where drug traffickers and migrants blend together and have become more difficult to separate. Given how many resources we could save by focusing law enforcement efforts away from economic migrants and more toward violent criminals crossing illegally, making this distinction has become more crucial than ever. Allowing the illegal immigration issue to be settled at the policy level rather than the enforcement level could save the US government a substantial amount of money, and could ultimately save the lives of thousands of northbound migrants every year.

"If you think drug dealers and terrorists are much more dangerous than maids and gardeners, then we should get as many visas as possible to those people, so we can focus on the real threat," said David Shirk, director of the Trans-Border Institute at the University of San Diego. "Widening the gates would strengthen the walls."[39] To be sure, this is the crux of the ongoing debate over comprehensive immigration reform. But it's clear that as long as the United States is safer than Mexico—which will be the case for the foreseeable future—Mexican and Central American citizens will go to great lengths to come and stay here, no matter what border enforcement actions we take or laws we pass. It's also guaranteed that as long as the American demand for illegal drugs continues, Mexican cartels will exploit every aspect of cross-border migration for their own profit-seeking purposes.

CHAPTER 7

TERRORISM AND THE SOUTHWEST BORDER

These bad guys [cartels] are now routinely coming in very close contact with the likes of Hezbollah, Hamas, Al Qaeda, who are vying for the same money, the same turf and same dollars.... And my point being is, if anyone thinks for a moment that Hezbollah and Qods Force, the masters at leveraging and exploiting existing illicit infrastructures globally, are not going to focus on our southwest border and use that as perhaps a spring board in attacking our country, then they just don't understand how the real underworld works.[1]

—Michael Braun, former DEA operations chief,
Congressional testimony in 2012

There was no evidence of ties between Mexican criminal organizations and terrorist groups, nor that the criminal organizations had aims of political or territorial control, aside from seeking to protect and expand the impunity with which they conduct their criminal activity.... There was no indication that terrorist organizations used Mexico as a conduit for illicit activities.[2]

—US Department of State, 2010 Country Reports on Terrorism

Manssor Arbabsiar was a man who enjoyed the high life. He was born in Iran, but spent much of his childhood in Corpus Christi, a coastal city in South Texas where he then worked selling used cars. Arbabsiar had three weaknesses: women, whiskey, and expensive cars, and it seemed like the last two got him a considerable amount of the first. He told a psychiatrist during an interview that he couldn't count the number of women he slept with, and that he rarely slept with the same woman twice.[3] The fifty-seven-year-old with the piercing blue eyes and bushy mustache definitely lived as if he had few cares in his world.

Despite Arbabsiar's low-key job and carefree social life, he had very sinister connections in his country of birth. His cousin was a high-ranking member of the Iranian Qods Force, which is a special unit within the Iranian Revolutionary Guard Corps—essentially the army—responsible for extra-territorial operations, including terrorist operations and training.[4] In early spring 2011, Arbabsiar went to Iran and met with his cousin, who told him he was working on a plan to kidnap or kill the Saudi Arabian ambassador to the United States. Arbabsiar didn't blink when his cousin told him this. In fact, he thought he could help because he traveled frequently across the border into Mexico and knew people he thought were drug traffickers—and possibly contract killers. His cousin thought about that and found it useful. He told Arbabsiar to hire someone in the narcotics business to do the job.[5]

Arbabsiar got to work right away. Both his cousin and his cousin's deputy in the Qods Force, Gholam Shakuri, provided him with thousands of dollars to cover his expenses during the search. He then reached out to one of his many female conquests, who in May 2011 put him in touch with a drug dealer in Mexico. But this dealer was no average drug hawker; he was employed by the vicious Los Zetas cartel, capable of committing the worst imaginable atrocities. Arbabsiar met with the dealer twice in July 2011 in Reynosa, Mexico, which is directly across the border from McAllen, Texas. He passed on his cousin's instructions, and told the dealer the job needed to be done fast. He then waited expectantly. To Arbabsiar's relief, the dealer agreed to do the job for $1.5 million.[6]

The plan came together quickly. Arbabsiar and the dealer plotted—together with the cousin, Shakuri, and other Qods force associates in Iran—for the dealer to travel to Washington, DC, and blow up a restaurant while the ambassador was dining there. Arbabsiar later returned to Iran, where he met with his cousin and Shakuri to relay the plan. They also agreed to provide the dealer with $100,000 as a down payment. Arbabsiar promised the dealer that if he succeeded in killing the ambassador, the dealer could count on several future contracts with Arbabsiar and Co. The dealer did have some concerns—namely the collateral damage that would result from the deaths of many Americans either dining in the same restaurant or walking nearby. The cousin also preferred that no innocent bystanders be killed, but Arbabsiar assured him, "Sometimes, you know, you have no choice."[7]

For all of Arbabsiar's rush to complete the job, his cousin wasn't in a similar rush to pay the dealer. Arbabsiar tried to reassure the dealer by explaining the Iranian government was supporting his cousin, and paying him was just a matter of clearing up some red tape. In early August 2011, Arbabsiar finally sent the dealer his full down payment in two separate transfers from an overseas bank, through a US bank in New York, and into the dealer's account. But the dealer wasn't happy with that; he demanded Arbabsiar either pay half the full amount of $1.5 million or travel personally to Mexico as human collateral. This was actually typical of underworld contracts like assassinations, so Arbabsiar agreed to the trip in lieu of the additional payment. Little did he know he would never make it beyond the airport.[8]

On September 28, 2011, Manssor Arbabsiar was denied entry into Mexico and detained by authorities until he was put on a plane to New York City the next day. He was extremely nervous, not eating or watching the movie during the flight. His only thought on the five-hour trip was, "I'm finished." He would have been even more frantic had he known that an undercover FBI agent was watching him the whole time. As soon as he landed, FBI agents arrested him and took him to a nearby hotel to be interrogated. Although he waived his rights to an attorney and agreed to speak to the agents, he was initially not forthcoming with any details about the plot.[9]

But then agents pulled out their trump card: dozens of recorded conversations between Arbabsiar and the dealer, talking about the plot. It turned out the dealer wasn't a member of Los Zetas after all; he was a confidential informant working for the DEA. Arbabsiar's carefree life was over.

When the details of the plot were publicly revealed, both American and Iranian officials were furious. US Attorney General Eric Holder said the plot was "conceived, sponsored and was directed from Iran" by a faction of the government, and called it a "flagrant" violation of US and international law. FBI Director Robert Mueller said in an announcement that the United States would "bring the full weight of [the] law to bear on those responsible" and that "any attempts on American soil will not be tolerated." White House officials toned down the rhetoric somewhat by acknowledging they had no information indicating that either Iranian Supreme Leader Ayatollah Ali Khamenei or President Mahmoud Ahmadinejad necessarily knew about the assassination plot. On Iranian news outlets, government officials rejected the charges, calling the plot a "prefabricated scenario" and the start of a "new propaganda campaign against Iran."[10]

While the intent of Arbabsiar, his cousin, and his cousin's Qods Force associates was very real, the plot itself was proving to be very bizarre. Some media outlets, bloggers, and conspiracy theorists started pointing to it as evidence that terrorists and Mexican cartels were working together to carry out terrorist acts on US soil. Thomas Donnelly wrote on *The Weekly Standard*'s website that "perhaps the most disturbing aspect of the story is that Iran's thugs are developing a strategic partnership with Mexico's most violent thugs," and that "we underestimate the Qods-Zeta partnership at our peril."[11]

But as time passed, more and more people started realizing just how unlikely it was that this particular plot would have ever gotten off the ground. The key to this whole plan was the cooperation of a Mexican cartel—in this case, Los Zetas. Arbabsiar and his people made a big and amateur mistake in assuming that any Mexican cartel would be willing to undertake such a herculean and inherently risky task for the paltry sum of $1.5 million. The United Nations estimates that cartels make as much as $40 billion annually from a combination of drug trafficking, kidnapping for ransom, extortion, and other criminal activities. Just one drug load of cocaine or methamphetamine seized at a US port of entry can be worth $1.5 million or more, and cartels take the occasional loss of such loads into account as an overhead expense—the cost of doing business on the black market. Cartels are also very hesitant to kill their own people on US soil, let alone foreign dignitaries, preferring to conduct "domestic" assassinations on Mexican soil after the target has been kidnapped and brought south of the border.

So why would anyone believe Los Zetas, or any other cartel, would be willing to enter into such an agreement with the Iranians, or some Middle Eastern terrorist group? And why would these Iranians in particular think this plot was such a great idea?

The answer has many parts, but fundamentally, Mexican cartels have little interest in aligning themselves with terrorist groups for operational purposes. Tim Padgett wrote in *Time* magazine, "If Iranian government operatives really did try to contract a Mexican drug cartel to assassinate the Saudi ambassador to the United States, as the Obama Administration alleges today, then they weren't just being diabolical. They were being fairly stupid." Journalist Ioan Grillo told Padgett, "For the Zetas, political murder is done concretely to protect their own business interests inside Mexico. It's just not their modus operandi to carry out political murders in the US."[12]

Kenneth Katzman, a specialist in Middle East affairs for the Congressional Research Service, explained why the Iranian government likely knew little about the plot:

> The main element that falls apart dramatically is that the assassination of the Saudi ambassador in Washington was supposed to be carried out by Mexican drug cartel members. Iran has never used surrogates with whom they are unfamiliar. Non-Muslim proxy groups are never used. The Iranians have always used very well known, familiar groups that are

operationally trusted, well integrated into the Iranian strategy, like Hezbollah. It's illogical that they would subcontract a plot like this to the Mexican drug cartels. They're not Muslim . . . They would see the drug cartels as
vulnerable to making a deal with the United States that would lead to the
exposure of the plot.[13]

Just because Mexican cartels are unlikely to work with terrorist groups
at an operation level and Iranian extremists wouldn't hire Mexicans doesn't
mean the two groups don't have business interests with the potential to
overlap. To see how easy it is for these business relationships to form, it's
important to first understand the presence and purposes of Middle Eastern
terrorist groups in Latin America.

Hezbollah is one of the largest and more well-known Islamist terrorist
groups in the world. The group came into existence in Lebanon due to a variety of factors, including the Iranian (or Islamic) Revolution of 1979, Israel's
invasion of Lebanon in 1982, and the overall disenfranchisement of Shia
Muslims in Lebanon during this time. In the 1980s, Hezbollah began export-
ing operatives to different parts of the world, including Latin America. Their
ideal destination was the tri-border area (TBA) in South America, where the
borders of Paraguay, Brazil, and Argentina meet. In his book *The Merger,*
author Jeffrey Robinson describes Ciudad del Este, one of the TBA's cities in
Paraguay, as "a city of two-hundred-thousand hustlers, whores, hoodlums,
revolutionaries, thugs, drug traffickers, drug addicts, murderers, racketeers,
pirates, mobsters, extortionists, smugglers, hit men, pimps and wannabes."[14]

Part of why this location was so ideal was that for decades the TBA has
been home to tens of thousands of Arab immigrants. The majority of Muslims in the TBA emigrated from Lebanon during the 1970s as a result of the
civil strife, and the Muslim population now is estimated at around thirty
thousand people. Brazil is thought to be home to around one million Muslims, from countries like Lebanon, Syria, Palestine, and Egypt, who settled
there during the same migration wave.[15] Despite local Arab leaders' denials
that any terrorist activity or financing is occurring in the TBA, there is ample
evidence to the contrary.

A Library of Congress report in 2003 stated that terrorist groups like the
Islamic Resistance Movement, Hezbollah, and the Islamic Group "use the
TBA to raise revenues through illicit activities that include drug- and arms
trafficking, counterfeiting, money laundering, forging travel documents, and
even pirating software and music. In addition, they provide haven and assistance to other terrorists transiting the region." Furthermore, the report indicated "Al Qaeda reportedly also does considerable fund-raising in Ciudad

del Este." The two largest terrorist attacks in Latin America—against the Israeli Embassy in 1992 and a Jewish center in 1994, both in Buenos Aires, Argentina—were committed by Hezbollah, and the operational planning reportedly occurred in the TBA.[16]

Hezbollah's presence and fundraising activities have not been limited to TBA countries. But the important question for border security purposes becomes, *Is Hezbollah operating in Mexico, and do they plan to use our southwest border to launch terrorist attacks in the US?*

Trying to determine the number of Arabs and Muslims in Mexico is sometimes complicated, as population counts vary from source to source. For example, in 2010, Lebanese diplomatic personnel in Mexico estimated that roughly twenty thousand Muslims of Arab descent were living in Mexico. Mark Lindley-Highfield, author of *Islam in Central America,* estimates that population is closer to thirty-nine thousand.[17] However, opinions seem to vary regarding a Hezbollah presence within this community.

In July 2011, a federal deputy in Jalisco state, Mexico, for the Institutional Revolutionary Party (also known as the PRI, one of Mexico's largest political parties) said that Hezbollah had a presence in northern Mexico, where they were carrying out drug trafficking and training activities. However, that information didn't come from Mexican sources; the deputy cited a US House of Representatives report. Most likely, that report was Ambassador Roger F. Noriega's testimony before Congress, titled "Hezbollah in Latin America: Implications for US Homeland Security." In this testimony, Noriega referred to "several published reports, citing US law enforcement and intelligence sources, that Hezbollah operatives have provided weapons and explosives training to drug trafficking organizations that operate along the US border with Mexico and have sought to radicalize Muslim populations in several Mexican cities." However, he doesn't provide specifics about these reports or their contents because "the US and Mexican governments have declined to share information publicly on these cases."[18]

One document that raised several alarms among some US officials was a situational awareness report about Hezbollah, written by the Tucson Police Department and leaked to the public by LulzSec, an Internet hacking group. The report addressed the July 2010 arrest of Jameel Nasr—a possible Hezbollah operative—in Tijuana, Mexico, and cited his presence in Mexico as a significant reason for concern.[19] Unfortunately, the only publicly available report about Nasr's arrest and reasons for being in Mexico came from a Kuwaiti newspaper. *Al-Seyassah* reported that Hezbollah operatives had employed Mexican nationals with ties to Lebanon to set up a network in South America designed to target Israel and the West. A FOX News report that cited the Kuwaiti story stated that authorities in Mexico conducted a surveillance operation on Nasr, who traveled frequently to Lebanon to receive instructions from Hezbollah militants. However, the report went on to say that no government or law enforcement officials on either side of the border would confirm a man named Jameel Nasr had been arrested in Tijuana.[20]

The lack of credibility of the Tucson Police Department report didn't end there. On the third page, the author(s) posted several pictures of individuals with tattoos, calling the section "Identifiers" and explaining how the tattoos linked Hezbollah to Mexican gang members. The first picture is of an AK-47 tattooed on the inside of a man's left arm. Next to the picture is an image of the Hezbollah flag, which also bears a firearm, and a red arrow connects the two gun images as if to say "they're the same." The gun depicted on the flag is indeed an AK-47. However, the AK-47 is the weapon of choice for millions of terrorists and criminals around the world. There is nothing on the tattoo whatsoever, or elsewhere on the man's body, to indicate the individual wearing it in the photograph specifically chose the "AK-47 from the Hezbollah flag" as the report claims, as opposed to a generic image of the firearm.

There's another photo of a tattoo depicting two crossed guns that resemble AK-47s and the words "Dushman Kush." The report claims the crossed guns are a symbol of Hezbollah and that Dushman Kush means "enemy killer." It is a phrase of Persian origin and does indeed mean "slayer of enemies." However, crossed AK-47s are used in symbols for many organizations, including the South West Africa Counterinsurgency Unit and on the flag of the Liberation Tigers of Tamil Eelam (a now-defunct south Asian terrorist group). It also doesn't help matters that neither firearm in the tattoo is actually an AK-47.

The final nail in the coffin of this report is that some of the sources cited included Wikipedia, Examiner.com (a "citizen journalism" site), a news aggregation site rather than the original source. Despite all these inaccuracies, US officials have cited this report as a solid source of information and a reason to be concerned about a Hezbollah threat emanating from Mexico.

The Tucson Police Department report was never meant for public distribution, but there is no lack of publicly available media reporting on this subject. In March 2009, *The Washington Times* published a story with the headline, "EXCLUSIVE: Hezbollah uses Mexican drug routes into US." The story cited numerous unnamed US officials who agreed that Hezbollah is "using the same southern narcotics routes that Mexican drug kingpins do to smuggle drugs and people into the United States." It paints an alarming picture, quoting former DEA Assistant Administrator and Chief of Operations

Michael Braun as saying that Hezbollah relies on "the same criminal weapons smugglers, document traffickers and transportation experts as the drug cartels." The report later concedes that, "Although there have been no confirmed cases of Hezbollah moving terrorists across the Mexico border to carry out attacks in the United States, Hezbollah members and supporters have entered the country this way."[21] Unfortunately, the report provides no context whatsoever regarding exactly how cartels and Hezbollah work together or why Hezbollah members enter the United States.

Hezbollah has been involved in money laundering operations in the Western Hemisphere for at least a decade. Because of the large volume of cash that Mexican cartels need laundered on a regular basis, many people believe it's inevitable that these two organizations would eventually develop a business arrangement for this purpose.

In December 2011, US authorities accused a Lebanese drug kingpin of allegedly helping to smuggle large amounts of cocaine into the United States and laundering more than $250 million for Los Zetas. Ayman Joumaa worked with at least nine other people and nineteen entities to smuggle cocaine out of Colombia, then launder the drug-related proceeds from Mexico, Europe, West Africa, and Colombia through a Lebanese bank. Sometimes part of that money was sent to Mexico City in bulk-cash shipments, ostensibly to be delivered to Los Zetas.[22] This story caused a great deal of alarm, especially after it made the national news cycles. People saw the words "Lebanese" and "Mexican drug cartel" in the same sentence, which led some pundits to make the assumption that this was the smoking gun—valid proof that terrorists and cartels were working together. But the connection between the man's Lebanese descent and Hezbollah was premature; Joumaa was never suspected of being a member of Hezbollah or any other terrorist group, and his affiliation with Los Zetas was purely a business relationship.

As for Hezbollah members entering the United States through Mexico, few people dispute this. Mahmoud Youssef Kourani "was a member, fighter, recruiter, and fundraiser for Hezbollah," according to a criminal complaint filed in November 2003. It said, "Operating at first from Lebanon and later the United States, Kourani was a dedicated member of Hezbollah who received specialized training in radical Shiite fundamentalism, weaponry, spycraft, and counterintelligence in Lebanon and Iran . . . Among other duties, Kourani held the position of fundraising solicitor for Hezbollah."[23]

It was these fundraising duties that led Kourani to the United States via the southwest border. He entered the country illegally from Mexico in February 2001 and took up residence in Dearborn, Michigan. But he wasn't on his own; he was closely monitored by his brother, the Hezbollah chief of military security for southern Lebanon. While in Dearborn, Kourani made sure he stayed under the radar, namely by publicly disassociating himself with the Muslim faith by avoiding mosques and shaving his beard.[24] After his apprehension, Kourani admitted to raising over $400,000 for Hezbollah.[25]

While some Hezbollah members and associates use Mexico as merely a transit point, others call it home. The Café La Libanesa in Tijuana, Mexico, looked like any other storefront in a popular part of town. Salim Boughader Mucharrafille's little coffee shop catered to some of Tijuana's more affluent residents, including workers at the nearby US Consulate.[26] But as innocuous as Salim and his shop appeared, both were busy with endeavors reaching way beyond coffee. Until his arrest in December 2002, Boughader helped smuggle around two hundred Lebanese countrymen into the United States, including Hezbollah sympathizers. But the human smuggling activity didn't end with Boughader's arrest. A US immigration investigator said in Mexican court documents that other smugglers continued to help Hezbollah-affiliated migrants in their effort to illicitly enter from Tijuana.[27]

The main concern for US law enforcement and the American public is what these Hezbollah-affiliated individuals plan to do once they arrive in the United States. So far, the answer has been to simply raise money and send it back to their homeland. However, thousands of these individuals have lived and worked here in the United States for decades. Not only are they raising millions of dollars every year for the organization; we're willingly giving it to them through our love of accessories, shoes, and cigarettes.

In 2006, US Representative Edward Royce (R-California) testified before Congress that the FBI had over two hundred active cases in 2005 against people in the United States suspected of being associated with Hezbollah. He said, "The vast majority of this activity has been linked to fundraising, specifically to attempts to use Visa cards and MasterCards for fraudulent funds to support Hezbollah along with other criminal fundraising activities." The first World Trade Center bombing in 1993 was reportedly financed by the sale of counterfeit textiles from a store on Broadway in New York City. Three years later, a confiscation of one hundred thousand counterfeit Nike brand t-shirts intended for sale at the 1996 Atlanta Olympic Games uncovered a multi-million-dollar fundraising operation conducted by followers of Sheik Omar Abdel Rahman—a blind cleric later convicted of plotting to bomb New York City landmarks. Raids on counterfeiting operations in California have led to the discovery of Hezbollah flags, photos, and other memorabilia. In one case, a female cigarette counterfeiter was arrested at the Los Angeles airport en route to Lebanon with $230,000 in cash strapped to her body.

While the woman claimed to be traveling for vacation, it was presumed that the funds were being transported to Hezbollah leaders.[28]

As disturbing as all this Hezbollah presence and activity within our borders is, no violence directed at US interests has occurred as a result—and there are good reasons for this. During her Congressional testimony in July 2011, Melani Cammett, an associate political science professor at Brown University, said, "the notion that Hezbollah intends to launch terrorist operations against US interests, particularly in the Western Hemisphere, seems implausible at this juncture. Since the 1980s, Hezbollah has evolved into a mainstream actor in Lebanese politics and has opted to participate in the formal institutions of the state. As a result," Cammett continued, "the party has become more pragmatic and far more willing to make compromises than in the past. Hezbollah remains committed to its struggle against Israel, but confrontation with the US is a much riskier venture and is well beyond the scope of its domestic and regional priorities."[29]

Many people believe that Hezbollah associates who have been living in the United States and raising money for quite some time could automatically be "activated" by handlers in Lebanon if tensions between the United States and Iran were to flare up significantly. However, that's not how Hezbollah cells here operate, and logistically it's much more complicated than that. In July 2006, Jack Cloonan, a former FBI counterterrorism agent, told ABC News, "The more likely scenario will be that Hezbollah will target a US facility overseas."[30]

Every year, the US Border Patrol captures hundreds of individuals from countries associated with terrorism. This means that it's likely many more of these individuals successfully make it across. After the attacks of 9/11, the US government was understandably highly sensitive to visitors or immigrants arriving from countries host to terrorist groups intent on harming Americans. In 2003, DHS created a list of "specially designated countries" (SDCs); a May 2011 report from the DHS Office of the Inspector General explained that these are countries "that have shown a tendency to promote, produce, or protect terrorist organizations or their members." Policy stated that any visitors to the United States from these countries—referred to as "special interest aliens," or SIAs, would be detained by ICE and subject to a special security screening called a Third Agency Check. "The purpose of the additional screening," said the report, "is to determine whether other agencies have an interest in the alien."[31]

Especially after 9/11, it was easy to see why many of the countries made the cut. The list included Afghanistan, Iran, Iraq, Lebanon, Libya, Pakistan, and Yemen. DHS never went out of its way to advertise this list of countries or use the terms SDCs or SIAs, but the program's existence was not a secret. In fact, during a January 2012 panel discussion at the Woodrow Wilson Center in Washington, DC, former DHS Secretary Janet Napolitano told reporters, "With respect to Mexico, we've been working very closely with them—there's a whole category called SIAs—Special Interest Aliens is what it stands for," and added that DHS watches that category of foreign visitors "very carefully."[32]

In fact, DHS had already distanced itself from the list by then. The DHS Inspector General's Office's 2011 report "Supervision of Aliens Commensurate with Risk" was revised in December 2011, and the following text was inserted in place of the country list:

> The specially designated country list as described in Appendix D was created in 2003, is outdated and is being eliminated . . . The list was not based on any judgment that the states listed supported, sponsored or encouraged terrorism. Indeed, many of the states listed are important and committed partners of the United States in countering terrorism. As threats around the world evolve, the United States will continue to work closely with our international partners to ensure the safety and security of people around the globe.[33]

In addition to SIAs, US immigration authorities also take note of individuals apprehended along the US-Mexico border who are not Mexican. These immigrants are designated in statistical reports as "Other Than Mexican," or OTMs, and changing patterns in OTM and SIA migration into the United States can be very telling.

San Diego, California, is home to one of the largest communities of Iraqis in the United States; possibly second only to Dearborn, Michigan. Many, if not most, of these Iraqi migrants are Chaldeans, who form a branch of the Catholic Church that exists primarily in Iraq and Turkey. Long persecuted in Iraq, the Chaldeans began to seek refuge in the growing community of Iraqi expatriates in southern California following America's post-9/11 invasion of Iraq. The rise in the level of Chaldean persecution in Iraq was mirrored by the corresponding number of Iraqis coming through California's border ports of entry, as well as in the number of Iraqis requesting asylum in US immigration courts.

Similarly, for the last two decades, as Somalia's internal security has sharply deteriorated and the country has become a textbook example of a failed state, more Somali immigrants have been settling in San Diego. The city today is home to one of the nation's largest Somali immigrant communities.

A steady growth in Somali immigration statistics had been expected as a result of that nation's descent into chaos, and the number of border crossers and asylum requests has borne out those expectations.[34]

Normally, changes in migration patterns from any country can be connected to some sort of political or economic strife there. For example, from 1999 through 2007, the number of annual Border Patrol apprehensions of Nepalese immigrants at our land borders was mostly in the single digits. But between 2008 and 2010, the number of annual apprehensions rose to forty-five, fifty-seven, and sixty-two, respectively. This dramatic increase paralleled the rise in crime in Nepal (a non-specially designated country) and the nation's political instability from a decade-long civil war between communist Maoists (a US-designated terrorist group), separatists, and the Nepalese government.[35] However, it's the anomalies that crop up when analyzing these patterns that often warrant more attention.

In 2010, more than 1,600 Indians—most of them Sikhs from the Punjab region of India (also a non-specially designated country)—entered Texas illegally. Six hundred and fifty were caught at the border during the last three months of 2010. In 2009, Border Patrol arrested only ninety-nine Indians along the southwest border, according to homeland security officials. The *Los Angeles Times* reported that authorities believed there may be thousands more Sikhs who have entered the United States undetected. Those who were caught or declared themselves at a port of entry requested asylum, claiming religious persecution in India. Yet, there have been no documented instances of widespread persecution of Sikhs in India since the 1980s.

Consequently, immigration authorities and analysts are stumped by the dramatic shift in the numbers of Sikhs asking for asylum. Most believe the Sikhs who requested asylum were simply looking for economic opportunities in America, much like the majority of citizens of Latin American nations who have migrated to the United States illegally. It's possible that Sikhs are using Latin American human smuggling pipelines because the pipelines into the northeastern United States that they had been using until recently are being scrutinized more closely. What makes the large influx of Sikhs arriving along the southwest border a source of concern is India's proximity to neighboring Pakistan and Bangladesh, two countries that are on the SDC list. Homeland security officials are concerned that terrorists from these nations could try to sneak in with a large group of Sikhs, just as Iraqis and Somalis with terrorism ties could sneak into the United States with their countrymen seeking asylum.[36]

The real challenge to our national security is that terrorists can monitor these international trends and use instability in specific countries to their advantage. While a terrorist from Syria might not be able to blend in as a Somali or a Romanian, for example, he could impersonate an Iraqi. And if he studied Spanish well enough, and mastered a few accents native to Mexico or Guatemala, he might even be able to pass for a Central American migrant. Adding to this challenge is the US policy of offering temporary protected status (TPS) to individuals in the United States who hail from countries experiencing civil unrest, violence, or natural disasters. While TPS is only temporary—deferring the removal of an illegal immigrant until such dangerous situations are resolved—a foreign national who is granted TPS receives a registration document and an employment authorization for the duration of TPS. As of January 2010, the US government was providing TPS or "deferred enforced departure" to over three hundred thousand foreign nationals from a total of seven countries: El Salvador, Haiti, Honduras, Liberia, Nicaragua, Somalia, and Sudan—the last two of which are on the SDC list.

As devious as terrorists are, homeland security agencies have several things working in their favor to combat their tactics. First, migration anomalies always raise red flags, which leads to scrutiny and investigation—as in the case of the Sikhs apprehended at the Texas border. Analysts constantly monitor world events, so they know when a shift in a migration pattern does or doesn't correspond to an increase in a country's instability or a change in its political situation. They also often have country experts at their disposal who know exactly what questions to ask to sort out the "real" immigrants from terrorists or criminals who are trying to blend in.

But it's not always terrorism from the outside that concerns Mexican and American government officials and citizens. Based on the evolving behavior of Mexican cartels, some people believe we should all be worrying about narcoterrorism developing from within North America.

It was a warm Thursday afternoon in Monterrey, Mexico, on August 25, 2011. There were a few lazy clouds in the sky, but the 150 or so patrons and croupiers inside the Casino Royale San Jerónimo were oblivious to the weather. They were inside a windowless building gambling their cares away, mostly women playing bingo, roulette, and the slots. At 3:50 P.M., their lives would descend into a chaotic hell in less than three minutes.

Two hours earlier, a dozen members of the bloodthirsty Los Zetas cartel met at a nearby restaurant, where they were given orders to carry out an attack on the casino. The owners, Raúl Rocha Cantú and José Alberto Rocha Cantú, had failed to pay their monthly extortion fee to Los Zetas and needed to be sent a message.[37] On their way to the casino a few blocks away, the men pulled their convoy of vehicles into a Pemex gas station to fill several containers with gasoline. Little did they know that closed-circuit TV cameras were capturing their actions at the station—or maybe they knew and were completely unconcerned.[38] The men arrived at the casino at 3:50 P.M. in four vehicles. Most of them calmly walked into the casino—a few remained outside as lookouts—and began dousing the casino with gasoline before promptly setting it on fire. Less than three minutes later, they walked out and departed in the same vehicles in which they arrived.[39]

Accounts of the sequence of events that followed in the next few minutes vary, simply due to the chaos from the "fog of war." Most victims heard gunfire and men yelling, and some thought they heard the sound of grenade explosions. The yelling might have been the men telling the patrons they were all about to die, or urging them to get out of the building as quickly as possible. Regardless, a stampede ensued, with some gamblers managing to get out of the casino and some having to hole up in the bathrooms because the emergency exits they tried were blocked off. The fire spread quickly; many victims died in corners, stairwells, or burned alive on top of game tables. By the next morning, fifty-three people were dead and dozens more were recovering in hospitals.[40]

Until that day, President Calderón and other Mexican officials had always been careful to insist that cartels were organized crime groups and nothing more. President Obama and US officials were usually careful to toe this line as well, particularly after former US Secretary of State Hillary Clinton embarrassed Obama by declaring at a Council of Foreign Relations event in September 2010 that Mexico was witnessing an insurgency like the one in Colombia. This is despite the fact that Los Zetas executed seventy-two innocent Central and South American migrants in the town of San Fernando—a mere ninety-four kilometers from the Texas border—simply for refusing to join them or pay ransom for their release.

So Calderón stunned many when the day after the attack, he called the murders of the casino patrons an "aberrant act of terror and barbarity." His secretary of the interior (equivalent to our secretary of state) Alejandro Poiré echoed this sentiment when he said, "An unspeakable, repugnant, unacceptable act of terror has been committed."[41] It's hard to argue with their logic if you're a Mexican citizen, or worse, a resident of Monterrey witnessing in real-time the black and acrid smoke rising from the charred remains of a local business. While the attack certainly struck fear into the hearts of many Mexicans and surely terrorized everyone inside the Casino Royale that day, could the attack truly be classified as an act of terrorism, and could Los Zetas be rebranded as a terrorist group? If so, what would be the ramifications for both the Mexican and US governments, as well as our border security apparatus?

On March 30, 2011, US Representative Michael McCaul (R-Texas) introduced legislation in Congress to designate six Mexican cartels as "foreign terrorist organizations," essentially placing them on the same categorical footing as groups like al-Qa'ida, Hezbollah, and the Irish Republican Army. In a statement, McCaul said, "Mexican drug cartels are terrorist organizations, and this designation will provide the necessary tools to effectively advance the national security interests of both Mexico and the United States." Had it passed, the bill would have enabled prosecutors to levy up to fifteen additional years of prison time on each conviction of providing "material support or resources" to the six cartels listed in the proposal, and a federal death sentence if deaths resulted from the cartels' actions.[42]

McCaul wasn't alone in his desire to go the terrorism route with Mexican cartels. On November 9, 2011, US Representative Connie Mack (R-Florida) introduced H.R. 3401, called the "Enhanced Border Security Act," to the US House of Representatives. If passed, the bill would have treated Mexican drug cartels like terrorists and applied a counterinsurgency strategy to fighting cartels along our southwest border. The bill would also have doubled the number of Border Patrol agents assigned to the border and encouraged the construction of more sections of border fence. During the mark-up of the bill in the Western Hemisphere subcommittee of the House Foreign Affairs Committee, where Mack serves as chairman, he said, "A terrorist insurgency is being waged along our Southern border."[43]

Imagine for a hypothetical minute that both of these proposed pieces of legislation had passed. In effect, Mexico would have tens of thousands (or more) of newly designated terrorists living within its borders, and millions more supporters of terrorism—corrupt police and government officials accepting bribes or looking the other way as cartels conduct their business. In the United States, Mexican cartels have a presence in roughly 1,000 US cities, according to the US Department of Justice. We would then magically have thousands of terrorists or supporters of terrorism within our own borders. The implications of such a paradigm shift in the way we view cartels goes way beyond political or diplomatic difficulties, despite the increase in funding or personnel that would necessarily be directed toward border security efforts.

The sticky fact also remains that Mexican cartels still don't fit the true definition of terrorist organizations as the US government has laid it out— although Los Zetas come dangerously close. Even the Casino Royale attack and the San Fernando massacre, as tragic and horrifying as they were, had financial gain as their underlying motive. None of the cartels active in Mexico right now want to take over or subvert the government; they actually need a stable government structure in place they can manipulate through bribery and coercion to facilitate their criminal activities.

We know that members of Hezbollah and many individuals from countries associated with terrorism have entered the United States from Mexico. We also know that many of those individuals have helped raise millions of dollars for terrorist organizations in the Middle East, Africa, and other parts of the world. But how does that translate into a tangible terrorist threat along our southwest border?

For a moment, put yourself in the mind of a terrorist operative seeking entry into the United States to conduct an attack. Maybe you're on your own, or you have several other operatives traveling with you. Many factors are going to help you decide the best way to travel: whether or not you have a criminal history or are on the Terror Watch List, the authenticity of your legitimate passport and visa or the quality of your fraudulent travel documents, if you have any firearms or explosives that need to travel with you, how you look and what languages you speak, etc. Depending on your specific situation, there are many travel options available to you, from easiest to most difficult. For example, you could just board a plane from your location and fly to any city in the United States with your passport and visa. Or, you could pay tens of thousands of dollars to a series of specialized human smugglers who will make you hop from country to country before dragging you through the brutal Mexican desert to cross the border into the United States.

If you're like most travelers—and terrorist planners—you prefer to take the path of least resistance. The 9/11 Commission report details the travel planning for the nineteen hijackers involved in the plot, and it serves as an excellent example of why many terrorists don't make their own lives more difficult than necessary. The report explained that the 9/11 hijackers submitted twenty-three visa applications during the course of the plot, and all but one of these applications were approved. The hijackers applied for visas at five US consulates or embassies overseas, and most of them applied with new passports—possibly to hide travel to Afghanistan recorded in their old ones. They successfully entered the United States thirty-three out of thirty-four times, with the first arriving at Los Angeles International Airport in 2000. All others entered through airports on the East Coast, including eleven entries through New York area airports and twelve through Florida airports. The four pilots passed through immigration and customs inspections a total of seventeen times as tourists. This guaranteed them six months of legal stay, which was sufficient time for them to make preparations, such as obtaining the identifications some of them used to board the planes on 9/11. Fourteen of fifteen operatives and all of the pilots acquired one or multiple forms of US state-issued identification.[44]

Since 9/11, the methods consular officers use to verify a visa applicant's background have become much more thorough, and many believe the hijackers would never have been issued visas had today's checks been run on them at the time. But there are several recent examples of individuals attempting to carry out terrorist attacks on US soil who arrived from foreign countries legally.

On December 25, 2009, Nigerian Islamist Umar Farouk Abdulmutallab tried to detonate a bomb hidden in his underwear on a Northwest Airlines flight from Amsterdam to Detroit, Michigan. Abdulmutallab applied for and was granted a US visa in 2008, which was valid through 2010. According to a *Huffington Post* report, "Abdulmutallab appeared on the Terrorist Identities Datamart Environment database maintained by the US National Counterterrorism Center . . . Containing some 550,000 names, the database includes people with known or suspected ties to a terrorist organization. However, it is not a list that would prohibit a person from boarding a US-bound airplane."[45] Amine El-Khalifi is a Moroccan national who plotted to blow up the US Capitol building, until he was arrested in February 2012. He arrived legally in the United States as a teenager with a visitor's visa, and stayed as an illegal immigrant after his visa expired in 1999.[46]

Despite the gaping holes in the length of the US-Mexico border and the hundreds of thousands of migrants who slip across it undetected every year, it's still one of the most highly scrutinized and monitored borders in the world. The Mexican government knows its enforcement efforts are highly flawed with extensive corruption and incompetence at various levels, but their national intelligence apparatus is closely attuned to potential terrorist activity. It also knows some of the likely consequences of a terrorist attack occurring on US soil facilitated by travel through Mexican territory. While it's impossible to truly "shut down the border," as some politicians have called for in the past, such an attack would bring border traffic—and the billions of dollars in trade that cross the southwest border every day—to a virtual halt. Neither the US nor the Mexican government want that, nor do drug traffickers, citizens, students, or businesses along the border. Ultimately, it's in Mexico's best interest to do absolutely everything in its power to prevent such terrorist transit from happening.

So why would an operational terrorist choose Mexico as the best route for gaining entry into the United States? Going back to the factors listed above, perhaps the group in question is in dire straits and can't recruit a bomber either already in the United States, or with no criminal history and good travel documents. Maybe they're confident enough in the border security gaps that they can just sneak in with a larger group of immigrants with little fuss; it's always possible. However, our northern border with Canada is significantly more porous and easy to cross than our southern border, and there are many other ways that terrorist operatives can travel to the United States without having to jump through many hoops in Mexico. Logic dictates that terrorist operatives will choose those routes first.

But logic doesn't necessarily allay people's fears about terrorism. In July 2011, former Arizona GOP Congressional candidate Gabriela Saucedo-Mercer said in an interview that the only goal of Middle Easterners crossing America's southern border was to "cause harm to the United States."[47] Several items discovered in the Arizona and Texas desert thought by some to be linked to terrorism have included a 1982 book published in Iran, titled *In Memory of Our Martyrs* (and written in English, not Farsi), mats that ranchers believed were Muslim prayer rugs, and clothing patches containing an image thought to resemble a plane flying into a tower and the word "martyr." However, one of the patches from the same piece of clothing was from an international corporation that sells sport fishing products with corporate offices in eight countries.

There is no doubt that there are many terrorist groups and their sympathizers who would love nothing more than to see another 9/11 occur on American soil. There is also no doubt that members and sympathizers of some of these groups have a presence in Latin America, in Mexico, and in the United States. There is ample evidence to prove some of these individuals arrived in the United States by way of crossing the US-Mexico border, either legally or illegally, and the mere presence in our nation of these groups' affiliates is completely unacceptable and worthy of much concern. However, there is nowhere near enough conclusive evidence to demonstrate that operational members of terrorist groups—members coming not just to raise money, but to blow something up—are currently and actively seeking to enter the United States from Mexico, and especially not with the willing participation of Mexican cartels.

CHAPTER 8

THE INVISIBLE FIGHT AGAINST MONEY LAUNDERING

You get to a point where it gets very complex, where you have money laundering activities, drug related activities, and terrorist support activities converging at certain points and becoming one . . . And I keep underlining . . . following the money. When you do that the picture gets grim. It gets really ugly.[1]

—Sibel Edmonds, former FBI translator and whistleblower

'Tis money that begets money.

—English proverb, *Gnomologia*, 1732

It was late November 2009 in Grand Prairie, Texas, and it was a beautiful Saturday night for horse racing. Nine quarter horse colts and their jockeys lined up for the annual Texas Classic Futurity race at the Lone Star Park track, just west of downtown Dallas. It was a short sprint—only four hundred yards—but with hundreds of thousands of dollars on the line for people with a stake in each horse. After several tense minutes of waiting, the gun went off. Within seconds, the number seven horse clearly took the lead, his jockey clothed in bright pink and angling for the best position to the finish line. Over the next few seconds, Tempting Dash continued to pull ahead of the other horses, crossing the finish in 19.205 seconds—a new track record. It was his fourth victory in as many races, and Tempting Dash earned his owner almost half a million dollars in just that brief time span.[2]

After the win, there was a brief ceremony where the presenter interviewed the owner of Tempting Dash, a heavy-set Mexican man named José Treviño. He and all his team members on stage were dressed in classic Texas style—jeans and cowboy hats all around—and he seemed genuinely pleased at his horse's latest victory. He spoke a little bit about why his horse began racing later than usual, owing it to the fact that Tempting Dash was on the small side, but that it turned into a speed advantage. What Treviño didn't elaborate on—and what no one watching the ceremony that day could have suspected—was the sinister path on which Treviño had placed that horse.

The previous year, in December 2008, a man named Ramiro Villareal bought Tempting Dash for the modest sum of $21,500. In October 2009, the quarter horse won the Dash for Cash at Lone Star Park with Villareal listed as the owner. The next month, the American Quarter Horse Association received paperwork indicating ownership of the horse was being transferred from Villareal to Treviño, but Treviño backdated the transfer to make it look like it had happened in late September 2009. Also during that September, Francisco Colorado and other individuals working for Treviño purchased thirteen quarter horses at auction for $546,500, most of which was paid for by a check drawn on Colorado's bank account. Subsequently, ownership of those horses was transferred to Treviño and his companies, Tremor Enterprises and 66 Land.[3] If you're already lost, don't worry—you're supposed to be.

A few weeks after Tempting Dash's victory in the Futurity race, Treviño transferred $435,000 from his personal Bank of America account to his Tremor Enterprises business account. The next day, he wrote two checks from the Tremor account made out to himself—one for $100,000 and the other for $57,793—and deposited them into his personal account. One week later, he did the same thing, except this time the $157,793 came from his personal account and went into his Tremor Enterprises account, making it look like personal income.[4]

Over the next year, the purchase of multiple quarter horses—sometimes involving over $2 million per purchase—and these back-and-forth deposits and wire transfers continued between Treviño's associates and his business enterprises. Many of the horses bought by Treviño's organization were paid for by a Mexican business entity. His wife Zulema was involved in these transactions, as well as overseeing the ownership, training, care, and feeding of all these horses. Responsibility for the day-to-day operations and financial transactions was divided among at least a dozen individuals. Some of the horses were transferred to a facility called Zule Farms in Lexington, Oklahoma, which Zulema oversaw. During 2011, more bank deposits were made to different organization members' accounts (Bank of America was the primary bank used), and the deposits were never for more than roughly $9,000, since anything over $10,000 would trigger the creation of a currency transaction report—in other words, a paper trail that would raise red flags.[5]

Then in November 2011, Treviño started unloading several quarter horses at an Oklahoma City auction, selling four horses for prices well above market value, and all to members of his own organization. In reality this was extremely shady, but on paper in looked completely legitimate. This was a continuing cycle—buying and selling horses at auction, racing them and funneling the winnings into several accounts, structuring deposits, and making wire transfers between Mexican and US businesses and banks. By mid-June 2012, Treviño and his people had purchased over three hundred horses, won three of the most prestigious quarter horse races in the United States, and pocketed over $2.5 million in prize winnings.[6] And while the entire operation doled out its share of fun and excitement for Treviño and those involved, it had only one underlying and nefarious purpose—to launder money for Los Zetas, the most violent drug cartel in all of Mexico.

Money laundering, at its most basic level, is the way that criminal organizations make money that comes from illegitimate sources—like drug trafficking, terrorism, prostitution, etc.—look like it comes from legal business transactions. Thus the term "laundering," as money goes in dirty and comes out clean. All sorts of criminals and terrorists engage in money laundering in virtually every country in the world, but for the purposes of this chapter, I'm going to focus solely on the money laundering practices of Mexican drug cartels. Money laundering practices make the world virtually borderless, and money crossing our national borders electronically—and thus invisibly—is incredibly difficult to detect and track.

Money—obscene amounts of it—is the reason cartels are in business, yet our government pursues cartel money with considerably less enthusiasm than it does the drugs they sell for that money. Cartel cash flows through US banks, which historically have only received a slap on the wrist for having weak anti-money laundering (AML) programs. Hiring experienced and competent compliance officers and digging too deeply into suspicious transactions are afterthoughts for banks who fear those actions might diminish profits. If politicians spent one-tenth of the time complaining about a lack of effective AML enforcement than they do about a lack of sufficient border security measures, money laundering activity in the United States might look a bit different.

Finding convenient ways to manage money is critical for drug traffickers. It's a cash-only business, and many people don't realize the sheer volume of paper bills involved in drug transactions on a daily basis. At the street level, drugs are generally paid for with small bills. When bulk cash shipments are caught at the border heading south into Mexico, it's not wads of hundred-dollar bills like you'd see in a movie. The tightly wrapped bales usually consist of smaller denominations and are large and unwieldy, which is why they're called "bulk cash." These heavy loads increase the chance that burdened border crossers will be targeted and caught, putting profits at risk.

This risk is inconvenient enough that cartels are willing to pay a premium to have drug proceeds returned to them in a manner that's quicker, safer, and less detectable by law enforcement agencies. To do this, they go through three basic steps of money laundering: placement, layering, and integration.

The placement step involves making cash deposits at legitimate banks. Usually, cartels will direct depositors to use several different banks spread across a large geographic area. They'll also instruct depositors to keep deposits below $10,000, and sometimes well below that, since a deposit for $9,893 can trigger just as much suspicion because it's *almost* the amount requiring a currency transaction report. After the initial deposits comes the layering step. During layering, cartel money is moved across the globe to make it as difficult as possible to track. Layering can take the form of wire transfers, withdrawals and deposits in varying amounts, currency exchange, and the purchase of high-value items like yachts and diamonds.[7]

The third and final stage is the integration phase, during which traffickers use the drug proceeds that have made their way around the world to "invest" in legitimate businesses or other enterprises, essentially making it look like they're engaging in a legal financial transaction. This could involve the purchase of a relatively inexpensive item for thousands of dollars or payment for services that were never actually performed.[8]

A recent case that serves as an example of how this process works involved a global financial titan. London-headquartered HSBC is one of the largest banking and financial services organizations in the world. It has a subsidiary in Mexico, and in the mid-2000s it was responsible for approximately half of the dollar cash transfers from Mexico to the United States, despite the fact it wasn't nearly the largest bank in the country. Guillermo Babatz, president of Mexico's National Securities and Banking Commission, said regulators started detecting an unusual swell in cash flow around 2007 and 2008, and although they notified HSBC management about the irregularities, they got little response. They even contacted top bank managers, which wasn't an ordinary action for regulators to take.[9]

Then in 2010, the US government started poking around, both through a US Senate investigative committee and a Department of Justice AML task force. The committee report, published in mid-2012, stated that HSBC Mexico had shipped north approximately $7 billion in bulk (that is, physical) cash, much of which originated in the pockets of Mexican drug traffickers.

It said, "Bulk cash shipments could reach that volume only if they included illegal drug proceeds." In the face of overwhelming evidence, HSBC Mexico acknowledged that "it failed to strictly comply with banking regulations, and with the standards that regulators and clients expect of our institution." The bank took corrective actions such as no longer conducting cash dollar transactions (like deposits) and refusing to do business with suspicious customers, but the Mexican government still levied a fine on HSBC Mexico of $28 million.[10]

HSBC also faced steep fines in the United States, agreeing to a $1.92 billion settlement with the government in December 2012. However, not a single HSBC employee would face any jail time. State and federal authorities decided against issuing a criminal indictment against the bank or any of its employees "over concerns that criminal charges could jeopardize one of the world's largest banks and ultimately destabilize the global financial system." In the months leading up to the settlement, there was considerable debate among authorities over the message a lack of criminal charges would send, how badly the company's reputation would be tarnished, and how much real damage an indictment would cause to the global financial sector.[11] In the case of HSBC, it looked like an abundance of caution—or fear—won out over justice.

Sadly, there seems to be a pattern of allowing large banks to get away with ignorance and a lack of compliance with merely a slap on the wrist. In 2006, whistleblower Martin Woods was working for London-based Wachovia Bank. He was the director of an AML unit for Wachovia, and started noticing suspicious activity originating from Mexican money exchange houses, known as *casas de cambio*. He informed his supervisors about the unusual transactions, and even contacted officials at Britain's Serious Organized Crime Agency. All of Woods's concerns were rebuffed or ignored, and he resigned shortly thereafter, claiming he was bullied out of the company, although Wachovia officials said his performance was below average.[12]

Regardless of his job performance rating, Woods was definitely onto something big. Less than a year after he notified his bosses about the transactions, Mexican authorities raided one of the exchange houses Woods had looked into, called Casa de Cambio Puebla. Authorities learned that a senior member of the Sinaloa Federation had purchased four airplanes for the purpose of drug trafficking with money that was laundered through both Wachovia Bank and Bank of America. But that was just the tip of the iceberg; the investigation uncovered that between 2004 and 2007 Wachovia had processed almost $400 billion in funds for Mexican currency exchange houses, at least $110 million of which belonged to drug cartels.[13]

In the Wachovia case, the US government did initially bring criminal charges against the bank as a whole, but the case never went to court. Wachovia settled in the case and avoided criminal charges, but not before paying federal authorities $110 million in forfeitures "for allowing transactions later proved to be connected to drug smuggling." It also incurred a $50 million fine "for failing to monitor cash used to ship 22 tons of cocaine." Authorities levied sanctions against Wachovia for weak AML measures that allowed the transfer of $378 billion into dollar accounts from *casas de cambio* in Mexico.[14]

How is it that these large financial services companies can't detect suspicious financial activity more effectively? Maria Saffold is a certified AML compliance expert who started out as a state financial regulator. She explained that after 9/11, the number of investigations into the finances of terrorist groups like al-Qa'ida went through the roof, as did the attention paid to money laundering activities and bank compliance. "It was there, but [before 9/11] it wasn't a priority. It wasn't something regulators were overly concerned about; it was just something to do," she said. One of the types of financial groups that Saffold oversaw was money transmitters. "You had your traditional money service businesses, or MSBs, like Western Union and Ria. eBay had only just started PayPal, so we were seeing the dawn of Internet financial transactions being licensed and regulated under state statutes. The statutes weren't originally written to cover these kinds of transactions, but we found that they needed to be regulated because people were already laundering money through PayPal."[15]

After the 9/11 attacks occurred, investigators determined that the hijackers had wired money through Western Union. "All of a sudden, the Patriot Act comes about, the Bank Secrecy Act gets updated, and we have this big new focus on AML," said Saffold. "And the new focus wasn't necessarily on the big banks; it was on Western Unions, the MoneyGrams, etc." Saffold's division was quickly overwhelmed as they were charged with getting out to inspect all the MSBs in the state—an impossible task, considering there were over ten thousand in her state alone.[16]

It wasn't long before MSBs across the United States started feeling the heat of the increased government scrutiny, and started worrying about potentially enormous fines being levied against them for non-compliance with the new AML rules. "The banks are doing a pretty good job. They're filing their currency transaction reports, and they have more sophisticated monitoring systems than the ones at the agent level at MSBs," said Saffold. "Theoretically, they're detecting activity and filing suspicious activity reports, etc. But is that where most money laundering activity is happening now? In my opinion, no. I think most of it is happening at the agent level at MSBs."[17]

While traffickers are certainly still engaging in making structured deposits and moving money across borders through financial giants like Bank of America and HSBC, Saffold walked me through the process that Mexican cartels typically go through when using MSBs to transfer large amounts of cash. "You could take your money and go to fifty different Western Union locations and use fifty different individuals to do it, but honestly, the structuring would probably be detected. The computers record the transactions, which are all funneled up to the company's 'mother ship' monitoring system that should pick it up. But if you take a chunk of that money and divide it up among just a few Western Union locations, then take another chunk and divide up at MoneyGram . . . those transactions are not connected." This is the main weakness of the MSB system—the computer systems are proprietary, and there is no easy way to connect the dots if a Mexican cartel is sending people to various locations of five different MSBs across several states.[18]

One hope for identifying this kind of behavior is if the dollar amount or nature of the transaction would cause agents at two different MSBs to initiate a suspicious transaction report. The Financial Crimes Enforcement Network, more commonly known as FinCEN, monitors these reports at the federal level, and some MSB agents do work in a dual capacity for more than one company. "It's still a really difficult thing to detect," said Saffold. "You feel wonderful when you find something, but when you do, you think the perpetrators had to be stupid. There are so many ways to get around the rules. It's so easy to launder money in this day and age, but that's why people in my field have job security. Every time they find a new way to launder money, we have to figure out ways to stop it."[19]

Saffold acknowledged that money launderers will still use large banks if they see a weakness in their monitoring systems. Some banks won't spend the money to hire an employee whose sole duty is to act as the bank's compliance officer. "Some of these banks are holding out, and they'll have a vice president in charge of sales who is also their chief compliance officer. That's a clear conflict of interest. How can you expect someone who's responsible for sales to monitor all this activity coming through, then stop something when it won't benefit their bank financially? You have a lot of banks who just refuse to hire the AML professionals, the people with the background. Then you have people in dalliance with money launderers; you're always going to have that. I think the banks are just trying so hard to avoid the cumbersome expense of compliance that they get individuals who are not qualified, experienced, or motivated to comply with their internal systems and prevent what they need to prevent."[20]

Money laundering activities by Mexican cartels certainly aren't limited to the banking sector, and cartels know how to get creative to evade financial monitoring systems. Mexico may be famous for its beaches, jalapeños, and tequila, but few people outside the country know it's one of Latin America's richest sources for minerals. Mexico is a major copper and silver producer, and deposits—and usually mines—for those metals, iron ore, zinc, coal, bismuth, and lead can be found in twenty-six of the country's thirty-two states. In 2010, Mexico exported $15.5 billion worth of minerals, and that figure is projected to grow over the next several years. The coal industry in Coahuila state alone—home to 95 percent of Mexico's coal deposits—is worth $3.8 billion annually.[21]

It may not seem like mining would be of any interest to drug traffickers, but cartels look at the industry and they see dollar signs. In the last few years, they've been targeting mines and the people who work in them for extortion, kidnapping for ransom, and theft. In some cases, cartels like Los Zetas are running their own mines. In May 2012, the Mexican government announced it had discovered several illegal coal mines in Coahuila being run by criminal gangs.[22]

Cartels can make big money by just stealing gold and silver from mining operations and selling it on the black market. But in some cases, they'll use the commodity as a way to launder drug proceeds. Michoacán is a small state in southwestern Mexico that is extremely rich in mineral deposits. It's also home to La Familia Michoacana and the Knights Templar, two violent and warring cartels that used to be united as one organization. During that time, a money launderer for La Familia Michoacana found a way to sell iron ore that was illegally extracted in Michoacán to China, of all places. When Ignacio López was arrested in October 2010, authorities discovered he was working with "at least three important, established international companies in Mexico" to export over a million tons of iron ore to China worth roughly $42 million.[23]

"Investing" in minerals is a great way for drug cartels to launder drug money. During the layering step, they can purchase large amounts of gold, silver, coal—essentially any of the more common minerals frequently exported from Mexico. Given the large size of the market and the dollar amounts involved, combined with extensive government corruption and the tendency of authorities to avoid digging too deeply into suspicious transactions, these purchases don't seem out of place. The minerals can then be shipped to almost anywhere in the world through arrangements with corrupt companies. According to Jesus del Campo, an official at Mexico's Ministry of Economy, some foreign mining companies encourage illegal mining so they can operate in Mexico without having to obtain permits.[24] At the mineral shipment's final destination, the sale is completed and the dirty drug money comes out clean.

Fruit and fabric are two popular commodities that cartels are now trading in through the licit business sector in an effort to hide their drug profits. Teams of launderers working for Mexican cartels will purchase goods in the United States using dollars—commonly fruit, bolts of fabric, and toys—and then export them to Mexico or Colombia, which is why this activity is known as trade-based money laundering. By doing so, the launderers create a paper trail that makes the exchange look legitimate. The goods are then sold in stores or on the street using pesos, which solves the problem for traffickers of needing to convert large amounts of currency.[25]

For several years, Mexican cartels have been using prepaid gift cards, like the ones with the VISA and American Express logos you find at the supermarket and other stores, to launder money and significantly reduce the physical volume of bulk cash they need to smuggle from the United States into Mexico. US authorities eventually caught on, and in late March 2012, FinCEN imposed new rules requiring retailers who issue store cards for more than $2,000 to collect customer information and maintain transaction records. Retailers who issue gift cards that can be used anywhere have to follow these procedures if they issue more than $10,000 to the same person in one day.[26] Given how easily one can find these gift cards almost anywhere, however, it's easy to see how one person can buy up tens of thousands of dollars (or more) in VISA or American Express prepaid cards in one day without having to provide any personal information.

We've already seen how creative cartels can be when trying to smuggle drugs north into the United States, and that same creative spirit applies to their efforts to launder money derived from drug sales. It's safe to say they are constantly looking for new ways to hide millions (if not billions) of narco dollars as well as launder them, and US authorities will likely always be trying to keep up with these new methods. One of these new methods is baffling to even seasoned AML experts.

If you're not into virtual worlds or online gaming, it's unlikely you've heard of bitcoin. However, its influence in financial markets—while small at the present time—has the potential to grow significantly, as does its potential for use by money launderers. Bitcoin is a cyber-currency that was invented in 2009 by Satoshi Nakamoto (probably a pseudonym). Essentially, it's a peer-to-peer system through which bitcoin owners can buy things online and transfer money between each other securely without having to go through a "normal" financial institution. Bitcoins are different from traditional dollars and cents in that their value isn't static; they behave more like a stock in this manner, and their value is highly volatile.

In April 2013, the value of bitcoin in global circulation was valued at $1.4 billion. While the volume of bitcoin transactions is growing very slowly, the demand for it is growing much more rapidly. This shouldn't come as a surprise, given an annual rise in cashless transactions using debit and credit cards, as well as an annual increase in online purchases. But bitcoin poses an enormous challenge to governments across the globe. Bloomberg.com asked an important question: "How do governments collect taxes on transactions in Bitcoin? The answer is they don't, and they can't. Crypto-currency's strong protections on anonymity make it impossible for any state to know who is buying what, who is paying whom, who earns what, and who has what in savings. That poses a direct challenge to the power of states to levy taxes."[27] If the US government can't find bitcoin users to levy taxes on them, how can it be expected to find drug traffickers using bitcoin to launder drug money?

To be sure, not just anyone can easily buy or use bitcoins anonymously. It takes a certain degree of technical skill to completely mask the Internet protocol address of the computer a trafficker is using, and any real-world transactions using bitcoin as payment can lead authorities to the bitcoin user if the trafficker's computer is seized.[28] That being said, bitcoin is ideal for laundering money during the layering phase because cash can be deposited in a bank account, transferred multiple times through one of the seven bitcoin exchanges, and finally withdrawn by a different individual, possibly even in a different currency (although bitcoin value tends to be mostly tied to the US dollar).

Access to bitcoin accounts has evolved in a way that makes it extremely difficult not only for normal people to hack into online funds, but also for AML investigators. Bitcoin locations are identified by online addresses, which are encrypted (i.e., long and complex). The development of the "brainwallet" allows bitcoin users to secure their cyber stash through a memorized (and usually silly) pass phrase. Using a few different websites, users can convert their pass phrase into an address where their bitcoins can be found. Unfortunately, federal law hasn't kept pace with brainwallets; there is no legal precedent that requires owners to divulge their pass phrases yet, and legal analysts are examining how the refusal to divulge this information might be protected under the Fifth Amendment.[29]

The US government sees bitcoin as a threat to its AML efforts. As of March 2013, firms that issue or exchange bitcoin are being regulated the same way as MSBs like Western Union and Coinstar; they're now required to meet new bookkeeping requirements and file currency transaction reports just like banks. In addition, entities that receive "normal" money in exchange for cyber currency or anyone conducting such a transaction on behalf of another person will be subject to higher scrutiny under new AML rules imposed by FinCEN. These rules wouldn't apply to people who use bitcoin for legitimate purposes, like paying for Domino's pizza deliveries or blog service on Wordpress.com, but part of the problem is that it's difficult to distinguish between these people and those using bitcoin for illegitimate purposes.[30]

Currently, it appears the volatility of bitcoin will work against money launderers. The risk is high that they could lose a decent amount of money if the value of their investment decreases rapidly while their money is in the system. The size of the bitcoin market is also small relative to the large amounts of cash drug traffickers need to launder on a regular basis. Finding enough bitcoins to buy and being able to easily sell them later on could prove to be a difficult task. However, the new FinCEN rules had an unintended consequence—it added more legitimacy to the bitcoin system, which could encourage more widespread use. But while the bitcoin system is still something of an unknown, other digital currency markets have been in solid use for several years, and recent investigations demonstrate that the future of money laundering lies in characters and hashtags, not bills and coins.

Almost everyone who has ever purchased something online has heard of PayPal, but very few have heard of Liberty Reserve. Created in Costa Rica in 2006, Liberty Reserve worked more or less like PayPal, allowing users to send money back and forth between accounts for purchased goods or services rendered. The biggest difference between the two systems is that PayPal is completely legitimate, requiring numerous user verifications, whereas Liberty Reserve allowed account owners to use fake names and whatever email address they wanted. It essentially operated as a "black market bank."[31]

According to Manhattan US attorney Preet Bharara, during the span of its seven-year existence, Liberty Reserve processed 55 million transactions, worth approximately $6 billion, that were related to criminal activity, including "credit card fraud, identity theft, investment fraud, child computer hacking, child pornography, and even narcotics trafficking." The system worked differently than bitcoin in that users still had to use a traditional bank to get money into the system. They would wire money to an "exchanger," which "tended to be unlicensed money-transmitting businesses without significant government oversight or regulation, concentrated in Malaysia, Russia, Nigeria and Vietnam," according to the indictment. Only after that would the wired "real world" cash be converted into digital currency and put into a Liberty Reserve account. From there, the money could be withdrawn—minus a small fee, of course—and sent anywhere in the world without a trace of where it came from.[32]

Then in May 2013, the entire system came crashing down. US federal prosecutors announced the indictment of seven people associated with Liberty Reserve, including the founder Arthur Budovsky, who was arrested in Spain a few days before the announcement. US law enforcement officials said it was the biggest online money laundering case in history, partly because Liberty Reserve had millions of customers around the world—including roughly 200,000 just in the United States. Richard Weber of the Internal Revenue Service's investigative division in Washington, DC, said the case heralds the arrival of "the cyber age of money laundering," in which criminals "are gravitating toward digital currency alternatives as a means to move, conceal and enjoy their ill-gotten gains." Mr. Bharara said the exchange's clientele was largely made up of criminals, but he invited any legitimate users to contact his office to get their money back.[33]

Stopping money launderers is an uphill battle all the way. Available information suggests that US authorities currently seize less than 1 percent of illicit outbound cash flows along the southwest border.[34] Mexican cartels send between $19 and $29 billion annually to Mexico from the United States, and Mexico is currently the primary placement area for US-generated drug dollars.[35] American and Mexican AML efforts are not something that cartels spend time worrying about. Because of the abysmal record of these efforts, cartels view any losses that result from AML investigations as an overhead cost.

Currently, there are two ways to combat money laundering: passing new laws that impose limits or reporting requirements on certain kinds of financial transactions, and investigating and punishing launderers and compliance violations more aggressively. US authorities seemed more intent in 2013 on pursuing all available avenues due to the perception—and more often the reality—that terrorists and drug traffickers are flooding our financial system with dirty money.

The legislative route in the United States originates in the Department of the Treasury at the federal level, which oversees FinCEN and the Office of Foreign Assets Control. This office oversees the "kingpin list," which was created by virtue of the Foreign Narcotics Kingpin Designation Act being passed in 1999. In essence, when the president decides that an individual, business, or organization plays "a significant role in international drug trafficking," he can add that entity to the list. Once on the list, all US persons and businesses are prohibited from engaging in any commerce or financial transaction with that entity, or face serious fines and even prison time.[36] As of August 2013, the list was twenty pages long and included every major Mexican cartel and senior cartel player. While it's nice that the White House publicly recognizes these are bad people doing bad things, it's a testament to the Act's ineffectiveness that cartel money continues to flow across global borders.

The other major piece of AML legislation in the United States is the Bank Secrecy Act, which has been in effect since 1970 but has been amended several times. This Act is the source of bank reporting requirements, like currency transaction reports and suspicious activity reports. FinCEN is working hard to try to keep up with trends in money laundering, but the process of amending the Bank Secrecy Act is long and tedious. Excessive amendments and additional reporting requirements, while possibly more effective in detecting suspicious transactions, could also start to hamper legitimate business.

In October 2011, FinCEN proposed an amendment to the Bank Secrecy Act that would require prepaid gift cards, formally known in the proposed rule as "tangible prepaid access devices," to fall under the same declaration rules as cash. In other words, any combination of dollar bills and prepaid cards that added up to $10,000 or more would have to be declared at the border or an airport.[37] To enforce this new rule, DHS planned to roll out a "handheld reader with features that will, among other things, allow law enforcement to quickly and accurately differentiate between a traveler's debit, credit, and prepaid products."[38]

While these sound like good ideas on paper, there have been delays with their implementation. As this book goes to press, the rule is still pending, almost two years after it was proposed. As such, DHS still hasn't deployed the card readers it said it was working on because there's no finalized rule to enforce yet. There is also a question of whether or not prepaid cards can really be considered equivalent to cash.

Cynthia Merritt, assistant director of the Federal Reserve Bank of Atlanta's Retail Payments Risk Forum, wrote, "When law enforcement takes possession of a cash or monetary instrument at the border, they are effectively holding the funds, but not so with a prepaid card or other device. Holding the card does not provide access to the underlying funds."[39] Jon Matonis of *Forbes* also noted, "Other questions to be settled include how to determine mobile phone wallet and key fob balances that can function in a manner similar to card *swiping,* how to distinguish between reloadable and non-reloadable prepaid cards, how to distinguish between bank-issued and non-bank-issued prepaid cards, should closed loop gift cards be included in the cross-border reporting requirements, what to do about cards that clear customs with a minimal balance but are then subsequently reloaded with an amount in violation of the reportable limits, and what to do about a large number of non-personalized, unembossed cards."[40] Clearly, both FinCEN and DHS have some work to do in tackling the illicit use of prepaid cards.

If the legal battle against money laundering appears to be faltering in the United States, it has been a downright failure on the Mexican side of the border. Money laundering has only been a crime in Mexico for about twenty-five years. Up until 2009, Mexican authorities won only twenty-five money laundering convictions, and during the intense drug war years of 2009–2011, prosecutors only secured thirty-seven convictions for money laundering. Only the Finance Ministry has access to data that can be used to open investigations against launderers, but prosecutors can't proceed with cases that utilize that data unless someone at the Ministry files a complaint.[41] Organized crime expert Edgardo Buscaglia has said that three quarters of all financial transactions in Mexico are cash-only, and that drug money has infiltrated 78 percent of Mexico's formal economy. Mexican officials believe money laundering is a $50 billion-per-year business, and accounts for roughly 3 percent of the country's legitimate economy.[42]

That being said, some legal measures have been taken in the last few years. In 2008, the Mexican Congress approved an asset-forfeiture law that allows authorities to seize the property and accounts of traffickers and launderers. However, that law has rarely been enforced because of concerns that it threatens the due-process rights of legitimate landowners. Then in 2010, the government began restricting the dollar amount of US cash deposits into Mexican banks to $4,000 per month. But traffickers responded by sending money to other nearby countries.[43]

If new legislation in either the United States or Mexico isn't the way to go, then maybe investigative methods need to improve. In mid-2012, the US Department of Justice decided it needed to get more aggressive with AML investigations and penalties, and started ramping up the number of criminal cases it was opening against banks under the Bank Secrecy Act. Historically, punishments against banks that failed to meet compliance standards have amounted to nothing more than fines, even though the one levied against HSBC was unprecedented in dollar amount. New punishments could include financial penalties equal to the illicit funds moved and prison sentences between five and ten years for bank employees. But there's a reason individuals at larger banks don't go to prison; responsibility for failing to stem money laundering activity is usually spread out across an organization, and unless complicity can clearly be demonstrated—as opposed to a simple failure to comply or low standards—the punishment is almost always financial.[44]

However, if this shift in federal investigations of banks holds true, then banks will have to modify their compliance plans to not only help them meet AML standards, but also avoid any criminal charges that could potentially be brought against them. This could cause some friction between bank regulators, who are more interested in imposing sanctions and extracting settlements, and federal investigators, who want to see successful prosecutions. But the Department of Justice isn't interested so much in pursuing non-compliant banks based on historical activity as they are in going after institutions with recent and ongoing illicit activity. In 2010 it actually created a money laundering and bank integrity unit within its asset forfeiture section to go after what it calls professional money launderers, as opposed to just tacking a money laundering charge onto a criminal case with a different focus.[45]

Despite this more aggressive approach toward combating money laundering, progress has been very slow. The FBI has an AML unit that specializes in asset forfeiture and dismantling money laundering organizations. In fiscal year 2011, they ran a total of 303 cases that resulted in 37 indictments and 45 convictions. They recovered only $809,414 and levied just under $1 million in fines. To echo the Woodrow Wilson Institute's report on domestic AML efforts: "Given the vast amount of money laundered in the United States and size of the economy, these statistics on AML investigations, prosecutions, and restitutions are woefully low."[46]

One recommendation made by the US Senate Caucus on International Narcotics Control in April 2013 was to renew our focus on customs inspections by increasing the number of CBP agents assigned to ports of entry. The report pointed out that the number of Border Patrol agents has roughly doubled since 2004, but the number of CBP agents has only increased by 12 percent during the same time frame. It also recommended the expansion of Trade Transparency Units to more locations. These units are a collaborative effort among Homeland Security Investigations, CBP, the State Department, and the Treasury Department to work with certain foreign countries to exchange financial and trade data relevant to AML techniques. As of April 2013, these units had relationships with nine different countries—including Mexico and Colombia—with the creation of two more units in progress. The report noted that trade-based money laundering was becoming more common, and at the low cost of $200,000 to stand up each unit, new units would be ideally poised to combat this trend.[47]

As long as US law enforcement agencies and financial regulators fail to pose a real threat to banks and MSBs, many of those institutions will continue to lack the motivation to hire enough well-trained compliance officers or dig too deeply into their own operations. Banks are often accused of ignoring red flags because the discovery of suspicious activity in their accounts might cause them to lose a lot of interest income when accounts have to be frozen or closed. Successful AML laws would need to make the potential loss of that money look miniscule in comparison to the enormous fines a bank would have to pay and jail time its employees would have to serve.

Another challenge to American AML initiatives is that money laundering is a global practice. You can't stop dirty money from crossing our borders in either direction when that money is being anonymously transmitted through bitcoin purchases and PayPal transactions. You can also have the strongest AML program on the planet, but if the countries where that money is going to or coming from have weak or no AML programs, the effectiveness of any domestic efforts is automatically limited.

US authorities have long known that going after cartel money is an intrinsic part of fighting the drug war, but few people view it as an aspect of border security—perhaps because virtual money transfers render our manmade borders completely useless. Cutting off the flow of money to Mexican cartels hurts them much more than seizing drug loads, yet the border security rhetoric in the United States continues to focus on drug interdiction rather than strengthening the enforcement of AML regulations. Cartels exist for the sole purpose of making tons of money, but there is no clamor by the public or members of Congress to pay more attention to the flow of that money. US authorities are stopping a miniscule fraction of cartel money invisibly crossing our borders every day, but GAO reports and Congressional testimony center more on statistics related to operational control and immigrant apprehensions than on how poorly we're hitting cartels where it really hurts—their wallets. In the absence of major drug policy reform or a significant reduction in US drug demand, the fight against cartel money laundering deserves a much bigger share of the border security spotlight.

CHAPTER 9

TAKING MATTERS INTO THEIR OWN HANDS

We pull up in our trucks, set up lawn chairs and pull out the binocu-lars, . . . If we observe anything, we report it to the Border Patrol and lo-cal law enforcement. No contact, no taking the law into our own hands.

—Chris Simcox, co-founder of the Minuteman Civil Defense Corps

Coverage of the border has now been reduced to the vigilantes coming to the border and those who protest against them.

—Christian Ramirez, American Friends Service Committee

Texas Governor Rick Perry is not a fan of the federal government when it comes to border security policy. In September 2009, he sent a contingent of Texas Rangers to the state's border with Mexico "to fill the gap that's been left by the federal government's ongoing failure to adequately secure our international border with Mexico."[1] In August 2011, Perry told CNN, "Matter of fact: $400 million we spent on border security in Texas since '07, and that's a shame because that's a federal responsibility."[2] In July 2012, he wrote in an op-ed: "If border security were a sinking ship, Washington would ignore the rising water and then write tickets to people who tried to bail it out."[3]

It's easy to understand why state officials like Governor Perry, border state residents, law enforcement officers, and other public officials are frus-trated with the federal government. Border state residents deal with border issues on a daily basis, whereas most policymakers in Washington, DC, only see those problems on paper. They're not the ones whose fences are being destroyed so drug traffickers can trespass on their land. They're not the ones counting illegal immigrants passing through their front yards by the hundreds in a typical week. They're also not the ones seeing their hard-earned city, county, and state tax dollars being spent on programs that benefit people who knowingly broke the rules. Texas is one of the two state epicenters—Arizona being the other one—for these frustrations.

Americans and foreigners alike picture the Lone Star state as a collection of iconic images: cowboy hats and boots, horses and cattle, and lots of wide open spaces where ranchers and farmers tend to their land and animals with pride. Many ranches and farms in Texas were established shortly after the Civil War, and their ownership has been passed down from generation to generation. Being a Texas rancher or farmer is a way of life, with deep roots in the region's history.

Most of the state's border land is privately held in the form of ranches and farms. These homesteads have been in operation for decades, so their owners have pretty much seen it all. When Texas Agriculture Commissioner Todd Staples—whom you read about in Chapter 3—took office in 2006, he was mildly aware of the security situation in Mexico and along the border. But then he started getting some disturbing phone calls from his constituents.

These ranchers and farmers living on the border pleaded with Staples to be their unified voice at the state, and possibly national, level. So in March 2011, the Texas Department of Agriculture created a website called Protect YourTexasBorder.com. A few months later, department staff conducted video interviews with various Texas landowners, law enforcement officers, and public officials, who spoke about their personal experiences with the dangers of living and working so close to the border. From these videos, a sixteen-part series was created, and the videos were posted on the site, one at a time, over the course of a few months.

"There's no better evidence than personal testimony from an individual who has been harmed," said Staples. "There's none better than farmers and ranchers living along the border telling their stories. We created the Protect Your Texas Border website to be a venue for landowners to tell their stories, and we created the Texas Traffic series so we could put together repeated information from real Texans who are living the nightmare. And there's no better way to tell it than in their own words."[4]

Staples was dismissive of those who were critical of the site's intent. "I believe some people think that if you ignore a problem, it will go away. I also think this is a major breach of national sovereignty, and to secure our border and to defend our sovereignty will require enormous resources and strategic cooperation, and recognition that drug cartels are narcoterrorists. We also have a resistance to recognizing the problem for what it is from Washington politicians, who are afraid or incapable of tackling big issues because of political pressure."[5]

Adding fuel to the fire was a study commissioned by the Texas Department of Agriculture that provided a military perspective of the border security problem in Texas. The 182-page report, titled *Texas Border Security: A Strategic Military Assessment,* released in September 2011, was written by retired four-star Army general Barry McCaffrey, former director of the Office of National Drug Control Policy under President Bill Clinton, and retired Army major general Robert Scales, former commandant of the United States Army War College. The authorship is evident in the report's language. In several places, the report characterized the Texas-Mexico border as a war zone, which led some journalists to say that Staples had indeed declared war on the border and was irrationally pushing to militarize border security efforts.[6]

Despite the criticism, the Protect Your Texas Border website has stayed up and continues to draw a regular amount of Internet traffic. The Scales/McCaffrey report has been repeatedly cheered and jeered by politicians on both sides of the aisle, but that still serves a purpose: drawing attention to the plight of Texas residents—namely ranchers and farmers—living close to the border. But their role in the state's border security plan didn't end with the videos or the study.

In January 2012, the Texas Rangers—part of the Texas Department of Public Safety (DPS)—came up with a plan called Operation Drawbridge, through which they partnered up with the Texas and Southwestern Cattle Raisers Association to place cameras on the properties of participating ranchers. The cameras are inexpensive (about $300 apiece), but have the capability to operate in low light and activate via motion sensors. When movement is detected—specifically, the movement of drug smugglers or illegal immigrants—alerts are sent to the Border Patrol, the sheriff's office, the state Fusion Center (a joint interagency unit), and other border law enforcement agencies. The system that sends the alerts was created in-house by DPS information technology staff.[7]

The initial results of Operation Drawbridge were promising. The early testing phase consisted of the placement of only twenty cameras on Texas ranchland, but they led to over three hundred arrests of both immigrants and smugglers. The program expanded to three hundred cameras, and by June 2012, they resulted in over two thousand arrests and the seizure of more than five tons of illegal drugs, according to DPS.[8] Seeing the operation's success, in October 2012, the Texas Department of Agriculture awarded a $225,000 grant to DPS to extend it even further. By the time of the grant award, the number of arrests and seizure tonnage had doubled from just four months earlier.[9]

"Operation Drawbridge provides undeniable photographic proof that private landowners are constantly dealing with the dangers of deadly drug cartels and the negative consequences of illegal human trafficking. [It's] a smart way to secure our border by using low-cost technology that enhances our boots on the ground," said Staples. "We've had great success, and we're looking for ways to get more cameras deployed."[10]

Operation Drawbridge cameras aren't the only camera systems on private property along the border. Another system is run by the private company BlueServo, which created a network of cameras along the Texas-Mexico border that streams a live feed to their website. People can sign up to monitor the feeds as "Virtual Texas Deputies" and report any sightings of illegal immigrants or drug smugglers to authorities via email only. BlueServo calls it the Virtual Community Watch and describes it as "an innovative real-time surveillance program designed to empower the public to proactively participate in fighting border crime." The BlueServo system began as a private endeavor in cooperation with the Texas Border Sheriff's Coalition, but management of the program shifted to Texas DPS in September 2011.[11]

It's easy to see BlueServo's appeal to Texas residents who are angry with the federal government for not doing what they perceive as enough to stop cross-border traffic. According to the website, the system "will allow the public to directly participate in reducing crime and improving their communities." BlueServo also makes the feel-good assertion, "This service will provide millions of dollars in benefits to local border Sheriffs." Adding to the feeling of active participation is the ability for individuals to connect their own cameras on their property to the Watch system.[12]

WHILE THE STATES MAY NOT be exact neighbors, Texas and Arizona have a lot in common—high rates of cross-border drug smuggling and illegal immigration. They're also both home to large border farms and ranches, and a similar attitude that border security is up to them because the federal government can't get the job done. In 2010, Arizona set off one of the biggest legal firestorms in the state's history when it attempted to stifle illegal border crossings on its own through legislation.

The name Krentz goes back a long way in southern Arizona. The 35,000-acre family ranch has been around for over a century, the legacy of Julius and Emma Krentz. The fourth generation of the Krentz family has continued the tradition of raising purebred Hereford and Charolais, as well as cross-bred cattle. In recent years, Robert Krentz ran the entire cattle operation and was also very active in the Douglas, Arizona, community, serving as president of the Cochise-Graham Cattle Growers Association. In March 2008, the Krentz

Ranch and family were inducted into the Arizona Farming and Ranching Hall of Fame.[13]

Like many cattle ranchers in southern Arizona, Krentz was concerned about the impact of drug smuggling and illegal immigration on his business operation and the security of his property. In 2005, he told local media, "We're being overrun, and it's costing us lots and lots of money. We figured it up over the last five years, and it's cost us over $8 million. Cattle don't like people walking through, so they move. So, cattle weight loss, destruction of fences, breaking our pipelines, [immigrants] break them in two and [the pipes] run for two or three days before we find it."[14] But despite his frustrations with border crossers, he always helped those who were in need. Krentz told a PBS interviewer in 1999, "If they come and ask for water, I'll still give them water. You know, that's just my nature." He would only call the Border Patrol if the immigrant needed more help than Krentz could give.[15]

The morning of March 27, 2010, Krentz was working outside on his ranch on his all-terrain vehicle, with his loyal dog Blue in tow. He suddenly saw an individual on his property that looked like he needed serious help, so he radioed his brother Phil. "I see an immigrant out here and he appears to need help," he told Phil. "Call the Border Patrol." That would be his last transmission. Authorities didn't find Krentz's body until the end of the day, before midnight. He and his dog had both been fatally shot, but Krentz managed to drive away before losing consciousness. He was found slumped over in his ATV, which still had its lights and engine on. His gun was still in its holster, and nothing had been removed from his body or clothing.[16]

When the authorities arrived on the scene, they soon noticed a set of footprints heading in what they said was the direction of the US-Mexico border. However, the border is roughly thirty miles south of the ranch, and a direct route would take someone on foot through very difficult terrain. Despite this, the mention of the footprints immediately stirred fears (and assumptions) that the killer was an illegal immigrant.

Krentz's tragic death was immediately politicized in Arizona. Governor Jan Brewer and Senator John McCain (R-Arizona) called on DHS to deploy National Guard troops to Arizona's border with Mexico. The Krentz family issued a statement that said, "We hold no malice towards the Mexican people for this senseless act, but do hold the political forces in this country and Mexico accountable for what has happened. Their disregard of our repeated pleas and warnings of impending violence towards our community fell on deaf ears shrouded in political correctness. As a result, we have paid the ultimate price for their negligence in credibly securing our borderlands." J. D. Hayworth, McCain's opponent in the 2010 Arizona senate race, accused

McCain of not doing enough to protect US citizens from growing border violence.[17] In early April 2010, the Pima County Republican Party accused US Representative Gabrielle Giffords (D-Arizona) of using the Krentz killing for political gain. On April 4, *The Arizona Star* ran an editorial that placed partial blame for the Krentz killing on the federal government for not doing enough to secure the border.[18]

Krentz's murder, which still remains unsolved, couldn't have come at a better time for advocates of tougher immigration laws in Arizona. In January 2010, State Senator Russell Pearce (R-Mesa) introduced Senate Bill 1070 (a.k.a. SB 1070), a sweeping bill that would grant unprecedented authority to Arizona law enforcement officials to check on the immigration status of individuals suspected of being in the state illegally. The Arizona Senate passed the bill on February 15 by a vote of 17–13. Popular support for SB 1070 skyrocketed after the Krentz killing on March 27, and the House passed the bill by a vote of 35–21 on April 13. Governor Brewer signed the controversial bill into law on April 23, and the lawsuits began within days.[19]

In late July 2010, just days before SB 1070 was set to take effect, a US District Court issued an injunction against the implementation of the law, and the appeals process took the matter all the way to the US Supreme Court. In one of the most highly anticipated court decisions in recent years, on June 25, 2012, the Court finally handed down its ruling on SB 1070. Three parts of the law were struck down, but one part—a part that supporters call critical to the intent of the law—was upheld in a ruling that filled dozens of pages, along with the court members' opinions. While news of the controversial law and ensuing lawsuit have circulated for over two years—and similar laws have been passed in several other states—many Americans in non-border states don't understand the practical details, implications, and potential impact on US law enforcement agencies.

Numerous federal laws lay out the definition of a crime with regards to immigration. Federal immigration laws also explain different requirements that visitors to the United States must meet, such as having certain forms of identification, visas, etc. The federal government states that it alone has the jurisdiction to enforce these laws and regulations.

The State of Arizona, particularly under current governor Brewer, has been very vocal in denouncing the federal government's inability—and perceived unwillingness—to enforce federal immigration laws. Statistics show that roughly half of all illegal immigrants who come to the United States from Mexico cross through Arizona, making it the epicenter of immigration controversy along the border. In its decision, the Court more or less confirmed the state's troubles, saying, "Accounts in the record suggest there is an 'epidemic of crime, safety risks, serious property damage, and environ-mental problems' associated with an influx of illegal migration across pri-vate land near the Mexican border."[20] Fed up with complaints from ranchers, concerned citizens, and law enforcement officers, Arizona decided to take immigration matters into its own legislative hands.

SB 1070 contains fourteen sections and dozens of subsections, but only two full sections and two subsections were blocked in July 2010. The Court upheld the part of the bill that says that state and local law enforcement of-ficers in Arizona are authorized to determine the immigration status of any-one they reasonably suspect might be in the United States illegally. It struck down the sections that made it a state crime for undocumented immigrants not to carry an alien registration document, look for a job in Arizona, or perform work in Arizona. The Court also struck down the section that would have allowed a state or local police officer to conduct an arrest without a war-rant when police have probable cause to believe an individual committed a felony, a misdemeanor, or a crime that would make them removable from the United States. The focus of the ensuing controversy—and scrutiny by Arizona citizens, civil rights groups, and Americans in general—would be on how state and local police officers in Arizona would enforce the section that was upheld without engaging in racial profiling.

While advocates of immigration reform and migrants in general were mostly happy that parts of SB 1070 were struck down, it was too late to re-strain the national sentiment that states had to take immigration matters into their own hands because the federal government was unwilling to help them. Public opinion polls taken the week after Governor Brewer signed the law indicated most Americans had not only heard of SB 1070, but the major-ity of those polled supported such anti–illegal immigration measures in their own states.[21]

But with the widespread talk in the spring of 2013 about comprehensive immigration reform—and the bashing the Republican party took over its unwillingness to budge on illegal immigration in the 2012 elections—some states have started to back down on the issue. According to the National Con-ference of State Legislatures, the number of proposed state immigration bills dropped by 44 percent in 2012, and no omnibus bills at the state level were introduced through at least March 2013.[22]

This doesn't mean that border states, or states elsewhere that are con-cerned about border-related issues, won't try to take such matters into their own hands again at the legislative level. These actions depend a lot on the national political temperature, and events that transpired at the local level had a lot to do with SB 1070's passage. Future flare-ups of drug and human smuggling activity may motivate ambitious legislators to make a political statement with controversial bills in the future.

After reading an entire chapter on the pros and (mostly) cons of the almost seven hundred miles of border fence that have been erected along the southwest border, it may come as a slight surprise that there is no shortage of people wanting to construct even more miles of fencing, regardless of cost. Some of the most vocal fence supporters live in Arizona, home to the busiest smuggling corridors along the entire southwest border. Most of this border section already has either a pedestrian fence or vehicle barrier, but there are some gaps in a few places, as you saw in Chapter 3. Based on seizure and apprehension data, many people and illegal drugs are managing to get through these gaps.

On July 20, 2011, an Arizona law went into effect that permitted the use of private donations to complete border fence construction in that state. Supporters created a website where donations could be made, and in its first day alone, the program raised over $58,000 from almost 1,300 donors. By August 2012, organizers had raised around $273,000, which sounds like a good start, but the ultimate goal of these private fence builders was to construct an additional two hundred miles of barrier. That comes at the very conservative estimate of $2.8 million *per mile*.[23]

All these plans started when the Arizona state legislature created a border security advisory committee in 2010. Members included Republican state lawmakers, county sheriffs, and state department heads, and the legislature tasked the committee with making recommendations to the governor about how to handle the border. Despite this tasking, no recommendations have been made to the legislature since the committee started meeting in March 2011. They were also supposed to file monthly reports, which they stopped producing in April 2012. The committee did not convene once in 2013. Despite the bureaucratic red tape, and the fact the planned fence would have to cross federally owned land, tribal reservations, and private property, State Senator Steve Smith (R-Maricopa) was optimistic, telling the *Arizona Republic* in August 2012 that he believed more private donations would come in once construction began—something he felt could happen by year's end.[24]

This was a bold statement from Smith, considering the construction materials hadn't been acquired, the prison labor hadn't been arranged, and the land where the fence would go hadn't been designated. It's pretty clear the privatized fence project is never going to get off the ground—or into the ground, as it were—but it did seem to have some sort of value. State Representative Russ Jones (R-Arizona), a chairman of the Legislature's advisory committee, told the Associated Press, "I don't think with the money that's [been] raised that it's going to be a large area [of fencing]. It may be more symbolic than anything. But it will be something."[25]

Despite the obstacles, both financial and logistical, efforts to raise money, support, and awareness continue. The state has created a website called "Build the Border Fence" where people can make donations and read more about the endeavor. It even assures visitors to the site that "online donors will receive an official numbered certificate from the State of Arizona thanking you for your support." However, the website hasn't been updated since mid-2012, and the last donation was made in February 2013. There is no indication as to whether or not the certificates are still being handed out.

In August 2013, the *Arizona Daily Sun* reported that the Legislature's border security advisory committee was trying to figure out how to spend the $275,250 in donations they had gathered, since state law clearly says the money has to be used to "construct and maintain a secure fence." Roughly $11,000 of that money was spent on software, office supplies, and postage, but nothing fence-related. Smith said a plan to spend the rest of the money was being formulated and would be put into action in a few weeks' time; he offered no specifics on what that plan might be.[26]

In late July 2013, I made the two-hour drive from Tucson to the small Arizona border town of Hereford to visit probably the most controversial individual involved in the private border watch movement. I had been reading quite a bit about Glenn Spencer in the previous months, but I still wasn't quite sure what to expect as I neared his 104-acre ranch that abuts the border fence in this part of town. I was just praying that my car would survive the ruts, dips, and holes in the two-mile-long dirt road that had been thoroughly abused by the season's heavy monsoon rains, but was a necessary hazard to get to his property. Then I smiled a bit when I saw a sign advertising American Border Patrol (ABP), Spencer's non-profit organization, that read, "Drug smugglers/addicts don't like us." They are certainly not the only ones who feel that way.

The Southern Poverty Law Center is a non-profit organization that monitors hate groups in the United States. They have a large staff that includes attorneys who routinely file lawsuits against people or organizations they perceive are violating the civil rights of their clients. Their self-proclaimed mission is to eradicate radical extremism through "innovative lawsuits," advocacy, and education. It's an understatement to say the Center dislikes Spencer, and their website describes him as "a vitriolic Mexican-basher and self-appointed guardian of the border."[27] Stephen Lemons of the *Phoenix New Times* called him "a serious nutbar who has attended white supremacist

events in the past and who likes to peddle the phony, racist 'reconquista' conspiracy theory."[28] Numerous blog writers and forum posters over the past
dozen or so years have repeatedly used the terms "racist" and "anti-Semite"
when referring to Spencer. So how is it that virtually an equal number of
bloggers and posters call him a patriot and tireless border defender, and there
is clear evidence that he has thousands of supporters?

Spencer has an interesting history. He has what he describes as a "broad
background" in everything from systems engineering and statistical analysis
to computer modeling and seismic exploration of oil deposits. He knew little
to nothing about the southwest border and illegal immigration in general
until he moved to Los Angeles in the mid-1980s for his work. His wife worked
in the school system there, and based on things she observed, he became dis-
illusioned with the various social services—including free education—being
provided to illegal immigrants in the city. Through press reports and a friend
in law enforcement, Spencer was also becoming hyper aware of shootings in
the city involving illegal immigrants.

He soon became involved with the right-wing Federation for American
Immigration Reform, then formed his own anti-illegal immigrant group
called Voice of Citizens Together in the early 1990s. The attendance at the
group's monthly meetings slowly grew, and they started to get some local
press coverage. Spencer came to consider himself a full-blown activist, and in
1994 he aggressively backed California's Proposition 187, which would have
banned any public funding of social services for illegal immigrants in the
state. Even though the bill passed in 1994, it was essentially nullified a few
years later after several legal challenges. Spencer, angry and frustrated with
the legislative gridlock in California, decided in 2002 to move to southern
Arizona—a place where he felt he could more effectively combat illegal immigration. "I had been through a lot, and I had seen a lot," explained Spencer.
"I couldn't let it go. I decided that I couldn't do anything about California.
There were so many powerful forces at the state level, at every level, in the city
council . . . everywhere. All the media would try to defeat any attempt to stop
illegal immigration into California. I just quit."[29]

Before the move, however, Spencer dug himself a pretty deep grave with
several public comments that earned him the labels of racist, anti-Semite,
and white supremacist. In 1996, he wrote a letter to the *Los Angeles Times*
that said, in part, "Mexican culture is based on deceit" and that "Chica-
nos and Mexicanos lie as a means of survival." He also posted an article to
his ABP blog in late 2008 titled "Is Jew-Controlled Hollywood Brainwash-
ing Americans?"[30] He has been linked to former Minuteman member and
convicted murderer Shawna Forde, various white supremacist groups, and

anti-Semites, sometimes just by virtue of his attendance at meetings where they also happened to be present, or because he interviewed them for his radio show.

He brought all this baggage with him to southern Arizona, where he created the non-profit ABP and the for-profit company Border Technology, Inc. "I came out here and I laid out a plan," Spencer said. "I wanted to use border technology to look at the border." So he got to work making sensors and small unmanned aerial vehicles that would detect illegal border crossers, ostensibly more effectively and more cheaply than systems being used by DHS. He routinely scheduled demonstrations of his creations for tech company executives, politicians, and journalists. He also posted videos of his experiments and trials on the ABP website, as well as live video streams of cameras he had deployed in various parts of the southwest border so viewers could observe illegal crossings. One of his biggest website projects was flying along the border in his private plane and photographing the construction of the mandated sections of border fence as it progressed.

I've seen his technological creations in action, and the unexpected thing is that they really do work. He and his team have made refinements that have been praised by others in the industry as revolutionary, and the cost to implement his systems is well below that of tech giants like Boeing and Honeywell. But despite the VIPs who come to see his work and the journalists who come to visit and interview him, he has yet to make a major sale of any of his systems, and very few media outlets have written about him in a way that encourages readers to take him seriously. The negative publicity he has generated—including a March 2012 walkout by two Arizona state senators during a hearing where he provided testimony—has completely overwhelmed any positive buzz that could emerge from his work.

Spencer believes his biggest hindrance comes from the US government, which he says doesn't want the American public to know the truth about illegal immigration. "I found that nobody wanted to know about it. A little bit at the beginning, but that was from all the media coverage in the first couple of years. But when they started getting really serious about [illegal immigration], they really came after me." Spencer then cited the negative reactions he received on the FOX News show *The O'Reilly Factor,* in meetings, and in other media interviews, where he claimed he was merely quoting racist-sounding comments made by others. However, he said that any anti-immigrant comments he made—including his theory that Mexicans wanted to reconquer and take back a huge chunk of the United States—were always attributed to him in bad context, and that accusations of racism increased right around the time the Southern Poverty Law Center designated ABP as a hate group.

"That is a side of me that I left eleven years ago. I haven't posted any videos since, I haven't given any talks about [the *Reconquista*] since; I've just focused on the border. But there is that history out there where people come after me for doing this," Spencer said. "But I believe I'm right—I know I'm right—and that everything I say is true."[31]

But for all the criticism of Spencer's technological work and personal philosophy, he has no shortage of supporters. After we finished chatting in his guesthouse, I followed him to the part of his property where he demonstrates his various sensors and drones to visitors. Visible from quite some distance were two walls, positioned about fifteen yards north of the brown bollard-style border fence. Both walls had a blue background, were about fifteen feet high, forty yards long, and were separated by a twenty-foot gap. In white letters, the sign on the left read "SAVE THE UNITED STATES," and the one on the right read "SECURE THE BORDER"; the word "FIRST!" was added at the end shortly after the immigration reform debate started in earnest in early 2013. From a distance, the words look painted on. However, close up, the letters tell a completely different story.

In 2008, Spencer (via ABP) started a program called Flags Along the Border, where supporters would send him small American flags with attached tags where they would write their names, sometimes former military units, and often words encouraging him to continue his work. The first few years of the program, Spencer would tie the flags to the old barbed wire border fence. After the new fence went up, he stapled the flags to long wood planks that he would attach to the bollards. Border Patrol agents started tearing the planks down, so Spencer built his own walls for the flags, with thousands of tiny holes placed in each letter. At the time of my visit, there were over ten thousand little flags filling those holes, all sent to him from supporters across the country and around the world. Most of the writing on the tags was faded from monsoon rains and the scorching desert sun, but Spencer had several boxes in his workshop filled with thousands more flags. He was saving them for placement in the wall right before a major demonstration of his sensor and drone system in mid-August 2013—a demonstration that went well enough to earn him an invitation by CBP to speak with Mark Borkowski, the DHS technology acquisitions guru.[32] Getting a seat in front of Borkowski is the Holy Grail for any vendor in the border technology business, and it will be interesting to see if DHS can look past Spencer's reputation and make use of the systems he's developed over the years.

Despite the controversy surrounding Spencer and the ABP, his activities are largely limited to the technology he develops on his property and the personal interaction—love it or hate it—that he has with the media and

Glenn Spencer and his personal border wall, filled with flags bearing messages from supporters.

government agencies. But no conversation about border residents taking security matters into their own hands would be complete without taking a look at the various watchdog groups that physically patrol the border (usually with weapons). Some are known as "Minutemen" and others (more derisively) as vigilantes. One of the more well known of these groups is the Minuteman Civil Defense Corps (MCDC). Much like Spencer, Chris Simcox, the group's founder, has what one might call a "colorful" personal history. When he was younger, he attempted to become a pro baseball player and a drummer. After neither panned out, he moved to California and became a teacher for thirteen years, then later a private tutor. During this time, he came across a lot of Latino immigrant students who could not speak English, an issue that disturbed him as more and more time passed.[33]

During the attacks of 9/11, Simcox's concerns over illegal immigration expanded to a fear of terrorism. That day, he left a disturbing message for his second wife on their answering machine: "I purchased another gun. I have more than a few weapons and I plan on teaching my son how to use them. I will no longer trust anyone in this country. My life has changed forever, and if you don't get that, you are brainwashed like everybody else." His African

American wife, with whom he had a son, at the time thought he had suffered a breakdown because of this and other apocalyptic and racist statements he was increasingly making. As a result, she divorced Simcox and gained full custody of their son.[34]

Simcox tried to join the Army in the wake of 9/11, but was denied because of his age. He later moved to rural southern Arizona and was disturbed by how porous he felt the border was, particularly because he was living near Organ Pipe Cactus National Monument, one of the busiest smuggling corridors in the country. He applied for a job with the Border Patrol, but was again turned down because of his age. While living in the Arizona town of Tombstone, he got a job as the local newspaper's assistant editor, and in 2002 he used his retirement earnings to buy the *Tombstone Tumbleweed* for $60,000. He then used the paper to chronicle border problems associated with illegal immigration.[35] Two months after he bought the paper, the front page read, "ENOUGH IS ENOUGH! A PUBLIC CALL TO ARMS! CITIZENS BORDER PATROL MILITIA NOW FORMING!"[36]

After this announcement, Simcox formed a militia called Civil Homeland Defense and claimed he had hundreds of volunteers joining him on his border watch in Cochise County. The locals mostly viewed him as an eccentric who could, in reality, only round up a few people to help him out. However, Simcox had his sights set on something bigger. In October 2004, Simcox joined up with former Marine, reporter and retired accountant Jim Gilchrist, to form the Minuteman Project. As with Simcox, the 9/11 attacks had a profound impact on Gilchrist, who was "outraged that most of the Saudi attackers were in the country illegally, having overstayed their visas." Gilchrist also "blamed the federal government for allowing the tragedy to happen."[37]

In April 2005, Simcox and Gilchrist launched the Minuteman Project with a demonstration in Tombstone that drew only about 150 people, despite their claims that they had recruited closer to 1,300 volunteers. US Representative Tom Tancredo (R-Colorado), founder of the Congressional Immigration Reform Caucus, was the keynote speaker at the event. The previous month, then President George W. Bush had condemned the Minuteman Project at a joint press conference with former Mexican President Vicente Fox, saying "I'm against vigilantes in the United States of America." Tancredo replied to that condemnation at the rally by announcing to attendees, "You are not vigilantes. You are heroes!" He then described Simcox and Gilchrist as "two good men who understand we must never surrender our right as citizens to do our patriotic duty and defend our country . . . and stop this invasion ourselves."[38]

However, Simcox and Gilchrist went their separate ways in December 2005—just a few short months after the Project's founding—due to conflicts over financial issues. In fact, two years later, Project members accused Gilchrist of using $300,000 to help promote a book he co-wrote and to fund an unsuccessful bid for a Congressional seat in 2005.[39] Gilchrist kept the Minuteman Project name and Simcox founded the MCDC in the wake of the split. Simcox immediately began aggressively pursuing opportunities to expand the MCDC's reach, announcing that patrols would start along the Canadian border in places like Vermont and New York.

Despite Simcox's attempts to emphasize MCDC's standard operating procedure of not engaging with immigrants and just reporting border crossings to the authorities, the group developed a reputation as racist, anti-immigrant, and violent. The common image of these citizen border watchers became one of old white men grilling brats and swilling beer on the border while looking through binoculars and comparing rifles. While there was some truth to that stereotype, not every MCDC volunteer was like that. However, the bad apples in the bushel tended to paint a generally negative picture for all border watch organizations, which are invariably labeled as vigilante groups.

In 2010 there was a surge in violence across the border and a rise in anti-immigrant sentiment in Arizona; despite this, the MCDC ceased to exist that year, largely due to a serious miscalculation of member sentiment. On March 16, 2010, MCDC president Carmen Mercer sent out a "call to action" via email to MCDC members, telling them to come to the border "locked, loaded and ready" and urging people to bring "long arms." Moving away from the group's longstanding procedures, she proposed a rule change that would allow members to track illegal immigrants and drug smugglers instead of just reporting the activity to the Border Patrol: "We will forcefully engage, detain, and defend our lives and country from the criminals who trample over our culture and laws."[40]

Just one week later, Mercer sent out another email completely dissolving the organization. Her previous email had very much polarized members, with some more than ready to hit the border "locked and loaded," and others vehemently opposing any rule change that would so dramatically alter the group's standard procedures. In the email, Mercer said, "It was obvious that many had decided to return to the border who had tired of the sometimes futile watch and observe methods. It showed me that people are not willing to be silenced anymore. It also showed me that people will be less likely to follow the rules of engagement in a desperate attempt to stop the criminals who violate our borders every day. That is not what we want and we cannot take responsibility for this."[41]

But other citizen watch groups—or vigilante groups, if you prefer—continue to operate along different parts of the border with varying levels of membership, commitment, resources, and infighting. In 2005, private investigator and bounty hunter Shannon McGauley partnered with Gilchrist to expand the Minuteman Project into Texas, where he founded the Texas Minutemen. In 2006, Dr. Mike Vickers and his wife Linda formed the Texas Border Volunteers, which sprang from the Minutemen organization. The Volunteers seem to be a more mellow and well-reputed organization, as border watch groups go. Border Patrol agents were initially concerned that armed members would get into violent confrontations with immigrants or smugglers, but they now welcome the reports of illegal border crossings the Volunteers detect during their patrols.[42]

Anti-illegal immigrant groups are not the only ones who are keeping watch over the desert, however. Organizations such as the non-profit group Humane Borders offer humanitarian assistance to border crossers through the deployment of emergency water stations on well-used routes. Since its creation in 2000, the group's "sole mission is to take death out of the immigration equation." The water tanks Humane Borders uses to help immigrants in trouble are deployed on both public and private land with permission from landowners. They're the only such group that has secured all the permits and permissions necessary to place the barrels, and as such, have legal recourse if they are vandalized or removed.[43]

In addition to the water stations, Humane Borders also partners with the Pima County medical examiner's office to keep track of immigrant deaths and plot their locations on a map available online to the public. The goal of the program is to "raise awareness about migrant deaths and lessening the suffering of families by helping to provide closure through the identification of the deceased and the return of remains." Indeed, the graphic is unsettling. Since January 2001, over 2,100 immigrants have perished in the Pima County jurisdiction alone. The red dots indicating a migrant's death completely obscure a triangle roughly from Douglas northwest to Mesa, then southwest to Cabeza Prieta National Wildlife Refuge, then east down the borderline back to Douglas.[44]

In August 2013, I met with Joel Smith, the operations director for Humane Borders, at their office in South Tucson before heading out to see one of the roughly fifty water stations they have deployed in Arizona and Sonora. He has been with the organization since 2009, and said he wanted to get involved because he was getting tired of reading about all the migrant deaths in the desert: "I live out here, I work out here, and I love going out in the desert. I saw all the migrant trails and all these caution signs, but the death toll kept climbing. That's how I came to Humane Borders."[45]

The biggest criticism leveled at organizations like Humane Borders is that the availability of potable water in the Arizona desert only encourages more illegal immigrants to make the trek north. Joel and other volunteers used to distribute flyers in Mexico so migrants would know how to find the stations, but both DHS and the Mexican government made them put an end to that—not because it would encourage illegal immigration, but because they were concerned that armed militia groups would ambush migrants at the water stations. Coyotes know where the stations are and how to find them by the blue flags flying on thin poles above them. However, Smith scoffs at the notion that migrants are increasingly encouraged to brave the dangers of the desert because of the water supply.

"That's false; it's misinformation that's been parroted for years. When I go down to Sonora [in Mexico], these migrants in the camps I visit have never even heard of us," Smith explained. "These are simple people. Radio is extravagant for them. They come from little villages where maybe they hear

Joel Smith, Operations Chief for Humane Borders, and one of the organization's water stations near Three Points, Arizona.

a couple of hours of radio a week. They're not on the Internet, they're not watching TV or reading books. They have no idea who we are, or that there's even somebody doing this. It's easy to say we're luring them across, but that's not true at all. They've never even heard of us."[46]

I was curious about how the Border Patrol views the Humane Borders operation, and there seems to be a relationship of mutual respect between the two organizations. Smith explained that local Border Patrol leadership has had a positive impact on the physical integrity of their stations. After the sector chief announced at a meeting a few years ago that agents were to stay away from the water tanks (except in the event of an enforcement action), Smith noticed that incidents of vandalism and the disabling of the tanks dropped significantly. Volunteers don't often interact with migrants, who sometimes think the resupply trucks belong to law enforcement. But when they do get a chance to talk, the volunteers will just ask questions like if anyone in their group is injured or if anyone is hiding from them who needs water. If someone needs immediate medical attention or wants to turn themselves in to Border Patrol, the volunteers will call the closest station or use a Spot GPS beacon to summon assistance.

After a 45-minute drive to the small town of Three Points southwest of Tucson, we took Highway 286 south toward Sasabe before turning off onto a gated dirt road. The land where Humane Borders had secured permission for this particular tank was under a state trust and leased out to ranchers. After driving about a quarter mile into this portion of the Altar Valley, it was hard to see what ranching could be accomplished there, but quite easy to see how any migrants who somehow made it that far north on foot would be desperate for water. The expanse of hot sand was interrupted only by the occasional creosote bush or teddy bear cactus, and the triple-digit heat was stifling.

The bright blue of the water tank stood out in its surroundings, and the blue flag was relatively easy to spot above the sparse vegetation. Ironically enough, I saw that the Border Patrol had set up a rescue beacon only a few yards from a water source that would reduce the need for migrants to ask for a rescue. After a quick chuckle over that, Joel and I got out of the truck to check out the drum. Joel and other volunteers have a way to check the water levels inside each fifty-five-gallon drum to see if people have been using them, but because they don't remotely observe the stations with cameras, they have no way of knowing how many migrants find and use them. "It's basically one of those intangibles," said Smith. "If we're not seeing migrant deaths around our stations, then we're counting that as a success because there are enough bodies out there right now."[47]

BY THIS POINT, YOU KNOW that DHS and other government agencies don't have the resources to prevent all illegal border crossings; in reality, no country does. But due to gross financial mismanagement and an inability to prioritize threats, our federal government is not effectively using the resources it does have. Therefore, DHS cannot say with any degree of credibility to the border states that "we're doing the best we can." As a result, the states and individuals within those states have decided to take action while they wait for DHS to man up.

This doesn't mean that every state- and individual-based initiative is going to be a good one. Some border watch groups like American Border Patrol have earned "fringe" status and are viewed as dangerous rather than helpful, whether those characterizations are accurate or not. But most Americans don't just sit around and wait for the government to figure out what to do, and this is especially true in the enterprising "red" states of Arizona and Texas.

Controversy will always surround any organization that takes a government matter into its own hands. But taking care of business is the American way, and as long as border residents feel the US government is failing in its duty to protect them from harm, they'll continue to do what they feel is necessary.

CHAPTER 10

THE BIG BUSINESS OF BORDER SECURITY

It's a world where billions of dollars are potentially at stake, and one in which nothing is more important than creating, testing, and even flaunting increasingly sophisticated and expensive technologies meant for border patrol and social control, without serious thought as to what they might really portend.[1]

—Todd Miller, CBS News reporter, June 2012

If we're going to live with the border day to day and all its problems and issues, why shouldn't we get the economic benefit from it?[2]

—Bruce Wright, associate vice president, University of Arizona, Office of University Research Parks

On a sunny and generally gorgeous March afternoon in Phoenix, I walked into the exposition hall of Border Security Expo (BSE) 2013 after a morning of keynote speeches and informational sessions. The sights and sounds were overwhelming in the cavernous space inside the Phoenix Convention Center. I was immediately assaulted by enormous corporate signs bearing the logos of technology companies large and small, known and unknown, hanging from the ceiling and even spinning at the top of elevated displays. As I started walking down the dozen or so aisles of roughly 180 exhibitors, I saw the hallmarks of every security-themed conference I've ever attended: huge professional graphics, computer displays, brightly colored brochures and pamphlets, and the indispensable candy bowls and freebies. If you're a pen collector, this was the place to be. Interspersed throughout the booths were an enormous armored vehicle with digital camouflage paint, a three-story

enclosed stairway used for tactical training, and scale models of surveillance
blimps and unmanned aerial vehicles. There was even a booth for a human
waste disposal kit for the Border Patrol agent with no access to a portable
toilet.

Just the sheer number of tools, widgets, gadgets, weapons, and video
screens on display was overwhelming. It's almost impossible to contemplate
a dollar figure for all the research and development money that went into creating these prototypes and fully functional systems. And every single vendor
in the building was hoping that at least one person from an agency involved
in border security would see their company's gadget and think it's the most
amazing thing they've ever seen. Maybe someone in acquisitions would look
the gadget up on the company's website and agree with the conference attendee. A phone call might be made to the company to set up a demonstration. And perhaps a year or two (or more) down the road, that company just
might secure a multi-million-dollar contract to provide hundreds of those
gadgets to the Department of Homeland Security.

It seems like an incredibly long shot for these vendors, and surely there
must be a more effective and efficient way to bring these technological mar-
vels to the attention of the agencies that can benefit from them most. But

The exposition hall at Border Security Expo 2013.

every year, hundreds of corporate giants and small businesses invest tens of thousands of dollars to attend these conferences, display their wares in a tiny booth, and pray the homeland security contracting gods are smiling down on them for just a couple of days while agency executives meander down the aisles. This is because the payday that could remotely result from such a conference will likely be large enough to keep many companies afloat for years. The market for border security–related goods is growing by 5 percent every year, and could become a $25 billion industry by 2020.[3]

BSE 2013 is only one of several annual conferences that focus almost exclusively on border issues like drug trafficking, human smuggling, immigration, and border violence. The lineup of keynote speakers, presenters, and panelists for these conventions is usually a "who's who" of senior officials and executives in CBP, Border Patrol, DHS, state and local law enforcement, FBI, DEA, ICE, and private industry. They offer their expertise on issues like the latest technological advances being used along both US borders, drug-related violence, human trafficking, border technology, illegal immigration, and cross-border cooperation. There's no doubt there is an abundance of useful information provided to attendees over the course of the two or three days of these conferences, and the networking opportunities are incredibly valuable.

But there is more to these conferences than the vast majority of lanyard and nametag-wearing attendees ever see: behind the scenes, hundreds of thousands of dollars change hands in order to put a conference together, and some of the money is provided by US taxpayers.

Most conferences have tiered registration fees based on how early you register and what sector you're a part of. For example, the standard non-"early bird" fee for government civilians, military personnel, and students for BSE 2013 was $215. However, the fee for industry registrants—meaning the self-employed (this would be me) and those working for private corporations and small businesses was a whopping $1,075. The 2012 Border Management Conference and Technology Expo run by the Institute for Defense and Government Advancement (IDGA) set each attendee, regardless of sector, back $1,835 for access to the summit and all associated events, and the fees remained the same for its Southwest Summit in May 2013. The main Government Security (GovSec) Expo in May 2013 was a bargain in comparison, with fees ranging from $99 for law enforcement officers and first responders to $455 for government contractors.

The attendance at each of these varies from year to year depending on budgets, the allure of keynote speakers, and the perceived quality of the sessions. However, even the lowest attendance I've seen has still been over one hundred people for a debut effort and well over one thousand for an established and reputable convention. Conservatively speaking, multiplying those attendance fees by just a few hundred attendees . . . well, you get the picture.

But registration fees aren't the only way conference organizers bring in money. The famed Expo Hall, printed conference programs, and corporate logos on every white space in the building are even bigger moneymakers, and organizers charge hundreds and often thousands of dollars for advertising and display space. The exhibitor prospectus for the 2013 Border Security Expo announced: "The 2012 Border Security Expo attendance grew more than 20 percent, with a SOLD-OUT Exhibit Floor. Within 90 days following, BSE 2013 is already more than 60 percent sold, and remaining space and sponsorships opportunities are selling fast! Last year, over 70 companies waited too long and were placed on a 'wait list.' Don't get locked out! Secure your space and sponsorships now!" It also listed well-known corporate sponsors like Motorola, Raytheon, and General Dynamics to assure potential exhibitors that they would be in the company of the elite.

Exhibitor information pamphlets are very professional marketing products, showcasing all the attending agencies and how companies could benefit from demonstrating their products to hundreds of knowledgeable executives and decision makers. But that exposure comes at a steep price. A modest 10 × 10-foot exhibit booth at BSE 2013 cost $2,800, although organizers did offer a discount of one dollar off the $28 per square foot price for anything over four hundred square feet. At BSE 2013, there were about 180 booths of varying size. Again, multiplying a conservative estimate of 180 small booths (many are much larger) in a sold-out situation by roughly $3,000 per booth means many zeros at the end of the final sum. If you merely wanted to advertise and not demonstrate a product, you could hang your company's banner in the convention center lobby for $5,500, stamp your company's name on a canvas bag given to all attendees for $4,500, or sponsor a networking reception for $20,000.

While there's a lot of money going into these security conventions and to the event companies that put them together, there's also a lot of money going out. It isn't cheap to rent out space at a premier convention center or resort. Guest speakers and panelists usually aren't paid or reimbursed for travel expenses, as most of them are employed by an agency or company that covers that. However, keynote speakers like General Stanley McChrystal and Joe Theismann (both were scheduled for GovSec 2013) don't come cheap, often commanding tens of thousands of dollars for appearances. Session rooms, exhibit booths, stages, and sound systems need to be set up and skilled people paid to do it. Food and beverages for breakfast, coffee breaks, luncheons, cocktail parties, and awards dinners need to be purchased (if a company isn't sponsoring them), and employees paid to prepare, serve, and clean up afterward.

The upside of all this spending is that it's good for the economy, and particularly for the cities in which these conferences are held. Many attendees will play golf at local courses, eat at local restaurants, drink at local bars, and stay in local hotels. This is all above and beyond the educational and networking benefits provided by attending the conference itself. Professional connections made this way are invaluable, and word of mouth about innovative technologies demonstrated in expo halls can help the companies that make them and the border agencies that can afford to purchase them.

The downside is that the majority of people who attend these security conferences are federal, state, or local government or law enforcement officials, with some military personnel sprinkled in. That means the person who ultimately pays for someone to attend one of these conferences—including their airfare, hotel, registration fee, and per diem (daily expenses)—is the American taxpayer. I believe that most people who go to these conferences sit through most sessions and go for the actual intended purpose, but some "attendees" use the trip as a free vacation and only show up for the social events. It happens, and unless those people have supervisors or coworkers in attendance who care enough to scold them, there's really no way to control that.

Ultimately, I believe border security conferences and other related conventions with a border security track are valuable and worthwhile to attend for the often useful and wide variety of information presented through briefings or panel sessions. You also just can't put a price on the networking. It is a wonderful thing when you need some crucial information from an agency or company where you didn't know a soul the week before, and all of a sudden you have a business card for a guy who you know loves rum and cokes and also happens to work there. But make no mistake—conference organizers like EagleEye, Clarion, IDGA, and 1105Media that put some of these conventions together are not charities.

Then in March 2013, a hydrogen bomb fell on the border security industry—sequestration. Even though the furloughs and major cuts weren't set to start until the following month, BSE 2013 was probably the first conference to really feel the pinch. Most of the scheduled keynote speakers, including Chief of the Border Patrol Michael Fisher, CBP Deputy Commissioner David Aguilar, and ICE Director John Morton, cancelled their appearances due to budget cuts. One panel session was cancelled because all of the panelists were no longer authorized to attend, and a number of attendees also had to cancel their travel plans at the last minute. Conference organizers did an incredible job of replacing speakers at the last minute, but the diminished attendance and prestige of presenters was notable. Most obvious—and slightly embarrassing—was the absence of Chief Aguilar since he was due to receive an Award for Excellence in Border Security Initiatives at a luncheon (sponsored by General Dynamics) being held in his honor. Fortunately, CBP had time to put together a really professional video of him giving an acceptance speech.

If award recipients and VIP speakers were being affected by sequestration and budget cuts, you can imagine the extent of reduced opportunities for lower and even mid-level officers and employees to attend these conferences. However, the organizers of GovSec West thought of a way to help these folks come to Dallas in November 2013 and bring in much-needed revenue: the "justify your attendance" letter to be provided to the attendee's travel-approving authorities. The fill-in letter allows plenty of opportunity for the employee to explain how their attendance at GovSec West will be an amazing benefit for his or her agency, closing with: "The opportunity for me to develop better contacts with industry experts and to gain knowledge in specific areas of government security makes my attendance at the GovSec conference a wise investment, which will yield rich dividends for [insert company/agency name here]."[4]

Reactions in the BSE exhibit hall to the diminished attendance and the potential impact of sequestration on business prospects were mixed. Some companies probably won't be impacted at all because their main customer base consists of state or local law enforcement agencies that don't receive a significant amount of funding from federal sources. For other companies, it was a different story. Lawrence Ottaviano of Hitachi Corporation told the Associated Press that the reduced attendance as a result of sequestration "basically killed the show. By these people not coming, it's basically like trying to sell them a car without having a test drive."[5]

Craig Laws, a program manager for Raven Aerostar, wasn't too concerned. The company he worked for made aerostats, which had applications internationally: "Even before sequestration, we were starting to see a slowdown on the US side because the surge had already taken place in Afghanistan, and the talk was about pulling out. We don't see [sequestration] as much of a threat as some of the other vendors would because we're a low-cost solution. We're [also] not the only country in the world that's concerned about border security. We get to see that as somebody who fields inquiries from around the world, and that's the other reason we don't feel threatened by the sequester. There's a lot of [international] potential, and we've just started to scratch the surface."[6]

That seemed to be a sentiment shared by many of his colleagues in the Expo Hall, simply because many of the other systems and gadgets on display also had international applications. Many had been tried and tested in places like Afghanistan by the Department of Defense and were being reconfigured and rebranded for homeland security uses. Michael Mackesy of Optellios, a small company in Pennsylvania that makes a fiber-optic intrusion detection system, thought the money would be there regardless of sequestration simply because the need for border security technological solutions was constant. "They're spending money they don't have now. [DHS] will say, *We really want your product. We can't afford your product.* But they can do anything they want. They can print money, or they [can incur] a CAPEX [capital expenditure]. Instead of paying in one lump sum they'll make monthly payments for three years."[7]

These conferences and expos are just the tip of the iceberg when it comes to the volume of money flowing across the United States in the name of border security. In the last decade and a half, an entire industry has exploded in a race to secure DHS contracts for fencing, sensors, cameras, staffing, and more. The question we need to ask is not whether enough money is being spent on securing our borders; it's already a multi-billion-dollar business. We need to ask if the choices our leaders are making about *how* existing funding is being spent are the best ones. Is the money going to the places and companies and universities where it can be best utilized, and where taxpayers can get the best return on their investment? Are there sufficient ways to determine if grant recipients are producing satisfactory results, and if not, is there a quick and effective way to cut off the money flow so it can be redirected? Most importantly, are there sufficient oversight mechanisms in place to minimize incidents of fraud, waste, and abuse? Unfortunately, the answers to these questions are grim.

One of the larger US government investments in the drug war is the Mérida Initiative. In 2007, then presidents George W. Bush and Felipe Calderón signed the initiative, a sweeping counterdrug assistance program that allocated money for efforts in Central America and the Caribbean, but mostly in Mexico. Between fiscal years 2008 and 2012, Congress appropriated $1.9 billion in Mérida assistance for Mexico, roughly $1.1 billion of which had been delivered as of November 2012. The big initial concern, of course, was that almost $2 billion was going to go to a highly corrupted government and its law enforcement agencies. Fortunately, the funding was designed to go straight into the US economy in the form of US equipment purchases and training packages for the Mexican military and police departments. In its

2013 budget request, the Obama administration asked for an additional $234 million in Mérida assistance for Mexico.[8]

In truth, since the Mérida Initiative was enacted in 2007, there have been some small improvements in law enforcement and military capabilities in Mexico, but corruption and violence levels have remained essentially unchanged. That may not be of much concern to the sellers of the surveillance aircraft and helicopters now, who get paid regardless of the drug war's progress. However, recently the flow of funding has shifted from aircraft and equipment to organizations that can provide training and support in the areas of institution building, which would negatively impact these manufacturers and sellers.[9]

The results and benefits of this training aren't likely to be seen for many years down the road. The changes in Mexico's justice system aren't set to take effect for a few years and are being implemented a few states at a time, not nationally. However, the American companies that provide this equipment and training benefit sooner rather than later.

Shortly after the creation of DHS in 2003, the agency created the Homeland Security Grant Program (HSGP). Per DHS, the grant program "is a primary funding mechanism for building and sustaining national preparedness capabilities . . . these grants fund a range of preparedness activities, including planning, organization, equipment purchase, training, exercises and management and administration."[10] The HSGP is currently comprised of three interconnected programs, one of which is called Operation Stonegarden. In a nutshell, state and local agencies can apply for DHS grant money through this program to help them conduct border security–related operations. The grants are designed to increase collaboration among agencies with similar missions, and provide them with the proper equipment and resources to accomplish their border-related tasks.

Annual funding for Operation Stonegarden grants has fluctuated, starting with $60 million in 2009, and reaching a low point of $46 million in 2012, before rebounding to $55 million for fiscal year 2013. Although agencies in all the southern and northern border states can apply for these grants, in July 2010, then DHS Secretary Napolitano announced that 80 percent of Operation Stonegarden funds would be allocated to southwestern border states.[11] However, DHS has specific criteria for how those funds will be distributed to those states: "OPSG funds will be allocated based on risk-based prioritization using a CBP Sector-specific border risk methodology to include, but not limited to: threat, vulnerability, miles of border, and other border-specific 'law enforcement intelligence.'"[12]

As is always the problem when millions of dollars in "free money" are up for grabs, the potential for misuse of funds and deceptive practices pops up.

In 2009, the Tucson-based *Arizona Daily Star* newspaper conducted an investigation of how Operation Stonegarden was being managed. The findings were disturbing; not only was the program being very loosely managed, but there seemed to be no mechanism in place for tracking how funds were spent, or any benchmarks written into the grants to determine success or failure of the law enforcement operations making use of the grant money.[13]

The investigation also uncovered several instances where Operation Stonegarden funds were being used for officer overtime hours without any limitations or oversight. In 2007 alone, one deputy police chief in Bisbee, Arizona, made $99,000 in Stonegarden overtime pay on top of his regular salary, and his colleague made $60,000 in overtime pay the same year. Technically this isn't illegal, but it raises several ethical and safety concerns. Working so many hours in a day and so many days in a row can leave an officer exhausted, and his or her work quality will suffer. And because officers sometimes work alone, it can be difficult for supervisors to determine if their Stonegarden overtime hours were actually spent doing border security–related work.[14]

After Bisbee city officials were alerted to the salaries these two officers were pulling in, they decided to cap all officers' annual salaries—including Stonegarden overtime pay—at $100,000. However, by then it was too late for local taxpayers, who would be feeling the effects of these overtime hours for decades. The city's police officers' retirement pay is based on their highest compensation level over the course of three consecutive years. Because of Stonegarden overtime, the deputy police chief's retirement pay increased by 53 percent, and his colleague's increased by 47 percent.[15] The grant money came from the federal government and the wallet pinch at the national level was probably minimal, but in the tiny town of Bisbee, those increased tax dollars make a big dent in local residents' budgets.

One county over in Arizona, Santa Cruz Sheriff's Office deputies were starting to make more money than their supervisors because of Operation Stonegarden overtime pay. Between 2008 and early 2013, the department received $2.5 million in overtime and mileage and more than $1 million in equipment through the grant program. However, a decade-old agreement made lieutenants exempt from receiving overtime pay, so that resulted in two problems: deputies who didn't want to move up the ranks for fear of losing the extra pay, and higher-ranking officers who were bitter that younger and less experienced colleagues were making more money. City officials are now reviewing the outdated policy to make officers in leadership positions eligible for extra pay.[16]

Defenders of the grant program staunchly believe that more law enforcement on the ground must necessarily result in crime reduction, but this common-sense approach isn't enough to assuage some critics. Raymond Michalowski, an Arizona regents professor in the Department of Criminology at Northern Arizona University told the *Daily Star,* "There is no clear agenda for the use of the Stonegarden money. There is no clear guidance as to how it will, in fact, improve border security. You don't know whether you have done due diligence with the people's money or whether you have squandered the people's money."[17]

The flip side of this argument is, of course, that at least some of the money is going to the right places. One of these examples is in plain view on the southern California coast, where the Harbor Unit of the Oceanside Police Department set aside almost half a million dollars of its $737,000 Stonegarden grant from 2010 to buy a boat. But it wasn't just any boat. In January 2012, it received a brand-new defender-class patrol ship with three outboard engines—totaling nine hundred horsepower and allowing it to clock in at forty-five knots—and a covered hull. It's twice as fast as their older boats, has infrared systems that allow officers to see in the dark, and the covered hull allows them to operate more comfortably in inclement weather.[18] Given the dramatic increase in panga boat drug smuggling traffic in these waters (see Chapter 1), the Harbor Unit will no doubt put this boat to good use in the coming years.

Other police department equipment purchases made with Operation Stonegarden funds show similar clear and evident benefits. For example, in September 2010, the Hill County (Montana) Sheriff's Office purchased two half-ton four-wheel-drive pickups and equipped them with standard law enforcement accessories using almost all of a $150,000 Stonegarden grant. Sheriff Don Bostrom said at the time, "I don't think this county could run without grants." And his county isn't alone; Border Patrol spokesman Tim Lamborne said all jurisdictions with a Northern border in the Havre Sector—from the US Continental Divide in Glacier County to the North Dakota border—have received grants.[19] In May 2013, the Imperial City, California, city council voted to purchase a $64,000 incident command/patrol unit for their police department. The vehicle was a four-wheel-drive Dodge Durango retrofitted with emergency-related equipment and was purchased from a local dealer, which resulted in a good financial investment for the community.[20]

The concept of Operation Stonegarden is fundamentally a good one. Sheriff Bostrom isn't alone in the feeling that his county couldn't run without grant money, especially in the light of budget cuts that have been going on for years at the state and local level. At least dozens of police departments and sheriff's offices along the border are in a similar situation, and the grants are usually viewed as a godsend from DHS. The problem is that a lack of federal oversight has resulted in several instances of financial mismanagement.

Because DHS hands out the grants and essentially washes its hands clean of responsibility for how they're used, the city councils and beneficiary departments are largely left to their own devices when it comes to preventing fraud. Stonegarden money continues to flow, and it should. However, DHS needs to rethink its strategy of abdicating all financial oversight of the program to grant recipients, and agencies receiving Stonegarden money need to maintain—or regain, in some cases—the public's trust by ensuring the grant money they receive is spent properly.

DHS grant money isn't limited to law enforcement agencies. For decades, many US universities have offered degree programs in cultural or international studies focusing on particular geopolitical regions or issues, and quite a few have undergraduate and graduate programs in Latin American, Chicano, and even Border Studies. However, some universities have established entire institutes and research centers completely dedicated to examining border issues and our cross-border relationship with Mexico, and DHS helps fund some of these. With one exception, the funded research centers have all been established within the last decade—a notable time in US history when the scrutiny of our borders increased significantly post-9/11. These centers started out as purely academic endeavors, but some have grown into entities with millions of dollars in public and private funding and are publishing research that wields a considerable amount of influence in both academic and government circles.

Without going into too much detail about each institute and research center, it's accurate enough to say their missions are very similar—generally, to increase cross-border understanding and cooperation through a variety of research projects and funded studies. They examine several aspects of the US-Mexico and US-Canada relationship, including immigration, security, and trade. Each organization publishes different kinds of newsletters, reports, and books, and regularly hosts border-themed conferences. Some are part of consortiums with over a dozen university members. Affiliated professors and advisory board members are often asked to testify before Congress regarding the complexities of cross-border trade with Canada, immigration issues, and the security situation in Mexico, just to name a few examples.

The sheer volume of material that US academia is spitting out every year about border security–related issues is mind-boggling, and unfortunately, some of it isn't easily digested by the casual reader; that's just the general nature of PhD-level writing. However, the research is incredibly valuable to students, other professors, journalists, and analysts and authors like me. But

the point of mentioning the role of academia in border security isn't to focus
on the research itself; rather, it's to highlight the enormous financial investment involved—much of it coming from US taxpayers via DHS grants.

What changed the landscape a bit with regards to the involvement of
universities and academia in border security was the creation of two National
Centers for Border Security and Immigration: the first in 2008 at the University of Texas at El Paso (UTEP) and the second in 2009 at the University
of Arizona (UA). The Arizona Center is host to BORDERS, "a consortium
of 16 premier institutions that is dedicated to the development of innovative
technologies, proficient processes, and effective policies that will help protect our Nation's borders, foster international trade, and enhance long-term
understanding of immigration determinants and dynamics." The mission of
BORDERS is completely different than those of the Trans-Border Institute at
the University of San Diego and other academically focused institutes. BOR-
DERS has the goal of researching concrete security issues that can provide
practical, ready-to-use border security solutions for DHS and DOJ agencies
like CBP, the Border Patrol, DEA, and the ATF.[21]

It should come as no surprise that this unique kind of research and relationship with government agencies comes with a high price tag. As such,
much of the funding for BORDERS and the two National Centers comes
from DHS through its Homeland Security University Programs Network.
Both the UTEP and UA programs have been designated as DHS Centers of
Excellence. Congress mandated the creation of these centers in the Homeland Security Act of 2002, and while funding for them has held steady at $40
million annually, the number of centers has increased and currently stands at
twelve. This means there are fewer dollars to go around for each center, and
the pressure to produce useful results increases every year.[22]

DHS funding for various BORDERS projects can range from tens of
thousands to hundreds of thousands of dollars, depending on the complexity
and resources required. Examples of projects in the center's work plan for July
2012-June 2013 included biometric identification, localization and tracking
of vehicles, border patrol checkpoint effectiveness, and post-apprehension
surveys of illegal immigrants. All of the money comes from DHS—and thus
taxpayer dollars—but the reports outlining the research being conducted,
the results of various experiments, and the proposed solutions emerging
from the results are some of the most transparent and understandable examples of our money at work.

I'm a huge proponent of learning, teaching, information sharing, dia-
logue, and idea exploration, so I will always have a hard time criticizing the
expenditure of money—yes, even tax dollars—on endeavors that pursue any

of those goals. I'm fortunate enough to be acquainted with many of the prestigious individuals who are a major part of these institutes, and the knowledge I've gained from reading their countless reports has been invaluable. We're very fortunate as a nation that it's these leaders in academia who are being summoned by our government to testify before Congress on issues related to border security, despite the fact that sometimes their advice goes unheeded.

The UA and UTEP Centers of Excellence are joined by ten others that focus on other non-border homeland security issues, and the solutions they're coming up with are truly cutting edge. Honestly, it's one of the best uses of DHS money anywhere in the country, and the potential for what BORDERS and its partner program at UTEP can produce is enough to lift the spirits of the worst border security cynic. The continuing challenge to researchers is the ability to traverse what they call the "Valley of Death"—the gap between problem/solution and realistic implementation. The universities can take care of the first two; we must rely on DHS and its component agencies to get their act together in order for the third step to happen, and for the researchers' time and effort to be worthwhile. Fortunately, there is a place in Arizona where dozens of companies, many in conjunction with the University of Arizona, are working feverishly to bridge that gap.

It's a cloudy and humid day in south Tucson, which isn't unusual during the summer monsoon season. I've been reading about how businesses cluster together into "parks" in this area, and how one in particular has been growing rapidly. As I leave central Tucson and head south of Davis-Monthan Air Force Base, I'm imagining in my mind that this business park will be just a few buildings in strip mall–like formation with a few dozen storefronts belonging to various tech companies. You can imagine my surprise as I'm confronted with a behemoth of a facility more reminiscent of something associated with NASA.

I had been hoping to just walk into one of the smaller businesses and ask the owner or manager what they liked about being clustered with companies in the same business, but nothing about this business park said *Come on in and say hello!* Many of the buildings were white, windowless, and identified only by a four-digit number. I took a wrong turn into the entrance to the Raytheon facility, where I was greeted by a kind security guard who showed me where I could make a U-turn and head back the way I came. Even the buildings for IBM and Citigroup had minimalist entrances with security keypads, and everyone I saw walking around was wearing security badges. This conglomeration of tech companies involved in some way or other with homeland and border security meant business, and they definitely didn't encourage curious visitors.

In 1994, the University of Arizona purchased this 1,345-acre technology park in southeast Tucson from IBM. It started out small and relatively empty, with only two tenants and roughly 1,200 employees. Currently, the facility (known as the UA Tech Park) is home to more than fifty companies and over seven thousand employees.[23] The key statistic noted on the park's website is that the facility contributes $2.7 billion annually to Pima County's economy, and is also one of the region's largest employment centers.[24] The two million square feet of space has been developed for these companies to help them develop, test, and deploy emerging border security technologies. The idea was mostly just on paper as recent as 2010, so the regional economic growth spurred by the park's tenant expansion has been considerable.

Bruce Wright directs the University of Arizona's Office of University Research Parks, and is the CEO of the UA Tech Park. "Three or four years ago, we decided we needed to figure out a better way to bring a value proposition into the park for technology-based companies," said Wright. "Why would they come to this park? Part of it is they want to affiliate with the University, they want to hire our students, they want to engage in collaborative research, they want to take advantage of our facilities, equipment and laboratories. But that isn't necessarily enough to either bring a company here from another part of the world or grow a small company here."[25]

That ability to test new technologies, however, is probably the Tech Park's biggest selling point, Wright explained. "There's a real need for a place to do third-party testing, evaluation and demonstration of new technology, whether you're a company that wants to present it to the government, or you have a government-sponsored technology and want to take it to industry. Somebody has to help test it, evaluate it, and demonstrate it for efficacy and figure out how to get it to market. That's what we've really focused on, along with business incubation." In the technology sector, starting up a small business takes a lot of investment, and even if a company has a gadget that could change the world, it may never see the light of day if the company that makes it can't get off the ground. Part of the UA Tech Park's mission is to help small businesses do just that.[26]

"Our strategy is really two-fold," said Wright. "One is, we want to play a meaningful role in developing technology and helping companies to present that technology, whether it's for industrial use or government use. But we'd also like to be the catalyst for creating a border/homeland security cluster based here in Tucson with a principal focus at the Tech Park. Here in Tucson, we're basically a border community with deep ties to the border because of trade and familial connections. But we also have all the attendant problems that come with being a border community. So the idea of creating an industry around this is like making lemonade out of lemons. Let's take advantage of the fact that the world needs border/homeland security technology. Why can't we be one of, if not *the* industry leader in that area? That's the concept we have in mind."[27]

The UA Tech Park is unique in that it's the only border security–related industry "cluster" organization in the world. However, there are countless companies, think tanks, consulting firms, and private individuals who play a part in the big business of border security. I just happen to be one of those individuals, and my income as a sole proprietor, consultant, and freelance writer very largely depends on the course of violent events in Mexico and the need for security along our southwest border. Law enforcement agencies pay me to train their officers, magazines and journals pay me to write articles for them, and immigration attorneys hire me to provide expert witness services for their asylum cases. My overhead costs are minimal—my "office" is a desk in our family room—and I'm a one-woman shop, so my fees are low compared to those of many other experts in my field.

However, organizations that need specialized training or information about Mexico's drug war and border security issues are often willing and able to pay top dollar for it. That's why more and more small business are cropping up in the border states and beyond to provide it. Many are created and staffed by former or retired law enforcement officers, government agents or analysts, or military members—often Special Forces–types. Bodyguard service companies are branching out beyond the Middle East and Colombia and into Mexico. Armored car manufacturers in the United States are expanding their contracts beyond the government and looking to sell to well-off Mexican businessmen, many of whom cross the border regularly. Private intelligence firms like Stratfor and Control Risks Group create and mold their Mexico reports to the demands of their subscribers and clients, and are able to charge higher fees because of their extensive network of in-country experts and sources.

In some cases, this need for border security expertise from outside sources has resulted in gross financial mismanagement of taxpayer dollars. In 2006, the State of Texas awarded a contract to Abrams Learning & Information Systems, Inc. (ALIS), "a consulting firm providing government and business clients with solutions and services in: workforce development, strategic planning, change management, program management, exercise support, and executive and management education."[28] Between fiscal years 2007 and 2011, ALIS received $22.7 million from the Texas Department of Public Safety (DPS) and the Governor's Office to manage border security operations for the state. ALIS was commissioned to improve border security strategy and operations along the US-Mexico border. The company's main objective was to "plan, coordinate, implement, and evaluate interagency border security operations to counter the threat of organized crime, terrorism, and the flow of contraband and human trafficking to foster a secure border region."[29] During this time, ALIS essentially created and managed the very foundation of the Texas border security program, including its vaunted Operation Border Star campaign, the management of its Border Security Operations Center, and the deployment of National Guard troops to the state's border with Mexico.[30]

In early 2012, the newspaper *Austin American-Statesman* began an investigation into the relationship between the Texas state government and ALIS. The contractor's involvement in the Texas border security apparatus was incredibly opaque. Minutes and agendas from state agency meetings had only passing reference to the contracts or none at all. Some state legislators were unaware of the extent of the commissioned work, and one called for an investigation. The initial contract was actually issued on an emergency basis, meaning it was granted without allowing other companies to bid on it. It was also repeatedly renewed under the same circumstances, with contract managers drawing reprimands from DPS "for [their] frequent use of emergency contracts and failure to solicit bids as required by state and federal rules."[31]

This *Statesman* investigation was published in March 2012. Two weeks later, the newspaper reported that DPS had diverted nearly $1 million in federal stimulus money that was earmarked for one ALIS contract to another—one that was not supposed to be paid for with that kind of funding—to cover the cost of a 2010 border security contract. The state's Compliance and Oversight Division explained in a review that DPS "had two contracts with ALIS, each of which involved similar deliverables. Texas DPS charged $936,509 of ALIS expenditures to the grant-related contract that pertained to the non-grant related contract because they were having trouble obtaining funds from the non-grant related funding source." The review also found that DPS "failed to post ALIS's $3.3 million TXMap award [a border mapping tool] on . . . a state website on which state contracts and solicitations are posted." DPS did reverse the stimulus payment using an unidentified funding source.[32]

The outsourcing of border security responsibilities to private companies isn't new; it's been happening since at least 2003, when DHS was created. In 2005, I began work as a contract intelligence analyst in one of California's state fusion centers and earned a paycheck from a company based out of the DC Beltway area. Every state along both our southern and northern borders has a fusion center, each with a different mix of contractors, law enforcement officers, and government employees. I can tell you firsthand that in some situations, it's virtually impossible for certain fusion centers to pull together several border security subject matter experts from existing state employees, or to hire people with sufficient expertise willing to work for a state government salary. Federal grant money is provided so state fusion centers can hire companies like ALIS (and dozens of others) to find that expertise and staff their analyst and management positions.

Border security is a big business because the demand for it—from government officials, politicians, and the American public—is huge. As taxpayers, we're generally okay with large volumes of our tax dollars going toward improving the security of our borders. As such, there is a rapidly growing industry of individuals, small businesses, and large corporations willing and able to meet that growing demand. Oversight of these contracts needs to continue, and in many cases needs to be strengthened to make sure grant money is not only being spent properly, but that taxpayers are getting a return on their investment. That is the crux of the problem; has our border really become that much more secure with all of these private companies and top universities involved? If not, then where is the disconnect between funding and result?

There is a huge constituency of "border hawks"—usually conservatives who advocate much stronger border security initiatives—who demand that hundreds of millions, if not billions, of additional dollars need to be allocated to border security efforts. What these politicians may not realize is that those billions of dollars are already out there, as you've seen in this chapter. All of that money may not be going toward the salaries of additional Border Patrol agents or port of entry upgrades, but they're being spent on developing new border technologies, educating thousands of government employees every year on border issues, and sharing information among academics, law enforcement officers, analysts, and the American public.

The problem is that we're not seeing a significant amount of progress by way of diminished cross-border drug and human traffic as a direct result of increased border spending. I'm not a conspiracy theorist by any stretch of the imagination, but one has to ask if the drug war needs the border security complex or if the border security complex needs the drug war. The American economy is surely benefitting from the influx of dollars into the technology sector, but most of those dollars are coming out of taxpayer pockets in the form of DHS grants and project funding. Good border security solutions cost big money, without a doubt, but just throwing money at the border will never be the answer. Our government ultimately needs to be smarter and more effectively manage its border security money flow.

CHAPTER 11

THE FORGOTTEN NORTHERN BORDER

The large amount of drugs that are freely coming and going across the northern border in our county is mind boggling.[1]

—Sheriff Frank Rogers, Okanogan County,
Washington State, March 2006

The Northern Border gets scant attention compared to the border with Mexico, but presents a significant threat to our security from illicit drugs and terrorism.[2]

—Sen. Charles Schumer (D-New York), January 2005

Ahmed Ressam was born in 1967 in a small, poor town just west of the Algerian capital of Algiers. Despite the poverty surrounding him, Ressam was able to go to school and was the first in his family—according to his brother Kamel—to get a "modern" education. As a teenager in the 1980s, he began dressing in American-style clothes like many of his peers. In 1984, he got sick with an ulcer and had to go to Paris for treatment. While he was in France, he took the opportunity to read some books that were banned back home. The books explained that military dictators had prevented democracy from taking hold in his country after it gained independence from France, and they led Ressam to believe his government was corrupt. At the young age of seventeen, he decided to take up the cause of Islamic rebels.[3]

Ressam returned to Algeria after his treatments and graduated from high school in 1988. He failed his college entrance exams and was denied employment with the Algerian police and security forces, so he ended up working with his father at a coffee shop until 1992. That year, he left for France to find work and ended up settling illegally in Corsica for two years, where he picked grapes and painted houses. In 1994, Ressam traveled to Montreal, Canada, on a fake French passport "to improve [his] life situation and improve [his] life in general."[4]

Canadian immigration authorities weren't buying Ressam's fake ID, so he switched gears and requested asylum, claiming he was persecuted and tortured in Algeria and had been falsely accused of arms trading and other terrorist activities. Oddly enough, immigration agents did buy this story, and without contacting Algerian, French, or Interpol officials, actually let Ressam go pending a hearing on his refugee status. He spent four years in Montreal, living off welfare payments and money he robbed from tourists. He was arrested for these thefts four times, convicted once, paid a fine and served no jail time, yet was still able to keep collecting welfare payments of $500 a month.[5]

During this time, Ressam met Mokhtar Haouari. They crossed paths several times at social events, and eventually Haouari starting talking to Ressam about different criminal activities he was involved in, like check and document fraud. Soon, Ressam started helping Haouari, sending him identity documents like social security cards and bank cards that a friend had stolen. Haouari, in turn, used these stolen documents to create false identities for terrorist associates around the world. In 1995, Ressam bailed on his immigration hearing, so Canadian authorities issued a warrant for his arrest. However, he was able to evade them because he used a stolen blank baptismal certificate to obtain a false Canadian passport in the name Benni Antoine Noris.[6]

Meanwhile, back in Algeria, the violent terrorist organization Armed Islamic Group (GIA) was wreaking havoc across Europe. The group orchestrated a series of bombings in Paris and Belgium between 1994 and 1996, and during a post-bombing investigation in 1996, police were led to a home in northern France. There they found an electronic organizer with the phone number to the Montreal apartment Ressam was sharing with several Algerian friends. The investigation then expanded to Canada, where Ressam was placed under surveillance for two years. Despite being watched by the Canadian government, Ressam used his fake Canadian passport in 1998 to buy a plane ticket from Montreal to Afghanistan, where he intended to train for jihad.[7]

First Ressam had to make a pit stop in Pakistan, where he had to get the green light from Osama Bin Laden lieutenant Abu Zubaida to continue on to the training camps in Afghanistan. Finally at his camp, over the course of several months Ressam received training in light arms, rocket-propelled grenades, the use of explosives and poison gas, and methods for assassination, sabotage, and urban warfare. At this point, he began to plan attacks on the United States. He and members of the European al-Qa'ida cell to which he was assigned agreed to meet in Canada, rob banks for funding, and launch an attack on the United States before the end of 1999. Zubaida told Ressam that after he arrived in Canada, he wanted Ressam to send him multiple Canadian passports for other network members.[8]

In February 1999, Ressam returned to Canada using his Benni Noris alias. He was able to bring with him chemicals, instructions for how to make explosives, and $12,000 in cash. He made temporary stops in Pakistan, Seoul, and Los Angeles. While Ressam waited in the Los Angeles airport (LAX), he was hit with inspiration for what his group's target in the United States should be. Placing a hidden bomb in a suitcase in the passenger waiting area would be the perfect plan. Ressam surveilled the airport, timed the security guard response to unattended luggage, then took a flight to Vancouver, British Columbia.[9]

From there he went back to Montreal. He began getting several identification documents in order—using his alias—so he could travel with minimal scrutiny after the attack was carried out. Ressam also started looking into opportunities to steal money and obtain weapons. There was a hiccup in the plan when other cell members were unable to join him in Canada because immigration authorities in London had detained them. Ressam looked for ways he could carry out an attack on the United States on his own, and in August 1999, he decided the target would be LAX.[10]

In September 1999, Ressam purchased several pieces of electronic equipment and constructed four timing devices in his Montreal apartment. In November, he started purchasing and stealing different kinds of chemicals that could be combined to make a TNT-like explosive. While all of these preparations were going on, Canadian security services were looking for Ahmed Ressam instead of Benni Noris; they had no idea Ressam was using an alias. It also took them six months to process an April 1999 French magistrate request to issue arrest warrants for Algerian terrorists in Montreal—including Ressam.[11]

During the summer of 1999, Ressam had reconnected with Haouari, who gave him some money and put him in touch with his associate Abdelghani Meskini. Meskini was to be Ressam's guide and assistant in the United States. In early December 1999, the two men made arrangements to meet in Seattle in a week's time. The afternoon of December 14, Ressam took a ferry from Victoria, British Columbia, to Port Angeles, Washington. US immigration authorities were initially suspicious of Ressam because he was hesitant in answering their questions. US Customs agents began searching his car, where they discovered the explosives (initially thought to be illegal drugs) in the trunk. Ressam tried to run, but was caught and arrested. Both Meskini and Haouari were arrested mere hours later.[12] From that point forward, he was known to most Americans as "the Millennium bomber."

One would think that after 9/11 it would be impossible for authorities to overlook this kind of activity. Sadly, it's happened several times since. In the spring of 2000, Somalia-born Mohammed Warsame traveled from his home in Toronto to al-Qa'ida training camps in Afghanistan. He returned to Canada a year later, all on al-Qa'ida's dime. He then moved to Minneapolis, Minnesota, where he maintained contact with people he met in Afghanistan and Pakistan. After 9/11, he communicated with al-Qa'ida operatives about border entries and the locations of jihadists. These communications ceased only after his arrest in December 2003. After pleading guilty to conspiracy to provide material support and resources to a foreign terrorist organization and serving seven years in prison, he was deported back to Canada.[13]

In August 2006, three Sri Lankan-born Canadians were arrested on Long Island, New York, after "engaging in negotiations with an undercover FBI agent to purchase and export twenty SA-18 heat-seeking missiles, ten missile launchers, five hundred AK-47s, and other military equipment for the Liberation Tigers of Tamil Eelam (LTTE), a designated foreign terrorist organization."[14] One of the three men ran a youth organization in Toronto that he acknowledged in 2009 was part of the LTTE. All pleaded guilty to terrorism and conspiracy.[15]

The threats that face us from the north are very different than those from the south. For that matter, almost everything about the northern border situation is different than our southern border. There is no drug war going on in Canada. Canada is a first-world country with an industrialized economy, poverty is relatively low, and almost all citizens are literate and well educated. There are some significant differences between the Canadian and US political and economic systems, but there are more similarities between them than there are between the Mexican and US systems. There also aren't hundreds of thousands of Canadian citizens trying to illegally cross our northern border every year, or millions of illegal Canadian nationals already living among us.

While there is plenty of cross-border drug trafficking activity happening between Canada and the United States (more on that later), it's not nearly as voluminous as it is in the southwestern states. Also, any terrorism-related activity going on in Canada that involves trips to the United States tends to be very under-the-radar and involve legitimate modes of transportation, not midnight border crossings in the woods using specialized human smugglers. Border security issues that crop up along our northern border rarely make headlines because there usually isn't any bloodshed or violence involved. As a result, we seem to have forgotten all about our northern border, even though crossing it—by air or on foot—seems to be one of the more likely ways an operational terrorist will attempt to enter the United States to do us harm.

In May 2011, former CBP Commissioner Alan Bersin testified at a hearing of the Senate Judiciary subcommittee on Immigration, Refugees, and Border Security that "in terms of the terrorist threat, it's commonly accepted that the more significant threat comes from the US-Canada border." Part of the reason for that, he explained, was the fact that the two countries do not share names on their "no-fly" lists. Because of this, a terrorist on the US list could legally fly into Canada without arousing suspicion, then drive across the land border into the United States through a port of entry. After the hearing, Bersin told reporters that CBP has recorded more cases of people with suspected terrorist backgrounds or links to terror organizations entering the United States from Canada than from Mexico.[16]

In 2012, the DHS-funded National Consortium for the Study of Terrorism collected data from FBI-designated terrorism cases conducted between 1984 and 2004. The study showed that during that time, 264 people with a direct tie to terrorism crossed the border either into or out of the United States in relation to a terrorist act. Out of the ninety-five people for which citizenship could be determined, 48 percent were US citizens and 18 percent were Canadian citizens. Their favorite way to travel was by airplane, with land and seaports used in only a few occasions. Also, only 13 percent of attempted border crossings were thwarted, and only 11 percent of these 264 individuals had criminal records.[17] With these statistics in hand, why are members of Congress and (mostly) right-wing pundits so hung up on the hypothetical prospect of a dirty bomb being smuggled into the United States from Tijuana and not Toronto?

David Biette, Director of the Canada Institute at the Woodrow Wilson International Center for Scholars in Washington, DC, offered up one answer. "The Canada-US border is a relatively open border, and I guess easier to get into, but the United States and Canada share a lot of intelligence," Biette explained. "You had that group of eighteen in Toronto and you had that guy in Montreal who was going to do some train bombings. They nipped those things in the bud. Even the Millennium Bomber was caught because we were connecting our dots. The Customs people knew what to look for, found it, and stopped it. There are a lot of people who, for political points, will try to say Canada's full of terrorists, we need to put up fences and stuff like that. We don't."[18] Then Biette told me a story that beautifully illustrated how US and Canadian authorities keep an eye on their shared border.

"There was a Canadian journalist who was traveling along the length of the Keystone pipeline, and he stopped—I think he was in Montana—and there was a road with a little fence that just said 'US Border.' There was no one around; he just pulled up and looked. He thought, *Do I cross? Do I cross?* He finally goes, *Mmmm, I don't think so.* So then he took some pictures, and there was still nobody around for miles. He got back in his car and headed south away from the border, but then got pulled over by the Border Patrol. The agent said to him, *I'm curious about why you stopped there.* The journalist couldn't figure out how the agent knew where he was since there was no one around for miles. It turns out he was seen from above and [the imagery was] relayed at once.

"So while there may be just this bright orange cone protecting us from terrorists in Canada, they're watching. In some instances, I think drones are probably okay because we cannot have people physically on every hundred feet along the border, nor should we. But it's a question of risk. And when you get in these little towns in Montana and Saskatchewan, there's nothing there, and people see what's different. You can't just be, to use the stereotype, a dark-haired Muslim going into a café in these little towns because you need something to eat or into a grocery store without being noticed. That's just the way it is."[19]

Cross-border drug trafficking is another issue where Mexico completely dominates the border security rhetoric, despite the fact that significant amounts of illegal drugs are entering the United States from Canada. The drugs are a little different, the organized crime groups and gangs are different, but the challenges posed to US law enforcement are the same.

Sandusky, Michigan, is a small rural town in the area of the state called the "Thumb" for the shape of the piece of land that juts out into Lake Huron. It sits about ninety miles north of Detroit and roughly two hundred miles west of Toronto, Canada, as the crow flies. The city airport is tiny, home to one runway, twenty-one single-engine aircraft, and one ultralight aircraft, and inbound and outbound flights average about sixty-three per week. Security used to be non-existent, but now it's just extremely low, with only a chain-link fence surrounding the runway to keep cars from meeting planes on the tarmac. The airport is not staffed at night, and neither are the several similar airfields that dot the Thumb region.

Matthew Moody and his nephew Jesse Rusenstrom knew this about Sandusky City Airport when they were hired in 2009 to work as couriers for an inbound shipment of 175 pounds of marijuana and four hundred thousand

A stone marker is all that greets hikers arriving in Glacier National Park, Montana, from Waterton Lakes National Park in Alberta, Canada. Photo by Alexander Cohen.

Ecstasy pills from Guelph in Ontario, Canada. Their job was to drive up from Detroit, meet the plane, then hand off the drugs to a local middleman. A pilot flew his Cessna airplane west across the invisible borderline that runs down the middle of Lake Huron and landed in Sandusky around midnight. Within ninety seconds, Moody and Rusenstrom offloaded the dope and the pills onto their truck, then loaded up the plane with sixty pounds of cocaine for the return flight. The unidentified pilot quickly took off and headed for Guelph. There wasn't any reason for Moody and Rusenstrom to think this job would be different from any others; they had met this plane before at other small airfields in the Thumb at least ten times and hadn't had any problems. Except this time, a Border Patrol helicopter was waiting for them.[20]

Moody and Rusenstrom pleaded guilty and testified at the 2011 trial of accomplice Robert "Romeo" D'Leone. Jurors were stunned at what they were hearing: these smugglers brazenly used small planes to transport drugs into unmonitored US airports. D'Leone testified he would look at hundreds of small airports in the area to determine if they had fences or cameras around their runways. Pilots can turn on navigation lights from their cockpits (a standard aviation practice) if they're arriving at an unmanned airport after hours, and can reduce their visibility by turning off their transponders and not filing a flight plan. At the time of the drug bust, Sandusky City Airport fell outside of US national radar coverage.[21]

As easy as this kind of air transport for drug smuggling purposes appears, the majority of drug traffic between the United States and Canada is vehicular. That's understandable, considering that 90 percent of Canada's population lives within one hundred miles of the US border, and over 120 land border crossings connect the two countries (compared to 46 with Mexico). Traveling between the United States and Canada has never been easier due to cross-border security cooperation and economic agreements. Currently, approximately 300,000 people and $1.5 billion in trade goods cross our northern border every day, and our two countries are each other's largest trading partner.[22]

While this close relationship and fluid cross-border traffic is beneficial for tourism and business, it's also beneficial for organized crime groups. Unlike our southern border, there is two-way traffic across the northern border when it comes to illegal drugs: high-potency marijuana and MDMA—more commonly known as Ecstasy—head south into the Unites States, and cocaine and tobacco products head north into Canada. Bulk cash shipments, which result from the sale of all of the above, travel in both directions.[23]

The face of drug smuggling in Canada is very different from that in Mexico, although Mexican cartels are the source of much of the cocaine moving north from the United States. One representative is Jimmy "Cosmo" Cournoyer, a French Canadian 33-year-old from Québec. He entered the world of drug trafficking as a youngster, and demonstrated early on that he had a lot of talent for maneuvering in this underworld. By the time he reached his twenties, he had built up an empire worth more than $1 billion and "included alliances with New York's Bonanno crime family, the Hells Angels, Mexico's Sinaloa cartel, as well as the Mafia's Rizzuto organized crime family and the West End Gang."

Cournoyer's operation was elaborate. He would coordinate the shipment of high-potency marijuana grown in British Columbia across Canada to Québec, getting some help along the way from the Hells Angels and the Montréal Mafia. The dope was then smuggled south into the United States and sent by truck to New York City. Once the dope was sold, the cash proceeds were flown by private jet from New York to California, then smuggled south to purchase the Sinaloa Federation's cocaine. The cocaine would then be transported to Canada for sale there, the profits from which would be used to fund the pipeline between British Columbia and New York.[24] Cournoyer pleaded guilty to drug trafficking charges and now faces a mandatory sentence of at least twenty years in prison since he was charged under "kingpin" statutes.

Marijuana is one of Canada's two largest drug exports, and a lot of groups have their hands in production and distribution. The main domestic production areas for marijuana in Canada are the provinces of British Columbia (famous for its "BC Bud"), Ontario, and Québec. Much of it is high-potency and destined for the United States, although Canadian dope accounts for only a small percentage of marijuana consumed by Americans. Similar to drug shipments entering the United States from Mexico, Canadian traffickers prefer to use cars and trucks and go through the land ports of entry. When taking advantage of the wide-open spaces between the ports, traffickers will use all-terrain vehicles, boats, hikers, and snowmobiles—a conveyance you definitely won't find in Mexico.[25]

The predominant crime groups in Canada that deal in cross-border drug smuggling are outlaw biker gangs (mainly the Hells Angels), the Italian-based Mafia groups, and South Asian crime groups and gangs. The latter are in charge of the marijuana trade in Canada, with the Vietnamese groups really running the production show. However, all of the above are involved in domestic distribution and cross-border smuggling, and even Indo-Canadian and Eastern European groups have a piece of the pie. Asian groups also control the production and smuggling of Ecstasy pills into the United States, which makes sense considering that the chemicals used to make the drug largely come from China and Southeast Asia. The sophisticated production of MDMA and its smuggling are centered in the more populated provinces of British Columbia, Ontario, and Québec.[26]

Selfridge Air National Guard Base is located near one of these populated areas, about twenty miles north of Detroit, and operates as a joint DHS and Department of Defense installation. The CBP Office of Air and Marine operates helicopters from Selfridge that patrol nearby Lake St. Clair, the St. Clair River, and the Detroit River. Air Interdiction Agent Jay Ferguson took a camera crew from the Discovery Channel on a flight with him to demonstrate some of the challenges involved in detecting—and stopping—drug smugglers who try to use these maritime routes across our northern border.

"The international border is pretty much a straight line that runs down the middle of the river," Ferguson narrated. "Take a look at the distance here [from shore to shore]; it's probably only a couple thousand feet. A lot of the activity we see happens in this stretch of river. If you've got a boat, it only takes you a few minutes to get across. They bring bodies across, people; guns going north, money coming south. The problem is, when a boat comes across, if they see our helicopter or see one of our boats in the water, they're just going to turn around and head back to Canada. There's nothing we can do about it."[27]

A lot of what Ferguson was describing sounded like something straight out of Sonora, Mexico. "They got guys that are spotting us; they're picking up cell phones and calling [their smugglers] to say, *Hey, there's a helicopter up today,* so nothing happens. They're doing just as much surveillance on us as we're doing on them." The busiest border crossing along the southwest border is in southern California, connecting Tijuana and San Ysidro. Its equivalent on the northern border is the port of entry spanning Detroit on the US side and the city of Windsor on the Canadian side. Ferguson said, "If you think like a bad guy, I mean, how easy would it be to cross this border and do stuff . . . bring drugs or weapons of mass destruction, something like that? My concern is," he continued, "if the terrorists are going to come across anywhere, it's going to be here." An undercover Border Patrol agent emphasized this with the comment, "Our southern border is just checkers, man; the northern border is chess."[28]

Trying to distinguish between pleasure boaters and drug smugglers on the waterways separating the United States and Canada is difficult enough. Adding to the challenge is the minimal amount of time the US Coast Guard or Border Patrol have to respond to an illegal border crossing. There is also no human presence at several official ports of entry in the Great Lakes region. For example, Ohio technically has eight official ports of entry along its Lake Erie coast. However, they're only manned with CBP videophones, called Outlying Area Remote Stations, located at these eight docks and marinas.

According to CBP procedures, if a boater from Canada arrives at one of these locations, all the boat's crew and passengers must report in to CBP with their identity documents using these videophones. If they want to report their arrival in Ohio to CBP in person, they have to call a certain phone number to make arrangements. If boaters fail to report their arrival and get caught, they're subject to fines ranging from $2,000-$10,000 and up to a year in prison.[29] It's easy to see how a drug trafficker could evade a border inspection this way. In a heavily populated area like Detroit, it's easy for smugglers to run across the river and drop off a drug load with waiting couriers. Some smugglers don't even bother with boats. In August 2013, US Border Patrol agents apprehended a man wearing scuba gear who was trying to pull an eight-pound bag of marijuana cross the St. Clair River—underwater.[30]

Fortunately, agents have technology at their disposal, like night vision cameras and infrared scopes, that allows them to identify suspicious activity. The technology package along the US-Canada borderline isn't too different from what's in place along the Mexico border, but the endurance requirements have to be modified to deal with extreme cold and snow, as opposed to extreme heat and blowing sand. The setup includes surveillance towers with cameras and sensors, mobile surveillance systems, underground sensors, and UAVs.

Karl Goguen was an electronics specialist for thirty-three years with the Royal Canadian Mounted Police and now runs his own technology company. He explained that radar coverage is sparse in some western border areas, which is problematic. "Ultralight pilots [carrying marijuana] can be found flying in the Rocky Mountains, through the Pacific Mountains, and even the Laurentians. They can find valleys to fly in there and do their [drug] drops, turn around and come back, and never be noticed," Goguen said. And that's not the limit of their airborne capabilities. He added, "[Smugglers] are not only using ultralights; they're flying small choppers and airplanes in there."[31]

Good technology solutions in northern urban areas are critical, but even more so in the remote and unpopulated areas of the Canadian Rockies and Big Sky Country—better known as the US state of Montana. Goguen explained that the technology used along our northern border is also dependent on the terrain and conditions. "On the prairies where the land is relatively flat, they can use standard alarms and video technology because it's easy to transmit a signal," he said. "But in the mountainous regions, they really don't have anything. But combining seismic sensors and video technology can give you a better idea of who's crossing from either side [of the border], as well as where they might be heading to do a drop."[32]

But sensor coverage is still sparse in many areas. Goguen estimated that from Washington state to Maine, there's an average of one sensor roughly every five miles with a range of only fifty to one hundred feet. But that was just an average. "There are many places where there are no sensors and no radar," he said.[33]

Not many people would suspect that Montana is a hub for drug trafficking activity, but the local demand for illegal drugs led parts of the state down that path. Mexican cartels oversee the shipments of methamphetamine north into the state, and Canadian smugglers hike south across the border with packs loaded with high-potency marijuana.

One such "bud runner" told the National Geographic Channel that smuggling dope into the United States from Canada is the biggest rush he's ever had. This particular smuggler, profiled on an episode of *Drugs, Inc.*, works in the forested areas of western Canada, where the only thing marking the forty-ninth parallel that defines the border is a sixty-foot wide cut in an endless sea of tall conifers. He makes about four border runs a year, which nets him anywhere between $15,000 and $30,000 each trip. While the geography and weather make it tough for US law enforcement to find smugglers, it's an equally difficult prospect for drug runners on foot to survive the elements without the benefit of a helicopter or heated vehicle.[34]

"I'm carrying sixty pounds of weed on my back, worth about $300,000," the smuggler told the camera. "My biggest fear is always seeing another human being. It's not so much the police I'm afraid of; it's the hillbilly, the logger, thinking *Oh, this guy's in the woods. He doesn't know the woods like I know the woods.* Seeing a big backpack on me and thinking *There's $300,000 worth of weed there, this guy is expendable.* I could be bear bait, really, and they'd walk away." He did express concern about getting arrested and spending time in an American jail, and noted that crossing that bare swath of cleared land was his biggest risk. He knows that drones are flying overhead looking for people like him, and said he tries to walk like a bear when he crosses so that he might be mistaken for a bear or other animal instead of a human.[35]

While police departments in the tiny towns dotting these remote border areas are sometimes inundated with illegal drugs and the crime that comes along with it, they can make a big dent in the security of their towns just by taking one or two major dealers off the street. It's hard for outsiders to blend in, and the small populations and wide-open spaces make smuggling activity more apparent to the trained eye. But Montana is a little different from southwest border states in that it serves more as a destination for illegal drugs than it does as a transit point. Its remoteness and long winters have helped create a strong local drug demand, and traffickers from both Mexico and Canada are more than happy to travel long distances and brave bad weather to meet that demand.

DHS seems to have realized that cross-border drug smuggling between the United States and Canada has become a problem, and that's reflected in personnel assignments. In 2001, there were only 340 Border Patrol agents working along our northern border. As of 2012, that number had increased to more than 2,200 agents. Similarly at the ports of entry, there were 2,721 CBP agents assigned in 2003, and that number increased to roughly 3,700 in 2012. It's interesting to compare personnel numbers in the north—as well as the volume of drug seizures—to those in the south. In 2012, there were over 18,500 Border Patrol agents assigned just to the southwest border. The same year, Border Patrol seized only 1,542 pounds of marijuana along the northern border, compared to almost 2.3 million pounds of dope along the southwest border.[36]

There is nowhere near the level of trafficking activity coming from Canada as there is coming from Mexico. That being said, while DHS can rely more heavily on technology to monitor the more remote areas of the northern border, there is still a high need for experienced agents in busy corridors like Detroit and Seattle. Fortunately, their jobs are made easier by their ability to work together with their counterparts across the border. US agencies can actually call their counterparts in Canada and expect a response. Agencies like the Royal Canadian Mounted Police and municipal police can be counted on to do their part to catch drug smugglers and potential terrorists.

"There's more trust on the northern border than there is on the southern border," explained Biette. "You have a lot of trade coming across both borders, but you don't have as many undocumented people coming in from Canada. You have the secure drivers' licenses, which some places did—Ontario/Québec and New York, British Columbia and Washington—because they had a lot of people coming and going, and it worked because they trusted each other. The legislatures of British Columbia and Washington State actually meet yearly, and that's something you don't see in other places."[37]

This level of cooperation is emphasized heavily in two recent US government reports: *Beyond the Border* from the White House, and the DHS *Northern Border Strategy* report (June 2012). In the introductory letter from former DHS Secretary Napolitano, she acknowledged, "until now, there has been no Department-wide strategy to guide DHS policy and operations at the northern border." Considering the number of investigations concerning potential terrorist activity stemming from Canada and the level of cross-border drug trafficking in the last decade, that's something of a stunning revelation. The strategy itself wasn't anything earth shattering, placing priorities on deterring terrorists and criminals, facilitating trade, and fine-tuning joint emergency response measures in the case of a terrorist attack or natural disaster. But that report—along with the *Beyond the Border* agreement that was drafted jointly by both governments—was an important step in codifying how the United States and Canada plan to work together to meet their security goals.[38]

While the US government's relationship with Canada is exceptionally strong, it's not perfect. In October 2011, leaders from both countries agreed to a perimeter security pact, which grew out of the *Beyond the Border* plan. Most of the pact's thirty points addressed increased intelligence sharing and joint investment in technology and border crossings. However, one little detail in the pact that was revealed by Canadian reporters in August 2013 riled up more than one Canadian official. While the pact allows for US law enforcement officers to work in Canada alongside their counterparts near the border, it also demands that US officers be exempt from Canadian laws. In return for the concession, the US government would allow Canadian trucks to cross the border more easily—an economic benefit that's hard to turn down.[39] While this aspect of the pact will continue to stir some controversy between the United States and Canada, at least the two countries are starting to implement parts of the border plan.

The relationship between the United States and Canada helps mitigate most terrorist and smuggling activity between the two—more so than sensors or physical barriers. The threat posed by both terrorists and drug traffickers along our northern border is very real, as is the fact that Border Patrol maintains operational control over only 2 percent of that border. However, the nature of the threat and how those individuals attempt to enter the United States need to be taken into account when formulating a strategy for keeping them out. In the past, terrorist operatives from Canada have used legitimate means of travel, and solid investigative work and intelligence sharing between US and Canadian agencies have thwarted those plots. Because we have that relationship, we don't need to build a fence that runs from Washington to Maine.

That being said, drugs and bad people are still getting through. The lack of complete radar and sensor coverage, as well as the infinite number of hiding places along the waterways of the Great Lakes, leaves traffickers a lot of open spaces to exploit. Two Predator B drones are currently operating out of Grand Forks, North Dakota, and are responsible for patrolling the area from their home base out to eastern Washington. Even though the drones have a 950-mile range, it's impossible for them to constantly cover every mile of the border.

Illegal drugs and immigrants might not be pouring over our northern border, in stark contrast to our southern border, but that doesn't mean there aren't significant threats there that need to be addressed. We can't afford to neglect those 5,500 miles. Terrorists and smugglers will know when we do, and won't hesitate to take advantage of any openings in the north we provide for them.

CHAPTER 12

CONCLUSIONS

THE FUTURE OF BORDER SECURITY

> *If this Nation really wants to create an effective border security policy, we need to have a debate that includes a discussion about actual solutions to our problems, which means taking all of the political grandstanding and baiting out of the equation.*
>
> —US Representative Raúl Grijalva (D-Arizona), December 2005

> *Going forward, as we work to strengthen our border in the interests of homeland security, we must also recognize the economic importance of immigration reform.*
>
> —U.S. representative David Reichert (R-Washington), May 2006

For each chapter in this book, I've carefully selected a pair of quotes that exemplifies the conflicting concepts of border security that exist in the minds of our leaders, elected officials, law enforcement officers, and everyday citizens. For this chapter, I found two quotes that could have been pulled right out of today's newspapers. However, they're from nine and eight years ago, respectively, which tells you exactly how much progress our government hasn't made when it comes to defining border security, prioritizing the threats along our borders, and establishing a solid border strategy that is free from political agendas.

That's not for a lack of trying. In early 2013, a bi-partisan group of eight US senators—four Republicans and four Democrats—came together to draft a much sought-after and long-awaited comprehensive immigration reform bill. These senators soon became collectively known as the "Gang of Eight," and put together the most thorough attempt to overhaul immigration policy in American history. The bill also courted a historic amount of controversy, and after it was introduced in April 2013, opponents wasted no time in trying to tack on a whopping 301 amendments during the committee process and 500 more after debate began on the Senate floor in June. The main goal of most was to elevate already strict border security requirements.

The immigration bill, formally known as S.744, provided several ways in which illegal immigrants already living and working in the United States could obtain work permits, apply for residency, and start on the path to citizenship. It also outlined a gradual transition process for DHS to streamline its detention and removal procedures and tackle the huge backlog of existing cases. It wasn't so much the immigration reform aspects of the bill that caused such a stir; even hard-core Republicans acknowledge that the current immigration system is broken. The thorn in the side of the bill—and many Democrats—was the "border surge" amendment that was approved and passed with the bill. Essentially, it mandates that our borders must be secured before the immigration reform aspects of the bill can go into effect. Based on what you've read so far, you can certainly understand why reform advocates are so disheartened with the parts of the bill that will never become a reality under those circumstances.

Some of the key components of the "border surge" amendment would require the deployment of an additional 19,200 Border Patrol agents to the southwest border, along with the construction of more reinforced fencing and Border Patrol stations. The bill itself created a fund of over $46 billion dollars to start paying for agent salaries, adding an alphabet soup of border technology solutions to every sector, expanding the electronic employment verification system, and purchasing and deploying more UAVs and mobile surveillance systems—just to name a few items on the list.[1]

Even more pie-in-the-sky was the requirement that the DHS secretary submit to Congress within 180 days a comprehensive border security strategy that would lay out a plan for achieving "effective control" of the border. This means that DHS has six months to figure out how to monitor 100 percent of the entire southern border 24/7 and apprehend 90 percent of all illegal crossers they detect. Better yet, if DHS can't accomplish this within five years, a committee that would be created after the bill's passage would find a way to keep funding DHS—with no apparent cap on that funding—in order to help reach those goals.[2]

Adam Isacson at the Washington Office on Latin America argues that these requirements are completely self-defeating. In an April 2013 report, he explained that the deployment of so much new technology to so many more parts of the border—especially the new VADER system that "can reveal every man, woman and child under its gaze from a height of about 25,000 feet"—would start to reveal many more illegal border crossings than previously estimated. For example, between October and December 2012, UAVs using the VADER systems detected 7,333 illegal border crossings during Arizona-based missions, but Border Patrol agents only made 410 apprehensions during that time. During one week in January 2013, the VADER sensor detected the on-foot movement of 355 people in Arizona near the border. Only 125 were apprehended, 141 got away, eighty-seven turned back to Mexico, and two were unaccounted for. Isacson wrote, "Deploying VADER and other technologies widely, as S. 744 proposes to do, will reveal how far from the goal of 'effective control'—a 90 percent effectiveness rate—US authorities are."[3]

Fortunately, both former DHS Secretary Napolitano and President Obama agreed that the 90 percent effectiveness requirement in the bill as originally drafted was "unacceptable."[4] However, there's still $46 billion in additional border security spending to consider. It's mind-boggling that Congress still hasn't learned that throwing money at the border is not the way to magically secure it.

The Senate also seems to have forgotten, or is completely ignorant, of what happened the last time DHS went on a CBP and Border Patrol agent hiring spree.

US law enforcement agencies have never been immune to corruption, and agents and officers working on the southwest border are particularly susceptible to the draw of big money because it's just everywhere. Narcotics officers working in other parts of the country consider seizures of a few pounds of cocaine or methamphetamine to be a big deal, and sometimes a months-long investigation involving several agencies and dozens of agents will round up less than a million dollars in cash, a dozen firearms, and a few hundred pounds of dope.

But in places like Texas and Arizona, seizures by CBP, Border Patrol, or sheriff's deputies working on border highways are measured in tons, with cash values of well over a million dollars. Cartels who successfully recruit these officers for their payrolls are handing off tens of thousands of dollars in bribes, expensive cars, and jewelry on a regular basis. And corruption issues extend well beyond inspection points and traffic stops; it affects the very foundation of border communities, like small businesses, elected officials, and the real estate market.

The number of corruption investigations opened against CBP and Border Patrol agents was historically relatively low until DHS went on a hiring binge in 2005 and brought in thousands of new recruits. In a report by the Homeland Security Studies and Analysis Institute, a DHS think tank, the authors stated CBP identified at least fifteen attempts by Mexican cartels to infiltrate the agency, and roughly 150 corruption cases have been opened against agents since 2004. The Government Accountability Office released its own report on the subject, which similarly concluded that CBP did not have a comprehensive strategy or sufficient internal controls to effectively address corruption problems. One hundred and fifty out of sixty thousand officers is an extremely low number, but still high enough for DHS to consider it unacceptable.[5] Those numbers were reached despite the fact that CBP started administering routine polygraph examinations in 2010 to comply with the requirements of the Anti-Border Corruption Act.[6]

Now the US Senate wants to almost *double* the number of Border Patrol agents working in southwest sectors. Where would they go, and what would they do? There is no logical justification for that kind of personnel increase, or reasonable process for recruiting, vetting, hiring, and training so many new agents. It's laughable to think that $46 billion will magically materialize just by raising visa issuance fees.

Then there's the fact that DHS is nowhere closer to quantitatively measuring the security of our borders than it was several years ago. For years the agency has been using levels of "operational control" to say what percentage of Border Patrol sectors agents can effectively manage through quick response times. You read earlier that Border Patrol maintains operational control of only 44 percent of the southwest border and only 2 percent of our northern border. The term "operation control" is going by the wayside, as DHS has worked since 2010 on developing something called the Border Control Index, or BCI. At that time, ICE official James Dinkins said, "We need not just to count outputs, and not all arrests are equivalent and don't have the same outcome. That is what we are in the process of doing now and we hope to . . . start a baseline and then move into 2012 a tool to measure border conditions and security."[7] In May 2013, US Representative Candice Miller (R-Michigan), Chairman of the House Border and Maritime Security Subcommittee, said that if the BCI cannot be ready within the next two years, Congress will need to reevaluate whether it will be a useful tool.[8]

Regardless of these inconsistencies, shortfalls, and shortsighted judgments, the US Senate passed its amended immigration reform bill on June 27, 2013. The bill was then sent to the House of Representatives for consideration, where it sits as this book goes to press. The Republican-controlled House quickly rejected the Senate's bill and is taking up individual components of the bill instead. A number of things can happen in the upcoming months as this process goes forward. The Immigration Policy Center explained, "Members of the House may introduce their own comprehensive package, which could be taken up; or the House may choose to consider a number of separate immigration bills that are packaged together for consideration. If the House passes a bill that differs from the Senate bill, the two bills will need to be reconciled."[9]

As Chairman of the House Committee on Homeland Security, US Representative Michael McCaul (R-Texas) is playing a vital role in how the House shapes its response to S.744. The bill he has crafted does not include a path to citizenship for the 11 million immigrants living in the United States illegally. However, it does contain a list of metrics that DHS officials need to regularly report to Congress in order to quantitatively measure the effectiveness of border security strategies.[10]

I had the chance to speak with Chairman McCaul about the House bill and his views on border security in general. "We've spent billions of dollars without any national strategy or plan, and it hasn't been very efficient," he said. "Programs like SBI*net* have been wasteful and have set us back a great deal, which is why one of the first things we do [in the House bill] is demand that the Department of Homeland Security write a national strategy. Once they provide that, then they're required to come up with an implementation plan. They haven't done that, and it's amazing that they've never had that. Then we have to look at the resource issue. We're not going to throw billions of dollars more at it, which is what the Senate [did] in their plan; that's not using taxpayer dollars wisely. Then we'll determine whether additional resources are necessary.

"We actually define what operational control is . . . they can't do that, define what a secure border is, what it looks like," McCaul continued. "We do that in our bill. We call for a 90 percent effectiveness rate, with regards to humans coming across the border, and a significant reduction in the amount of narcotics. If you can't measure that, then you don't have any way to know if you're being successful. So we talk about this concept of situational awareness where you know what you're apprehending and what you're not. This is why we call for [more] technology and aviation assets."

McCaul would like to see a good portion of military hardware returning from Afghanistan get redeployed to the southwest border. He believes military sensor technology is superior to what's being used now on the border, and likes the information being gleaned from newer systems like the UAV-mounted VADER.

Regarding where border security sits on the national priority list, McCaul agreed it's toward the bottom. "If you take the words of the [DHS]

Secretary, it's not a very high priority. Unless they can tie in immigration reform; then they get interested in it for political reasons. I think when [former Secretary Napolitano] says it's never been more secure, yeah, it probably is, but it's still not *secure*. Arizona may be more secure, but it's the whack-a-mole game and it's popping into Brownsville [in south Texas] and San Diego." At the national level, McCaul appreciates that President Obama and former Secretary Napolitano have engaged with the Mexican government through avenues like the Mérida Initiative, and by helping them deal with the cartels. However, he said, "In terms of resources on the ground, I don't think it's as high a priority as it should be for the Administration, given the threat we're seeing from the border."

Fortunately, McCaul also agreed that this threat comes from potential terrorists, their associates, and violent drug traffickers, not economic migrants. "I don't think [illegal immigrants] pose a threat," he said. "We can always have a guest worker program, which would help increase security. I think the biggest threat we see, from a national security standpoint, is the increase in OTM rates and special interest aliens, and of course the cartels. The nexus between them and some of these narcoterrorist organizations is still not clearly defined, but there's a lot of concern that there is a relationship there."

I still can't help but think that the goals set out in both the Senate bill and McCaul's House bill are not very realistic, especially given the limited time frame involved. However, McCaul believes it can be done. We talked a bit about former "border surge" attempts under the Secure Border Initiative, and I expressed my skepticism about the House bill's timetable. McCaul replied, "Your point is well taken. We're at only 44 percent [of operational control] five years later . . . we really haven't moved the dial on that. I mean, what have we done in five years? That's what we're trying to do with this bill: set a goal, prioritize [border security] for the nation so we can get it done."

"Frankly, I'm a little frustrated," McCaul continued. "I've been dealing with this issue since I was back at the Justice Department, and I'm still dealing with it in my fifth term in Congress and as Chairman of this committee. I'd really like to do something about it."[11]

One of the biggest obstacles to improving border security through legislation is that the US government at its highest levels has to first acknowledge that there is a problem. No president or government wants to look bad, and both the DHS secretary and President Obama have many political points to lose if they concede that they have underestimated the security situation along our southwest border. Elected officials at all levels want their constituents to feel safe and cared for, and few are willing to publicly describe any vulnerabilities we have that stem from the border. Then there's the little trick of being in denial.

In 2012, DHS requested that a panel of statisticians, economists, and demographers at the National Academy of Sciences conduct a study of illegal immigration patterns. The study found that roughly 75 percent of illegal border crossers keep crossing until they make it without getting caught. Other outside studies have shown that up to 90 percent of border crossers eventually get into the United States. Panel members told the media that their DHS-funded study was excluded from presentations made to the Senate during the immigration reform debate. Several researchers said they're frustrated that enormous decisions about future spending on border security are being made with little or no reference to research.[12]

Tougher immigration enforcement measures have made little to no difference in preventing migrants from repeatedly crossing the border. Operation Streamline was created in 2005 to harshly punish illegal immigrants with jail time—six months for first-timers and felony charges with longer sentences for repeat offenders. It started along part of the Texas border, expanded to Arizona, and is now in effect along most of the southwest border. Despite the fact that immigrants are averse to spending time in prison, researchers believe Operation Streamline has had no significant negative impact on migrant apprehensions. Wayne Cornelius, founder of the Center for Comparative Immigration Studies and a political science professor at University of California, San Diego, said, "Factors like family reunification trump fears of incarceration or prosecution. If you have children or spouses in the US, that's going to trump everything else. If you have a desperate economic situation in Mexico, and you can't feed your family, that's going to trump any fears of enhanced consequences." Cornelius also added, "US policy has consistently underestimated the sheer determination, the sheer tenacity of Mexicans once they have made that decision. They will find a way to rationalize the costs and the risks and to borrow the money to make the trip, and to persist until they succeed."[13]

Drug traffickers and terrorists are similarly driven to enter the United States with almost complete disregard for harsher consequences; they just have different motivators. For smugglers, the carrot and the stick are at the extreme opposite ends of the spectrum. The piles of cash involved in successfully crossing the border with a drug load keep them coming, and the prospect of being dismembered by cartel members in Mexico if they fail keep them from going back empty handed. Terrorists are driven by extreme ideologies that will keep the United States in their crosshairs for years, if not decades, to come. While an increasing number of these violent extremists are "homegrown" and don't have to worry about surreptitiously entering the country, groups like al-Qa'ida and Hezbollah will always want to send fund-raisers and operatives here.

Out of terrorists, drug traffickers, and illegal immigrants, the last group is the only one that poses no threat to our national security, and coinciden-tally is the easiest one to manage through legislation alone. Finding a way to convert illegal immigration from an enforcement issue to a policy issue is critical to improving border security across the United States. Members of Congress who believe our borders must be secured before tackling immigra-tion reform have the process completely backward.

Imagine a situation where migrants wishing to work in the United States could go through a standardized and streamlined process of applying for a guest worker visa (or similar temporary program) and go through all the background checks from their home countries. Or a situation where millions of immigrants who overstayed their visas and have been living here illegally for years can affirmatively apply for cancellation of removal and start paying income taxes.

This isn't to say illegal immigration would stop completely; plenty of people who don't get approved for entry into the United States will want to come anyway. But with significantly reduced numbers of economic migrants crossing our borders, DHS could prioritize threats and refocus its limited re-sources toward detecting and apprehending violent criminals and terrorists. Instead of having to double the number of Border Patrol agents in the field, manning levels could actually be reduced in some areas, with agents shifting to sectors where drug smuggling is more prevalent. Thousands of lives would be saved every year, since migrants would no longer have to travel on foot through the most forbidding parts of our southwest border. Cartels would take a financial hit as their income from involvement in human smuggling operations would substantially decline.

Even if comprehensive immigration reform somehow miraculously comes to pass in the next few years, it would be the same dysfunctional DHS running the border security show. The budget cuts will keep coming thanks to an enormous federal budget deficit, and DHS cannot afford to bleed money on contracts that are being inadequately scrutinized for waste, fraud, and abuse. Before it spends another red cent on technology, DHS needs a clear and standardized process for vendors to propose their tech solutions. Whenever DHS has a need, they issue a "request for proposal" and companies start to competitively bid for the contract. However, there is a lot of cost-effective technology available today that DHS isn't remotely aware of because the vendors don't know how to get it in front of the DHS decision makers. As for border technology currently in use, DHS has to ensure it's actually working and being fully utilized.

Moving beyond our physical borders, the Department of Justice must better comprehend the impact of letting big banks slide when they fail to detect money laundering activity. Too many US officials are walking on eggshells when it comes to potentially disrupting the financial sector in order to punish an institution for not complying with AML regulations. In the process, however, Mexican cartels, terrorists, and other criminals are sending cash all over the globe through bank deposits, wire transfers, and now cyber money with a low risk of ever being detected.

No country will ever be able to stop 100 percent of anything from coming across its borders, and we have to learn to be okay with that. But US government officials and law enforcement agencies also have to reach some sort of agreement and codify through legislation exactly what level of illicit traffic is acceptable, however unpleasant that concept might be. The border security portions of both the Senate and House reform bills are attempting to do this, but they're too laden with political agendas to be realistic. It's so crucial for the men and women on the ground performing the enforcement mission to have a clear goal and a finish line by which they can measure their levels of success.

Our nation truly has the ability to maximize the flow of legitimate trade and minimize the entry of terrorists and violent criminals across our borders. It also has the ability to change how it views and manages illegal immigration through legislative and policy changes. However, the political will to do these things is severely lacking, and the sheer size of the DHS bureaucracy means the agency just keeps tripping over its own feet every time it tries to implement a new border security strategy. Even after a decade of existence, DHS still has not produced a comprehensive border security strategy. It took the agency nine years to develop a security strategy for our northern border, and this is with the hearty cooperation of transparent Canadian agencies and a border region devoid of an astronomical body count.

It is time for President Obama and DHS officials to acknowledge that we have serious security problems along our southwest border, and that our northern border holds more national security significance than anyone gives it credit for. They need to figure out exactly what level of illicit cross-border traffic they can live with, come up with a clear plan to get there, and communicate the goals to other agencies involved in the fight.

We, as American citizens, have our own role to play. We have to understand that bad people and drugs will always find a way to come into this country, and that this cross-border traffic is having a disproportionate impact on people living in border areas. We also have to realize that just because most of us live in places far from our land borders, we're not remotely immune to the effects of cross-border drug trafficking, human trafficking and smuggling, and money laundering. Finally, we need to acknowledge that economic migrants living here illegally are not our enemies. They want to work hard, provide for their families, and just find some semblance of a happy life they didn't have where they came from. Finding a way for them to become law-abiding taxpayers instead of rule-breakers benefits our communities, our law enforcement agencies, and our nation as a whole. Doing these things will finally put us on the road to seeing what a truly, practically, and realistically secure border looks like.

ACKNOWLEDGMENTS

Writing a book for the first time is no small undertaking. Writing a second book, when you know exactly what to expect, can be even more daunting. It's impossible to write a full-length manuscript from start to finish in the span of six months without taking at least some time away from family, so first and foremost, I want to thank my husband and children for their infinite patience, understanding, and support. Somehow they always know how to help me keep a good perspective, and frequently remind me of what's most important in life.

Many thanks and *abrazos* go out to my literary agent, Diane Stockwell of Globo Libros, for helping me navigate the literary world a second time, in addition to all the projects that have popped up in between *Cartel* and *Border Insecurity*. I certainly couldn't have done any of it without her guidance and unfailing support. I'm also grateful for the unending professionalism and enthusiasm of the Palgrave Macmillan team, current and former, including Elisabeth Dyssegaard, Tracey Lillis, Karen Wolny, Luba Ostashevsky, Laura Lancaster, Victoria Wallis, Donna Cherry, Allison Frascatore, Siobhan Paganelli, and Christine Catarino.

Many individuals with extraordinarily busy schedules were kind enough to take time to speak with me about border security issues, and I'm incredibly grateful for their contributions. Very special thanks go to Chairman Michael McCaul, Commissioner Todd Staples, Sheriff Mark Dannels, and Sheriff Richard Wiles. I also had the opportunity to speak with dozens of US Border Patrol and Customs and Border Protection agents, as well as local law enforcement officers, many of whom couldn't go on the record or use their real names for security reasons or fear of losing their jobs. I can't thank these men and women enough for the sacrifices they make every single day to help protect our nation.

For their help in making this book a reality, whether it was just chatting with me, providing insight, or helping me make the right connections,

I would like to thank (in no particular order) Pendleton Parrish, Matthew Green, Bruce Wright, Eloisa Támez, "Miguel," Christof Putzel, Maria "Sarnoff," Brad Barker, Mark Tinker, Robert Lee Maril, David Silverberg, Dan Verton, Glenn Spencer, Joel Smith, Jason Modglin, Karl Goguen, Ralph DeSio, Sally Gall, Nick Stein, Natalia Baldwin-León, Angela Kocherga, Deputy Mike Magoffin, and David Biette.

I'm very fortunate I've had the opportunity over the last four years to write about border security issues for *Homeland Security Today* magazine, and I treasure the relationship I've developed with them. I'm also grateful for the platform I've been provided by FOX News Latino to regularly publish opinion pieces on drug war and border security issues, and to *Small Wars Journal's* El Centro for the opportunity to contribute to their amazing repository of work. I'm very lucky to have a fabulous and loyal following through my Mexico's Drug War blog, Facebook fan pages and Twitter feed, and I very much appreciate those of you who have read my work and pushed it out to others through these sites.

While it's not obvious in my headshots and media interviews, I have been living with multiple sclerosis for over nine years, and I volunteer for and strongly support the efforts of the National Multiple Sclerosis Society. If you ever see me in person at a book signing or speaking engagement, I'll be accompanied by my trusty walker or electric scooter. That sometimes surprises people, but I'm easy to spot at a busy conference. I'm very vocal about my MS as a former Ambassador for the Society, and very proud of and thankful for the support the NMSS has provided over the years to people like me who work hard to live full and active lives with this chronic, often debilitating, and incurable disease.

On a more personal note, many thanks and love to my parents, my brother and his family, all the Curbelos and Longmires (and extensions), Erin and Alana, the Griggs and Wiggs families, Paige, Aimee, and Danielle, Shae, Hayley, playgroup moms in O'Fallon and MOPS moms in Tucson. I always joke that I lead a double life, playing the role of suburban housewife and mother by day and writing about drug smugglers and weapons traffickers by night. But these people, along with my husband and kids, are the people who comprise my "real" life, and I can't thank them all enough for their love, friendship, and support.

NOTES

INTRODUCTION

1. Stephanie Condon, "Napolitano: Border Security Better than Ever," CBS News, March 25, 2011, accessed December 2, 2012, http://www.cbsnews.com/8301 -503544_162-20047102-503544.html.
2. Barry R. McCaffrey and Robert H. Scales, *Texas Border Security: A Strategic Military Assessment,* Texas Department of Agriculture, September 26, 2011, accessed December 2, 2012.
3. Brady McCombs, "Border is a clear line; 'control' is a gray area," *The Arizona Daily Star,* April 19, 2011, accessed December 17, 2012, http://azstarnet.com /news/local/border/article_bfe40b78-ef21-538c-93a3-9017c4163dab.html.
4. "Officials struggle to define border security," *Homeland Security News Wire,* April 21, 2011, accessed December 17, 2012, http://www.homelandsecurity newswire.com/officials-struggle-define-border-security.
5. *National Drug Threat Assessment 2011,* National Drug Intelligence Center, US Department of Justice, April 2012.
6. "Border Security: Preliminary Observations on Border Control Measures for the Southwest Border," Statement of Richard M. Stana, Director Homeland Security and Justice Issues, in Testimony Before the Subcommittee on Border and Maritime Security, Committee on Homeland Security, House of Representatives, Government Accountability Office, February 15, 2011, accessed December 11, 2012, http://www.gao.gov/new.items/d11374t.pdf.
7. Rex Hudson, "Marijuana Availability in the United States and its Associated Territories," Federal Research Division, US Library of Congress, December 2003, accessed December 16, 2012, http://www.loc.gov/rr/frd/pdf-files/Mar Avail.pdf.

CHAPTER 1: ENEMIES AT THE GATE

1. Telephone interview, August 15, 2013.
2. Ibid.
3. Ibid.
4. Ibid.
5. Ibid.
6. Ibid.
7. "A history of the drug trade in Mexico," History Department (lecture), Michigan State University, accessed March 18, 2013, http://webcache.google

usercontent.com/search?q=cache:-tMusHfyQIsJ:history.msu.edu/iss330c
/lectures/3-1/+&cd=3&hl=en&ct=clnk&gl=us&client=safari.

8. The term "cartel" by definition is a misnomer for drug trafficking organizations. Unlike true cartels (e.g., OPEC), Mexican organized crime groups don't
band together to set prices and stifle competition. However, the term became
well known during the 1980s when used in reference to the major drug organizations in Cali and Medellín, Colombia. A more accurate term—and one that
is used by most US agencies—is transnational criminal organization (TCO).
However, for readability and simplicity, the term "cartel" will be used throughout this book to refer to Mexican organized crime groups.

9. Olga R. Rodriguez, "Hugo Hernandez: Mexico Cartel Stitches Rival's Face On
Soccer Ball," *The Huffington Post*, January 8, 2010, accessed March 19, 2013,
http://www.huffingtonpost.com/2010/01/09/mexico-cartel-stitches-ri_n_417
326.html.

10. George W. Grayson, "La Familia: Another Deadly Mexican Syndicate," E-
Notes, Foreign Policy Research Institute, February 2009, accessed March 19,
2013, http://www.fpri.org/enotes/200901.grayson.lafamilia.html.

11. "CBP's 2012 Fiscal Year in Review," CBP.gov, February 1, 2013, accessed April 23,
2013, http://cbp.gov/xp/cgov/newsroom/news_releases/national/02012013_3
.xml.

12. "Apprehension/Seizure Statistics—Fiscal Year 2011," United States Border Patrol, CBP.gov, accessed April 23, 2013, http://cbp.gov/linkhandler/cgov/border
_security/border_patrol/usbp_statistics/usbp_fy11_stats/fy_profile_2011.ctt
/fy_profile_2011.pdf.

13. Penny Starr, "DHS Inspector General: '80 Percent Increase' in Cross-Border
Tunnels Since 2008," CNSNews.com, October 19, 2012, accessed April 23,
2013, http://cnsnews.com/news/article/dhs-inspector-general-80-percent-incr
ease-cross-border-tunnels-2008.

14. Email from Victor Brabble, CBP Office of Public Affairs, Southwest Border
Joint Information Center, dated March 11, 2013.

15. Starr, "DHS Inspector General."

16. Robert Beckhusen, "Border Patrol Seeks Hazmat Teams for Drugs Smuggled
in Toxic Waste," Wired.com, March 21, 2013, accessed April 23, 2013, http://
www.wired.com/dangerroom/2013/03/toxic-drugs/?utm_source=twitterfe
ed&utm_medium=twitter.

17. "Excavator Arm Packed with Marijuana," KRGV.com, April 23, 2013, accessed April 24, 2013, http://www.krgv.com/news/excavator-arm-packed-with
-marijuana/.

18. Nick Welsh, "America's Sea-Born Terrorism Challenge: The Panga Boat," *Pacific
Standard,* April 1, 2013, accessed April 24, 2013, http://www.psmag.com/legal
-affairs/panga-boat-mexico-california-marijuana-drug-trafficking-homeland
-security-54454/.

19. Dane Schiller, "DEA agent breaks silence on standoff with cartel," *The Houston
Chronicle,* March 15, 2010, accessed February 27, 2013, http://www.chron.com
/news/houston-texas/article/DEA-agent-breaks-silence-on-standoff-with
-cartel-1713234.php.

20. Monique Ching, "FBI agent recalls 1999 standoff," *San Angelo Standard-Times,*
August 22, 2012, accessed February 27, 2013, http://www.gosanangelo.com
/news/2012/aug/22/fbi-agent-recalls-1999-standoff/?print=1.

21. Schiller, "DEA agent breaks silence on standoff with cartel."

22. Ibid.

23. Ching, "FBI agent recalls 1999 standoff."

24. Dane Schiller, Dudley Althaus, and Susan Carroll, "Agent battled with his killers," *The Houston Chronicle*," February 17, 2011, accessed March 19, 2013, http://www.mysanantonio.com/news/local_news/article/Agentbattledwith-hiskillers-1017191.php#page-2.

25. "Jaime Zapata Told Gunmen 'We're Diplomats,'" FOX News Insider, February 17, 2011, accessed March 19, 2013, http://foxnewsinsider.com/2011/02/17/jaime-zapata-told-gunmen-"we're-diplomats"/.

26. Schiller, Althaus, and Carroll, "Agent battled with his killers."

27. "Cartel hit possibly behind US agent killing, congressman says," CNN.com, February 17, 2011, accessed March 19, 2013, http://articles.cnn.com/2011-02-17/world/mexico.ice.attack_1_zetas-task-force-cartel?_s=PM:WORLD.

28. "Mexican police attacked CIA officers, ambush likely: sources," Reuters.com, August 29, 2012, accessed March 19, 2013, http://www.reuters.com/article/2012/08/29/us-mexico-shooting-idUSBRE87S19K20120829.

29. Ibid.

30. Ibid.

31. Matthew Boyle, "Filmmaker creates full-blown re-enactment of Brian Terry's Fast and Furious murder," *The Daily Caller*, October 1, 2012, accessed March 25, 2013, http://dailycaller.com/2012/10/01/filmmaker-creates-full-blown-re-enactment-of-brian-terrys-fast-and-furious-murder-video/.

32. Personal account as told to the author by a US government official who wished to remain anonymous.

33. Greg Moran, "Third guilty plea in killing of border agent," *San Diego Union-Tribune*, January 25, 2013, accessed March 26, 2013, http://www.utsandiego.com/news/2013/jan/25/border-patrol-agent-killed-guilty-plea/.

34. Personal interview with a senior ATF official who wishes to remain anonymous.

35. Adriana Gómez Licón and Daniel Borunda, "Juárez massacre: Football players, honor student among 16 victims," *El Paso Times*, February 2, 2010, accessed February 27, 2013, http://www.elpasotimes.com/ci_14315072?r44b=no.

36. "'El Diego' Confesses, details Villas Salvarcar massacre, car bomb and more," BorderlandBeat.com, August 2, 2011, accessed February 27, 2013, http://www.borderlandbeat.com/2011/08/el-diego-confesses-details-villas.html.

37. E. Eduardo Castillo, "Mexico Horror: Suspected Drug Traffickers Dump 35 Bodies On Avenue In Veracruz," *The Huffington Post*, September 22, 2011, accessed April 24, 2013, http://www.huffingtonpost.com/2011/09/21/mexico-bodies-gunmen_n_973298.html.

38. "A Closer Look: Who Were The 35 Slaughtered in Veracruz?" BorderlandBeat.com, January 1, 2012, accessed April 24, 2013, http://www.borderlandbeat.com/2012/01/by-for-borderland-beat-part-1-two-weeks.html.

39. "MEXICO: The Killing of Innocents, by Cartels, Police, Military and Death Squads," BorderlandBeat.com, May 28, 2012, accessed April 24, 2013, http://www.borderlandbeat.com/2012/05/mexico-killing-of-innocents-by-cartels.html.

40. Ignacio Alazaga, "Captura Ejército a 'El Loco' presunto responsable de 49 ejecutados en Cadereyta, NL," *Milenio*, May 18, 2012, accessed April 24, 2013, http://monterrey.milenio.com/cdb/doc/noticias2011/8f5f3eb62bb61e396de9cd0eea3dc389.

41. "Were the Cadereyta 49 migrants? Plus Chronology of mass killings in Mexico since 2010," BorderlandBeat.com, May 14, 2012, accessed April 24, 2013, http://

www.borderlandbeat.com/2012/05/were-49-cadereyta-victims-migrants-plus
.html.

42. "International Narcotics Control Strategy Report: Volume I, Drug and Chemi-
cal Control March 2010," US Department of State, March 2010, p. 7.

CHAPTER 2: THE GUARDIANS

1. Public Papers of the Presidents of the United States: George W. Bush (2005,
Book II), October 22, 2005, pp. 1576-1577, accessed February 10, 2013, http://
www.gpo.gov/fdsys/pkg/PPP-2005-book2/html/PPP-2005-book2-doc-pg1576
.htm.

2. "Border Emergency," *The Washington Post* (editorial), August 26, 2005, accessed February 10, 2013, http://www.washingtonpost.com/wp-dyn/content
/article/2005/08/25/AR2005082501571.html.

3. Telephone interview, July 20, 2013.

4. Telephone interview, July 21, 2013.

5. "Border Patrol History," CBP.gov, January 5, 2010, accessed July 7, 2013, http://
www.cbp.gov/xp/cgov/border_security/border_patrol/border_patrol_ohs/his
tory.xml.

6. "US Border Patrol Sector Profile," CBP.gov, February 4, 2013, accessed July 7,
2013, http://www.cbp.gov/linkhandler/cgov/border_security/border_patrol/us
bp_statistics/usbp_fy12_stats/usbp_sector_profile.ctt/usbp_sector_profile
.pdf.

7. "Enacted Border Patrol Program Budget by Fiscal Year," CBP.gov, February
4, 2013, accessed July 7, 2013, http://www.cbp.gov/linkhandler/cgov/border
_security/border_patrol/usbp_statistics/usbp_fy12_stats/program_budget
.ctt/program_budget.pdf.

8. "Agents find 8 dead; seize nearly 6.5 tons of marijuana," KSAT.com, August
9, 2013, accessed August 18, 2013, http://m.ksat.com/news/agents-find-8-dead
-seize-nearly-65-tons-of-marijuana/-/15126192/21407526/-/fmkks5z/-/index
.html.

9. "US Border Patrol: Sequestration cuts hamper agents' efforts in hottest areas," *The Daily Caller,* June 15, 2013, accessed August 9, 2013, http://dailycaller
.com/2013/06/15/u-s-border-patrol-sequestration-cuts-hamper-agents-ef
forts-in-hottest-areas/.

10. Angela Kocherga, "Border Patrol agents running out of gas," WFAA8 News,
May 26, 2013, accessed August 9, 2013, http://www.wfaa.com/news/texas
-news/209025561.html.

11. Personal interview, July 30, 2013.

12. Ibid.

13. Personal interview, August 6, 2013.

14. Ibid.

15. Ibid.

16. Ibid.

17. Personal interview, February 28, 2013.

CHAPTER 3: THE BORDER FENCE

1. Edward Wyatt, "Cain Proposes Electrified Border Fence," *The New York
Times* (The Caucus blog), October 15, 2011, accessed January 25, 2013, http://

thecaucus.blogs.nytimes.com/2011/10/15/cain-proposes-electrified-border
-fence/?smid=tw-thecaucus&seid=auto.

2. Telephone interview, March 2, 2013.
3. Liz Goodwin, "The Texans who live on the 'Mexican side' of the border fence: 'Technically, we're in the United States,'" Yahoo! News, December 21, 2011, accessed April 26, 2013, http://news.yahoo.com/blogs/lookout/texas-americans -live-wrong-side-border-fence-christmas-183312787.html.
4. Richard Marosi, "Some angry Texans are stuck south of the barrier," *The Los Angeles Times,* February 28, 2011, accessed August 25, 2013, http://articles.la times.com/2011/feb/28/nation/la-na-texas-fence-20110228.
5. Joseph Nevins and Timothy Dunn, "Barricading the Border," *Counterpunch,* November 14-16, 2008, accessed January 31, 2013, http://www.counterpunch .org/2008/11/14/barricading-the-border/.
6. Ibid.
7. "Secure Border Initiative Program Guide," *Washington Technology,* August 31, 2006, accessed January 31, 2013, http://www.trezzamediagroup.com/uploads /sbi_supplement.pdf.
8. Ibid.
9. Secure Fence Act of 2006, Public Law 109-367, Government Publication Office, October 26, 2006, accessed January 31, 2013, http://www.gpo.gov/fdsys/pkg /PLAW-109publ367/pdf/PLAW-109publ367.pdf.
10. Nevins and Dunn, "Barricading the Border."
11. Consolidated Appropriations Act, 2008, Public Law 110-161, Government Publication Office, December 26, 2007, accessed January 31, 2013, http://www.gpo .gov/fdsys/pkg/PLAW-110publ161/pdf/PLAW-110publ161.pdf.
12. "US-Mexico border fence almost complete," NBCNews.com (Associated Press), January 27, 2009, accessed January 31, 2013, http://www.nbcnews.com /id/28878934/ns/us_news-security/t/us-mexico-border-fence-almost-com plete/#.UQrysqWJB7k.
13. H.Amdt.648 to H.R.4437, 109th Congress, December 15, 2005, accessed February 2, 2013, http://beta.congress.gov/amendment/109th-congress/house-ame ndment/648.
14. Blas Nuñez-Nieto and Stephen Viña, "Border Security: Barriers Along the U.S. International Border," Congressional Research Service, September 21, 2006.
15. Ibid.
16. Ibid.
17. Robert Lee Maril, *The Fence* (Texas Tech University Press), Kindle edition, March 1, 2011.
18. Ibid.
19. "Total Illegal Alien Apprehensions By Fiscal Year," U.S. Border Patrol, accessed February 4, 2013, http://www.cbp.gov/linkhandler/cgov/border_security /border_patrol/usbp_statistics/60_10_app_stats.ctt/60_11_app_stats.pdf.
20. Nuñez-Nieto and Viña, "Border Security."
21. "Closure of Refuge Lands Adjacent to the Border," Buenos Aires National Wildlife Refuge, US Fish and Wildlife Service, October 3, 2006, accessed August 19, 2013, http://www.azgfd.gov/pdfs/h_f/huntingunits/BuenosAiresAreaClosure .pdf.
22. "Uptick in Violence Forces Closing of Parkland Along Mexico Border to Americans," FOXNews.com, June 16, 2010, accessed on February 7, 2013, http://www .foxnews.com/us/2010/06/16/closes-park-land-mexico-border-americans/.

23. "Border Refuge Not Closed," Media Advisory, U.S. Fish and Wildlife Service, June 20, 2010, accessed February 7, 2013, http://www.fws.gov/southwest/docs /MediaAdvisory.BorderRefugeOpen.62010.pdf.

24. Telephone interview, March 6, 2013.

25. "Jeep gets stuck trying to drive over US-Mexico border fence," CNN.com, November 1, 2012, accessed February 2, 2013, http://www.cnn.com/2012/10/31 /us/mexico-border-jeep/index.html.

26. "Smugglers catapult pot over border fence," News4 Tucson (KVOA.com), January 26, 2011, accessed February 4, 2013, http://www.kvoa.com/news /smugglers-catapult-pot-over-border-fence/.

27. Jeff Tietz, "The US-Mexico Border's 150 Miles of Hell," *Men's Journal,* April 2012, accessed February 8, 2013, http://www.mensjournal.com/magazine /the-u-s-mexico-borders-150-miles-of-hell-20130103?page=1.

28. Daniel Gonzalez, "Nogales gets a more secure border fence," *The Arizona Republic,* June 30, 2011, accessed February 8, 2013, http://www.azcentral.com /news/articles/2011/06/30/20110630nogales-border-fence-replacement.html.

29. David Crowder, "Border fence gap to close," *El Paso Times,* October 21, 2012, accessed April 26, 2013, http://www.elpasoinc.com/news/local_news/article _eab8ab70-1b7d-11e2-87ab-0019bb30f31a.html.

30. Daniel C. Vock, "Arizona's Border Fence Still Faces Obstacles," *Stateline,* April 2, 2013, accessed April 26, 2013, http://www.pewstates.org/projects/stateline /headlines/arizonas-border-fence-still-faces-obstacles-85899465056.

31. *Secure Border Initiative Fence Construction Costs,* GAO Letter to Congressional Committees, January 29, 2009.

32. Ibid.

33. Julia Preston, "Some Cheer Border Fence as Others Ponder the Cost," *The New York Times,* October 19, 2011, accessed February 5, 2013, http://www.nytimes .com/2011/10/20/us/politics/border-fence-raises-cost-questions.html.

34. Reece Jones, "Something There Is That Doesn't Love a Wall," *The New York Times,* August 27, 2012, accessed February 5, 2013, http://www.nytimes .com/2012/08/28/opinion/Border-Fences-in-United-States-Israel-and-India .html.

35. Richard Marosi, "$57.7-million fence added to an already grueling illegal immigration route," *Los Angeles Times,* February 15, 2010, accessed February 6, 2013, http://articles.latimes.com/2010/feb/15/local/la-me-fence15-2010feb15.

36. Ibid.

37. Emergency Supplemental Appropriations Act for Defense, the Global War on Terror, and Tsunami Relief, 2005, Public Law 109-13, Government Publication Office, May 11, 2005, accessed February 6, 2013, http://www.gpo.gov/fdsys /pkg/PLAW-109publ13/html/PLAW-109publ13.htm.

38. Paul J. Weber, "Landowners on Border Say They Were Shortchanged," Associated Press, October 15, 2012, accessed April 30, 2013, http://bigstory.ap.org /article/landowners-border-say-they-were-shortchanged.

39. Melissa del Bosque, "Holes in the Wall," *The Texas Observer,* February 22, 2008, accessed August 24, 2013, http://www.texasobserver.org/2688-holes-in -the-wall/.

40. Margo Támez, "Open Letter to Cameron County Commission," *The Cut* vol. 2, no 1 (winter 2009): 110.

41. "Támez sues Chertoff," *The Rio Grande Guardian,* February 10, 2008, accessed August 24, 2013, http://www.texascivilrightsproject.org/203/tamez -sues-chertoff/.

42. Greg Harman, "Obama, guns, and Eloisa Támez," *San Antonio Current,* April 17, 2009, accessed August 24, 2013, http://borderwallinthenews.blogspot .com/2009/04/obama-guns-and-eloisa-tamez.html.

43. "Feds get last piece of Cameron County land needed for border fence," *The Monitor,* April 17, 2009, accessed August 24, 2013, http://www.freerepublic .com/focus/f-news/2236642/posts.

44. Goodman, "The Texans who live on the 'Mexican side' of the border fence."

45. "Woman at Odds with Feds over Border Fence," KRGV.com, April 17, 2013, accessed August 24, 2013, http://www.krgv.com/news/woman-at-odds-with-feds -over-border-fence/.

46. Telephone interview, August 28, 2013.

47. Ibid.

48. Ibid.

49. Telephone interview, March 6, 2013.

50. Ibid.

CHAPTER 4: TECHNOLOGY ON THE BORDER

1. Samantha Levine, "Next contract up for bid: border security," *The Houston Chronicle,* April 18, 2006, accessed January 28, 2013, http://www.chron.com /news/nation-world/article/Next-contract-up-for-bid-border-security-15808 89.php.

2. "High tech inspection systems hit ports this year," *US Customs Today,* CBP. gov, March 2000, accessed February 20, 2013, http://www.cbp.gov/custoday /mar2000/hitec.htm.

3. "Better Than X-Rays: The Z-Backscatter Scan-Van," *Defense Industry Daily,* October 21, 2008, accessed February 20, 2013, http://www.defenseindustrydaily .com/better-than-x-rays-the-z-backscatter-scan-van-04276/.

4. *Suggested Guidelines: Operation of License Plate Reader Technology,* New York State Division of Criminal Justice Services, January 2011, accessed February 11, 2013, http://criminaljustice.state.ny.us/ofpa/pdfdocs/finallprguidelines012 72011a.pdf.

5. Andreas Parsch, "Tethered Aerostats," Designation-Systems.net, 2005, accessed February 10, 2013, http://www.designation-systems.net/dusrm/app4/aerostats .html.

6. Christina Thompson, "Aerostat Balloon Crashes into Neighborhood, Power Lines," KOLD News, May 9, 2011, accessed February 10, 2013, http:// sierravista-fthuachuca.tucsonnewsnow.com/news/news/aerostat-balloon -crashes-neighborhood-power-lines/48817.

7. Adam Linhardt, "Keys icon deflated in name of progress," *Florida Keys News,* January 23, 2013, accessed February 10, 2013, http://keysnews.com/node/45129.

8. Mark Rockwell, "Aerostat system demonstration helps in arrests along Arizona border," *Government Security News,* April 5, 2012, accessed May 27, 2013, http:// www.gsnmagazine.com/node/26043.

9. David Bellow, "Obama Closing Air Defense System on U.S./Mexico Border: Texas & America Vulnerable to Attack from Low Altitude Missiles and Aircraft," TexasGOPVote.com, January 17, 2013, http://www.texasgop vote.com/issues/restore-families/obama-closing-air-defense-system-us /mexico-border-texas-america-vulnerable-005033.

10. Linhardt, "Keys icon deflated in name of progress."

11. Dennis Romboy, "Slain Border Patrol agent Nicholas Ivie opened fire first, investigators say," *Deseret News,* October 7, 2012, accessed February 19, 2013, http://www.deseretnews.com/article/865563971/Slain-Border-Patrol-agent -Nicholas-Ivie-opened-fire-first-investigators-say.html?pg=all.

12. Brian Bennett, "Border agents relying on outdated surveillance equipment," *The Los Angeles Times,* October 19, 2012, accessed February 19, 2013, http:// articles.latimes.com/2012/oct/19/nation/la-na-border-security-20121020.

13. Ibid.

14. David Gonzalez, "Radio woes put agents at risk on the border," *The Arizona Republic,* October 27, 2012, accessed May 27, 2013, http://www.azcentral.com /arizonarepublic/news/articles/20121025radio-woes-put-agents-risk-border .html.

15. "Detecting tunnels using seismic waves not as simple as it sounds," Sandia Labs News Releases, Sandia National Laboratories, December 6, 2012, accessed February 20, 2013, https://share.sandia.gov/news/resources/news_releases/sei smic_tunnels/.

16. Bruce Monk, "Using Threat Analysis and Technology to Improve Border Tunnel Detection," *Leading Edge Today,* October 2012, accessed February 20, 2013, http://www.nxtbook.com/nxtbooks/kmd/let_201209/#/6.

17. "Guardian UAS Maritime Variant Predator B," CBP Fact Sheet, CBP.gov, August 2012, accessed February 11, 2013, http://www.cbp.gov/linkhandler/cgov /newsroom/fact_sheets/marine/guardian_b.ctt/guardian_b.pdf.

18. Allya Sternstein, "Drones Outlast Narco Boats in Caribbean," Nextgov .com, July 12, 2012, accessed February 11, 2013, http://www.nextgov.com /defense/2012/07/drones-outlast-narco-boats-caribbean/56752/.

19. Jason Ryan, "Audit Finds Problems With DHS Drone Program Management," ABCNews.com, June 11, 2012, accessed February 11, 2013, http://abc news.go.com/blogs/politics/2012/06/audit-finds-problems-with-dhs-drone -program-management/.

20. "US Deploying Drones to Counter Caribbean Drug Traffickers," InSightCrime .org, July 17, 2012, accessed February 11, 2013, http://www.insightcrime.org /news-briefs/us-deploying-drones-to-counter-caribbean-drug-traffickers.

21. Brian Bennett, "U.S. plans more drone flights over Caribbean," *The Los Angeles Times,* June 23, 2012, accessed February 11, 2013, http://articles.latimes .com/2012/jun/23/nation/la-na-drugs-caribbean-20120623.

22. Chad C. Haddal and Jeremiah Gertler, "Homeland Security: Unmanned Aerial Vehicles and Border Surveillance," Congressional Research Service, July 8, 2012, accessed February 11, 2013, http://www.fas.org/sgp/crs/homesec/RS21698.pdf.

23. John Roberts, "EXCLUSIVE: Drones vulnerable to terrorist hijacking, researchers say," FOXNews.com, June 25, 2012, accessed February 11, 2013, http://www.foxnews.com/tech/2012/06/25/drones-vulnerable-to-terrorist -hijacking-researchers-say/.

24. "CBP's Use of Unmanned Aircraft Systems in the Nation's Border Security," Office of the Inspector General, US Department of Homeland Security, May 2012, accessed February 11, 2013, http://www.oig.dhs.gov/assets/Mgmt/2012 /OIG_12-85_May12.pdf.

25. Ibid.

26. Robert Lee Maril, *The Fence* (Lubbock, TX: Texas Tech University Press, 2011), pp. 101-103.

27. Ibid.

28. Ibid.

29. "Watching the Border: The Virtual Fence," *60 Minutes,* CBSNews.com, January 11, 2010, accessed February 21, 2013, http://www.cbsnews.com/8301-18560 _162-6067598.html.

30. Ibid.

31. Chris Strohm, "Appropriators skeptical of promised secure border initiative," *Government Executive,* April 7, 2006, accessed February 21, 2013, http://www .govexec.com/defense/2006/04/appropriators-skeptical-of-promised-secure -border-initiative/21530/.

32. Ibid.

33. Maril, *The Fence,* p. 449.

34. Ibid.

35. Ibid.

36. "Secure Border Initiative: DHS Needs to Strengthen Management and Oversight of its Prime Contractor" (GAO-11-6), US Government Accountability Office, October 2010.

37. "Arizona Border Surveillance Technology: More Information on Plans and Costs Is Needed Before Proceeding," US Government Accountability Office, November 2011.

38. Maril, *The Fence,* p. 183.

39. "Arizona Border Surveillance Technology," US Government Accountability Office.

40. Ibid.

41. Paul McLeary, "Is A Billion-Dollar Border Security Program Finally Due?," *Defense News,* May 14, 2013, accessed May 28, 2013, http://www.defense news.com/article/20130514/DEFREG02/305140009/Is-Billion-Dollar-Border -Security-Program-Finally-Due-.

42. Griff Witte, "Firms Vie to Provide the Future of Border Security," *The Washington Post,* September 18, 2006, accessed February 21, 2013, http://www.wash ingtonpost.com/wp-dyn/content/article/2006/09/17/AR2006091700847.html.

43. José J. Soto, "Sign Cutting and Tracking Methods Employed by the US Border Patrol," ITS Tactical website, April 18, 2012, accessed May 28, 2012, http://www.itstactical.com/skillcom/navigation/sign-cutting-and-tracking -methods-employed-by-the-us-border-patrol/.

44. Ibid.

45. "New border technology analyzes behavior to predict threats," KSAZ FOX10 News, October 12, 2012, accessed May 29, 2013, http://www.myfoxphoenix .com/story/19243250/2012/08/09/border-technology-can-predict-intent.

46. Richard Marosi, "Border drug enforcers award ultralight-detection-system contract," *Los Angeles Times,* August 18, 2012, accessed May 29, 2013, http:// articles.latimes.com/2012/aug/18/local/la-me-border-contract-20120818.

CHAPTER 5: BORDER VIOLENCE SPILLOVER

1. Gary Moore, "The Hunger for News of Mexican 'Spillover' Violence," InSightCrime.org, November 7, 2011, accessed December 2, 2012, http://www.insight crime.org/news-analysis/the-hunger-for-news-of-mexican-spillover-violence.

2. Ibid.

3. All the details of Martín Alejandro Cota-Monroy's murder and subsequent investigation were gleaned from the 170-page Chandler Police Department Incident Report (no. 10-11-1857), dated October 10, 2010, accessed December 20, 2012, http://narcosphere.narconews.com/userfiles/70/PoliceReport.pdf.

4. Kevin L. Perkins and Anthony P. Placido, US Senate Caucus on International Narcotics Control, Washington, DC, May 5, 2010, accessed December 21, 2012, http://www.fbi.gov/news/testimony/drug-trafficking-violence-in-mexico-implications-for-the-united-states.

5. "On the Border and in the Line of Fire: U.S. Law Enforcement, Homeland Security and Drug Cartel Violence," Opening Statement of Chairman Michael McCaul (R-TX) as Prepared for Delivery to the Subcommittee on Oversight, Investigations, and Management, May 11, 2011, accessed December 21, 2012, http://homeland.house.gov/sites/homeland.house.gov/files/05-11-11%20 McCaul%20Open.pdf.

6. John Burnett, "'Spillover' Violence from Mexico: Trickle Or Flood?" NPR .org, July 6, 2011, accessed December 21, 2012, http://www.npr.org/2011 /07/06/137445310/spillover-violence-from-mexico-a-trickle-or-flood.

7. Erika Flores, "Sheriff confirms deputy was shot in 'spillover' violence incident," ValleyCentral.com, October 31, 2011, accessed December 21, 2012, http://www .valleycentral.com/news/story.aspx?id=681024#.UNS66qU3t7k.

8. Brian Bennett, "Napolitano urges officials to stop exaggerating border crime," *East Valley Tribune,* January 31, 2011, accessed December 22, 2012, http://www .azcentral.com/news/articles/2011/01/31/20110131napolitano-says-stop-exag gerating-border-crime.html.

9. Brian Koenig, "CBP Director: US-Mexican Border Areas Are Among the Safest in US," *The New American,* May 3, 2012, accessed December 22, 2012, http:// www.thenewamerican.com/usnews/immigration/item/11218-cbp-director -us-mexican-border-areas-are-among-the-safest-in-us.

10. All statistics were pulled from the FBI's Uniform Crime Reports database at http://www.fbi.gov/about-us/cjis/ucr, accessed December 20, 2012.

11. Transcript of House Homeland Security Subcommittee on Oversight, Investigations and Management Hearing on US-Mexico Border Law Enforcement, May 2011, accessed December 24, 2012, http://www.micevhill.com/attach ments/immigration_documents/hosted_documents/112th_congress/Tran scriptOfHouseHomelandSecuritySubcommitteeOnOversight.pdf.

12. "Why Border Violence Spillover Needs to Be Defined," *Homeland Security Today,* January 17, 2012, accessed December 24, 2012, http://www.hstoday.us /briefings/correspondents-watch/single-article/why-border-violence-spillover -needs-to-be-defined/e4df3ebc4e28933d98b3c676cf2cb52f.html.

13. "Sources: Fatal gunshots on McAllen expressway point to Gulf Cartel," BorderlandBeat.com, September 27, 2011, accessed January 8, 2013, http://www .borderlandbeat.com/2011/09/sources-fatal-gunshots-on-mcallen.html.

14. "Two Zetas executed in Brownsville, Texas," BorderlandBeat.com, October 5, 2010, accessed January 8, 2013, http://www.borderlandbeat.com/2010/10/two -zetas-executed-in-brownsville-texas.html.

15. Brean Bierman, "Police arrest Mexican drug cartel member in Phoenix," CBS5Az.com, October 19, 2012, accessed January 8, 2013, http://www.kpho.com /story/19868294/cartel-member-lost-drugs-ordered-to-kill-or-be-killed.

16. "The Enemy Within," *Newsweek,* March 13, 2009, accessed January 8, 2013, http://www.thedailybeast.com/newsweek/2009/03/13/the-enemy-within .html.

17. "Bullets fired into SUV, family of three inside," ValleyCentral.com, October 6, 2012, accessed January 4, 2013, http://www.valleycentral.com/m/news /story?id=809921#.UOdFvqVnR7l.

18. "Home invasion leaves man dead, homeowner kidnapped," ValleyCentral. com, December 22, 2012, accessed on January 4, 2013, http://www.valleycentral .com/news/story.aspx?id=840242.

19. Dave Hendricks, "Shots fired from Mexico at water district employees near Hidalgo, official says," *The Monitor,* July 14, 2011, accessed January 8, 2013, http:// www.freerepublic.com/focus/f-news/2748505/posts.

20. Burnett, "'Spillover' Violence From Mexico: Trickle Or Flood?" NPR.org.

21. Personal interview, July 30, 2013.

22. Personal interview, August 6, 2013.

CHAPTER 6: THE EVOLUTION OF CROSS-BORDER MIGRATION

1. "Book by Minuteman founder & 'Unfit for Command' author to target illegal immigration," press release, Jim Gilchrist and the Minuteman Project, February 22, 2006, accessed January 28, 2013, http://powderbluereport.blogspot .com/2006/02/book-by-minuteman-founder-unfit-for.html.

2. Damien Cave, "Crossing Over, and Over," *The New York Times,* October 2, 2011, accessed June 21, 2013, http://www.nytimes.com/2011/10/03/world/americas /mexican-immigrants-repeatedly-brave-risks-to-resume-lives-in-united-states .html?pagewanted=all&_r=1&.

3. "Their Dreams Ended in The San Fernando Massacre," BorderlandBeat .com, August 24, 2012, accessed May 9, 2013, http://www.borderlandbeat .com/2012/08/their-dreams-ended-in-san-fernando.html.

4. Ibid.

5. Ibid.

6. Ibid.

7. The Mexican government tends to downplay any incidents that possibly involve the targeting of innocent people by drug cartels. It has historically preferred to portray the drug war as almost exclusively a cartel-on-cartel problem, so the San Fernando massacre posed a big public relations challenge. Government officials tried repeatedly to discredit Luis's version of events as not plausible, and establish possible (but ultimately non-existent) links between the victims and organized crime groups.

8. Gary Moore, "Unravelling Mysteries of Mexico's San Fernando Massacre," In SightCrime.org, September 19, 2011, accessed May 14, 2013, http://www.insight crime.org/investigations/unravelling-mysteries-of-mexicos-san-fernando -massacre.

9. "Survivor Details Massacre of 72 Migrants by Drug Cartel in Mexico," FOXNews .com (Associated Press), August 25, 2010, accessed May 14, 2013, http:// www.foxnews.com/world/2010/08/25/mexican-government-migrants-dead- ranch-killed-zetas-drug-gang/.

10. "Their Dreams Ended in The San Fernando Massacre."

11. Comisión Nacional de los Derechos Humanos (CNDH), *Special Report of the Human Rights National Commission over Kidnapping Against Migrants* (Mexico City: CNDH, 2011).

12. "Mexican Immigrant Labor History," PBS.org, accessed May 14, 2013, http:// www.pbs.org/kpbs/theborder/history/timeline/17.html.

13. Ibid.

14. Martin Brass, "The U.S./Mexican Border Has Become a Sieve of Death," *Soldier of Fortune,* vol. 29, no. 9 (September 2004): 58-61, accessed May 16, 2013, http:// www.military.com/NewContent/0,13190,SOF_0804_Mexico,00.html.

15. Steven Dudley, "Transnational Crime in Mexico and Central America: Its Evolution and Role in International Migration," Migration Policy Institute, Woodrow Wilson International Center for Scholars, November 2012.

16. John Burnett, "Migrants Say They're Unwilling Mules for Cartels," NPR .org, December 4, 2011, accessed June 20, 2013, http://m.npr.org/news/front /143025654.

17. Telephone interview, January 2013.

18. Cave, "Crossing Over, and Over."

19. Hannah Rappleye and Lisa Riordan Seville, "Deadly Crossing: Death toll rises among those desperate for the American Dream," NBCNews .com, October 9, 2012, accessed June 21, 2013, http://openchannel.nbc news.com/_news/2012/10/09/14300178-deadly-crossing-death-toll-rises -among-those-desperate-for-the-american-dream?lite.

20. Telephone interview, July 27, 2013.

21. "Life and Death on the Border," *Vanguard,* Current TV, aired on November 8, 2010, accessed July 28, 2013, http://current.com/shows/vanguard/videos /life-and-death-on-the-border-2/.

22. Telephone interview, July 27, 2013.

23. Sebastian Rotella, "The New Border: Illegal Immigration's Shifting Frontier," *ProPublica,* December 6, 2012, accessed June 21, 2013, http://www.propublica .org/article/the-new-border-illegal-immigrations-shifting-frontier.

24. Maria S. as next friend for E.H.F., S.H.F., and A.S.G., minors, plaintiffs v. Four unknown named agents of United States Customs and Border Protection and/ or Immigration and Customs Enforcement: "John Doe," "Mark Moe," Robert Roe," and "James Loe," in their individual capacities, defendants, US District Court for the Southern District of Texas, Brownsville Division, accessed June 19, 2013, https://www.documentcloud.org/documents/709515-lauras-1.html.

25. Ibid.

26. Ibid.

27. Ibid.

28. Melissa del Bosque, "Lawsuit Claims Woman's Deportation was a Death Sentence," *The Texas Observer,* June 6, 2013, accessed June 19, 2013, http://www .texasobserver.org/lawsuit-claims-womans-deportation-was-a-death-sentence /#.UbDEi6mN_Lw.twitter.

29. Ioan Grillo, "Mexico's drug-war refugees seek asylum," *Tucson Sentinel,* September 15, 2011, accessed June 19, 2013, http://www.tucsonsentinel.com/nation world/report/091511_mexico_asylum/mexicos-drug-war-refugees-seek -asylum/.

30. Ibid.

31. "Judge-by-Judge Asylum Decisions in Immigration Courts FY 2007-2012," Transactional Records Access Clearinghouse, Syracuse University, 2013, accessed June 20, 2013, http://trac.syr.edu/immigration/reports/306/include /denialrates.html.

32. Chris Vogel and Patrick Michels, "Asylum Denied: Unlike Refugees from Other Troubled Countries, Only a Fraction of Mexicans Seeking U.S. Asylum Are Accepted—No Matter Their Wounds or Stories," *The Phoenix New Times,* August 26, 2010, accessed June 20, 2013, http://www.phoenixnewtimes .com/2010-08-26/news/asylum-unlike-refugees-from-other-troubled-coun tries-only-a-fraction-of-mexicans-seeking-u-s-asylum-are-accepted-no-mat ter-their-wounds-or-stories/4/.

33. Personal interview, July 20, 2013.
34. Vogel and Michels, "Asylum Denied."
35. Ibid.
36. William La Jeunesse, "Agencies buying hotel rooms for surge of Mexican illegal immigrants, others released," FOXNews.com, August 9, 2013, accessed August 20, 2013, http://www.foxnews.com/us/2013/08/12/surge-mexican-illegal-immigrants-claiming-asylum-overwhelms-border-officials/.
37. Ibid.
38. Lauran Rabaino, "Infographic: US-Mexico border crossers not giving up," Center for Investigative Reporting, May 23, 2013, accessed June 21, 2013, http://cironline.org/reports/infographic-us-mexico-border-crossers-not-giving-4562?utm_source=CIR&utm_medium=social_media&utm_campaign=twitter.
39. Cave, "Crossing Over, and Over."

CHAPTER 7: TERRORISM AND THE SOUTHWEST BORDER

1. Congress, House Committee on Homeland Security Hearing, "Iran, Hezbollah, and the Threat to the Homeland," 112th Congress, March 21, 2012, homeland.house.gov/hearing/hearing-iran-hezbollah-and-threat-homeland.
2. *Country Reports on Terrorism,* US Department of State, August 18, 2011, accessed November 30, 2012, http://www.state.gov/j/ct/rls/crt/2010/170259.htm.
3. Vytenis Didziulis, "Behind Manssor Arbabsiar's Plot to Kill the Saudi US Ambassador," ABC Univision (online), October 22, 2012, accessed December 6, 2012, http://abcnews.go.com/ABC_Univision/mansour-arbabsiars-twisted-plot-kill-saudi-us-ambassador/story?id=17533527#.UMD59qU3t7k.
4. "Qods (Jerusalem) Force, Iranian Revolutionary Guard Corps (IRGC–Pasdaran-e Inqilab)," Federation of American Scientists Intelligence Resource Program, August 1, 1998, accessed December 6, 2012, http://www.fas.org/irp/world/iran/qods/.
5. United States of America v. Manssor Arbabsiar and Gholam Shakuri, US Magistrate Court, Southern District of New York, October 11, 2011.
6. Richard Esposito and Brian Ross, "Iran 'Directed' Washington, DC, Terror Plot, US Says," ABCNews.com, October 11, 2011, accessed December 6, 2012, http://abcnews.go.com/Blotter/us-iran-tied-terror-plot-washington-dc-disrupted/story?id=14711933#.UMEH5KU3t7k.
7. United States of America v. Manssor Arbabsiar and Gholam Shakuri.
8. Ibid.
9. Didziulis, "Behind Manssor Arbabsiar's Plot to Kill the Saudi US Ambassador."
10. Esposito and Ross, "Iran 'Directed' Washington, DC, Terror Plot, US Says."
11. Thomas Donnelly, "Quds and Zetas," *The Weekly Standard,* October 12, 2011, accessed December 7, 2012, http://www.weeklystandard.com/blogs/quds-and-zetas_595798.html.
12. Tim Padgett, "Hiring Narcos to Murder the Saudi Ambassador? If It's True, Tehran Is Pretty Dumb," *Time,* October 11, 2011, accessed December 7, 2012, http://world.time.com/2011/10/11/hiring-narcos-to-murder-the-saudi-ambassador-if-its-true-tehran-is-pretty-dumb/.
13. Bernard Gwertzman, "Mounting Questions on Iran Terror Plot," Council on Foreign Relations, October 13, 2011, accessed December 7, 2012, http://www.cfr.org/iran/mounting-questions-on-iran-terror-plot/p26185.
14. Jeffery Robinson, *The Merger* (New York: Overlook Press, 2000).

15. Bartosz Stanislawski, "Ciudad del Este and the Tri-Border Area of South America," *International Spotlights ON and OFF,* Syracuse University, accessed December 7, 2012, http://sites.maxwell.syr.edu/luce/Stanislawski2.html.

16. "Terrorist and Organized Crime Groups in the Triborder Area (TBA) of South America," Federal Research Division, US Library of Congress, December 2010 (rev.), accessed December 7, 2012, http://www.loc.gov/rr/frd/pdf-files/Terr OrgCrime_TBA.pdf.

17. Camila Pastor de Maria y Campos, "Being a New Muslim in Mexico: Conversion as Class Mobility," Islam in Latin America Workshop, Florida International University Applied Research Center, April 2010, accessed December 7, 2012, http://strategicculture.fiu.edu/LinkClick.aspx?fileticket=3ZO7yvT4G1E %3D&tabid=89.

18. "Hezbollah in Latin America: Implications for U.S. Homeland Security," Written Testimony of Ambassador Roger F. Noriega Before a Hearing of the Subcommittee on Counterterrorism and Intelligence Committee on Homeland Security, US House of Representatives, July 7, 2011, accessed December 7, 2012, http://homeland.house.gov/sites/homeland.house.gov/files/Testimony%20 Noriega.pdf.

19. "International Terrorism Situational Awareness: Hezbollah," Tucson Police Department (Tucson Urban Area Security Initiative), September 10, 2010, accessed December 7, 2012, http://info.publicintelligence.net/AZ-Hezbollah.pdf.

20. Joshua Rhett Miller, "US, Mexican Officials Say They Can't Confirm Arrest of Hezbollah Operative on Border," FOXNews.com, July 9, 2010, accessed December 7, 2012, http://www.foxnews.com/world/2010/07/12/hezbollah-arrest -mexico-lawmakers-terror-analysts-worried/.

21. Ben Conery, "EXCLUSIVE: Hezbollah uses Mexican drug routes into US," *The Washington Times,* March 27, 2009, accessed December 7, 2012, http://www .washingtontimes.com/news/2009/mar/27/hezbollah-uses-mexican-drug -routes-into-us/?page=all.

22. Jeremy Pelafsky, "U.S. indicts Lebanese man for aiding Mexican cartel," Thompson Reuters News & Insight, December 13, 2011, accessed December 7, 2012, http://newsandinsight.thomsonreuters.com/Legal/News/2011/12_-_ December/U_S__indicts_Lebanese_man_for_aiding_Mexican_cartel/.

23. United States of America v. Mahmoud Youssef Kourani, United States District Court, Eastern District of Michigan (Southern Division), Complaint No. 03-81030, November 19, 2003.

24. Ibid.

25. "Mahmoud Youssef Kourani," *Mother Jones* (Profiles), accessed December 9, 2012, http://www.motherjones.com/fbi-terrorist/mahmoud-youssef-kourani -hezbollah.

26. "Terror-Linked Migrants Channeled into US," Associated Press, July 3, 2005, accessed on December 9, 2012, http://www.foxnews.com/story/0,2933,161473,00 .html.

27. Pauline Arrillaga and Olga R. Rodriguez, "The Terror-Immigration Connection," Associated Press, July 3, 2005, accessed December 9, 2012, http://www .msnbc.msn.com/id/8408009/ns/us_news-security/t/terror-immigration-con nection/#.UMTE_aU3t7k.

28. "Hezbollah Presence in the United States is No Surprise," *Homeland Security Today,* January 10, 2012, accessed December 9, 2012, http://www.hs today.us/briefings/correspondents-watch/single-article/hezbollah-presence

-in-the-united-states-is-no-surprise/2e1af4c017be5f75d5a5da67329b6b91.
html.

29. Melani Cammett, "Hezbollah in Latin America—Implications for U.S. Homeland Security," Testimony before the Subcommittee on Counterterrorism and
Intelligence Committee on Homeland Security, U.S. House of Representatives, July 7, 2011, homeland.house.gov/sites/homeland.house.gov/files/Testi
mony%20Cammett.pdf.

30. Pierre Thomas, "Some Experts Fear Hezbollah Attack in United States," ABC
News.com, July 28, 2006, accessed December 9, 2012, http://abcnews.go.com
/GMA/Mideast/story?id=2246657#.UMTlvKU3t7k.

31. Edwin Mora, "U.S. Designates Israel as Country That Tends 'To Promote, Produce, or Protect' Terrorists; Also Calls Israel Anti-Terror Partner," CNSNews
.com, June 29, 2011, accessed December 9, 2012, http://cnsnews.com/news
/article/us-designates-israel-country-tends-promote-produce-or-protect-ter
rorists-also-calls.

32. Penny Starr, "Napolitano: DHS Is Working with Mexico on 'Special Interest
Aliens' Threat Along U.S.- Mexican Border," January 17, 2012, accessed December 9, 2012, http://cnsnews.com/news/article/napolitano-dhs-working
-mexico-special-interest-aliens-threat-along-us-mexican-border.

33. Supervision of Aliens Commensurate with Risk, Office of the Inspector General, US Department of Homeland Security, December 2011.

34. "What Can We Learn From Trends In 'Special Interest Alien' Migration Into
The US?" *Homeland Security Today,* May 11, 2011, accessed December 9, 2012,
http://www.hstoday.us/briefings/correspondents-watch/single-article/what
-can-we-learn-from-trends-in-special-interest-alien-migration-into-the-us/dd
e14d2e6e96cdb40a5ae5003d4002f2.html.

35. Ibid.

36. Ibid.

37. "Zetas planearon ataque al casino en conocido restaurante de Monterrey," *El
Diario,* August 28, 2011.

38. "Video captó cuando atacantes de casino cargaron gasolina," *El Universal,* August 29, 2011, accessed December 10, 2012, http://www.eluniversal.com.mx
/notas/789461.html.

39. Mike Jaccarino, "Gunmen set Monterrey's Casino Royale on fire, killing at
least 53 in latest Mexico violence," NYDailyNews.com, August 25, 2011, accessed December 10, 2012, http://articles.nydailynews.com/2011-08-25/news
/29947228_1_gunmen-alejandro-poire-three-other-casinos.

40. Ioan Grillo, "Burning Down Casino Royale: Mexico's Latest Drug Atrocity,"
Time, August 26, 2011, accessed December 2012, http://www.time.com/time
/world/article/0,8599,2090601,00.html.

41. Ken Ellingwood, "Mexico gunmen set casino on fire, killing at least 53," *Los
Angeles Times,* August 26, 2011, accessed December 10, 2012, http://articles.la
times.com/2011/aug/26/world/la-fgw-mexico-casino-20110827.

42. Stewart M. Powell, "Rep. Michael McCaul seeks to designate cartels as terrorists," *The Houston Chronicle,* March 30, 2011, accessed December 10, 2012,
http://www.chron.com/news/houston-texas/article/Rep-Michael-McCaul
-seeks-to-designate-cartels-as-1684882.php.

43. Elizabeth Harrington, "Republicans Propose Bill to Treat Mexican Drug
Cartels as 'Terrorist Insurgency,'" CNSNews.com, December 15, 2011, accessed December 10, 2012, http://cnsnews.com/news/article/republicans
-propose-bill-treat-mexican-drug-cartels-terrorist-insurgency.

44. Thomas Eldridge, Susan Ginsburg, Walter Hempel II, Janice Kephart, and Kelly Moore, *9/11 and Terrorist Travel*, Staff Report of the National Commission on Terrorist Attacks Upon the United States, August 21, 2004, accessed December 10, 2012, http://govinfo.library.unt.edu/911/staff_statements/911_TerrTrav _Monograph.pdf.

45. Larry Margasak and Corey Williams, "Nigerian man charged in Christmas airliner attack," *The Huffington Post*, December 26, 2009, accessed December 10, 2012, http://www.huffingtonpost.com/2009/12/26/northwest-airlines-flight_ n_403860.html.

46. Sari Horwitz, William Wan, and Del Quentin Wilber, "Federal agents arrest Amine El Khalifi; he allegedly planned to bomb Capitol," *The Washington Post*, February 17, 2012, accessed December 10, 2012, http://www.washington post.com/world/national-security/federal-agents-arrest-man-who-allegedly -planned-suicide-bombing-on-us-capitol/2012/02/17/gIQAtYZ7JR_story.html.

47. Sam Stein, "Gabriela Mercer, Arizona GOP Candidate: Middle Eastern Immigrants Want 'To Harm' The U.S.," *The Huffington Post*, August 28, 2012, accessed December 10, 2012, http://www.huffingtonpost.com/2012/08/28 /gabriela-mercer-arizona_n_1837358.html.

CHAPTER 8: THE INVISIBLE FIGHT AGAINST MONEY LAUNDERING

1. Jim Hogue, "Former FBI Translator Sibel Edmonds Calls Current 9/11 Investigation Inadequate," *Baltimore Chronicle & Sentinel*, May 7, 2004, accessed June 5, 2013.

2. "Texas Classic Fut & Derby," 440Post.com, November 28, 2009, accessed March 30, 2013, http://www.440post.com/node/789.

3. United States of America v. Miguel Ángel Treviño Morales, et al., United States District Court, Western District of Texas, Austin Division (A-12-CR-210-SS), May 30, 2012, accessed March 30, 2013, http://www.scribd.com/doc/96881023 /Trevino-Indictment#fullscreen.

4. Ibid.

5. Ibid.

6. "Brother of Z40 Takes a Fall For Money Laundering," BorderlandBeat.com, June 12, 2012, accessed March 30, 2013, http://www.borderlandbeat.com/2012/06 /brother-of-z40-takes-fall-for-money.html.

7. Julia Layton, "How Money Laundering Works," HowStuffWorks.com, accessed June 5, 2013, http://money.howstuffworks.com/money-laundering1.htm.

8. Ibid.

9. Mark Stevenson, "Mexico fines HSBC $28 million in laundering case," Associated Press, July 25, 2012, accessed July 17, 2013, http://finance.yahoo.com/news /mexico-fines-hsbc-28-million-laundering-case-152542240—finance.html.

10. Ibid.

11. Ben Protess and Jessica Silver-Greenberg, "HSBC to Pay $1.92 Billion to Settle Charges of Money Laundering," *The New York Times*, December 10, 2012, accessed July 17, 2013, http://dealbook.nytimes.com/2012/12/10/hsbc-said-to -near-1-9-billion-settlement-over-money-laundering/?ref=business.

12. Malcolm Beith, "HSBC Report Shows Difficulty of Stopping Money Launderers," *The Daily Beast*, July 19, 2012, accessed July 17, 2013, http://www .thedailybeast.com/articles/2012/07/19/hsbc-report-shows-difficulty-of-stop ping-money-launderers.html.

13. Ibid.

14. Ed Vulliamy, "How a big US bank laundered billions from Mexico's murderous drug gangs," *The Guardian,* April 2, 2011, accessed July 17, 2013, http://www .guardian.co.uk/world/2011/apr/03/us-bank-mexico-drug-gangs.
15. Personal interview, May 22, 2013.
16. Ibid.
17. Ibid.
18. Ibid.
19. Ibid.
20. Ibid.
21. Joseph Kirschke, "Drug Cartels Cash in on Coal Rush in Northern Mexico," *Coal Age,* March 21, 2013, accessed June 6, 2013, http://www.coalage.com /index.php/news/latest/2561-drug-cartels-cash-in-on-coal-rush-in-northern -mexico.html.
22. Tracey Knott, "Mexican Gangs Set their Sights on Illegal Mining," InSight-Crime.org, July 17, 2012 accessed June 6, 2013, http://www.insightcrime.org /news-analysis/mexican-gangs-set-their-sights-on-illegal-mining.
23. Ibid.
24. Ibid.
25. Tracy Wilkinson and Ken Ellingwood, "Cartels use legitimate trade to launder money, U.S., Mexico say," *Los Angeles Times,* December 19, 2011, accessed July 17, 2013, http://articles.latimes.com/2011/dec/19/world/la-fg-mexico-money -laundering-trade-20111219.
26. Rob Bates, "New Anti-Money Laundering Rules Apply to Gift Cards," *JCK Magazine,* February 10, 2012, accessed July 17, 2013, http://www.jckonline .com/2012/02/10/new-anti-money-laundering-rules-apply-to-gift-cards.
27. Evan Soltas, "Bitcoin Really Is an Existential Threat to the Modern Liberal State," Bloomberg.com, April 5, 2013, accessed June 5, 2013, http://mobile .bloomberg.com/news/2013-04-05/bitcoin-really-is-an-existential-threat-to -the-modern-liberal-state.html.
28. Jason Mick, "Cracking the Bitcoin: Digging Into a $131M USD Virtual Currency," DailyTech.com, June 12, 2011, accessed June 5, 2013, http://www.daily tech.com/Cracking+the+Bitcoin+Digging+Into+a+131M+USD+Virtual+Cu rrency/article21878.htm.
29. David Gilson, "How to Create a Brain Wallet," CoinDesk.com, June 10, 2013, accessed July 18, 2013, http://www.coindesk.com/how-to-create-a-brain-wallet/.
30. Jeffrey Sparshott, "Web Money Gets Laundering Rule," *The Wall Street Journal,* March 21, 2013, accessed June 5, 2013, http://online.wsj.com/article/SB1000142 4127887324373204578374611351125202.html.
31. Schuyler Velasco, "Liberty Reserve money-laundering case: five questions answered," *The Christian Science Monitor,* May 29, 2013, accessed June 8, 2013, http://www.csmonitor.com/Business/2013/0529/Liberty-Re serve-money-laundering-case-five-questions-answered/What-is-Liberty -Reserve.
32. Ibid.
33. Marc Santora, et al., "Online Currency Exchange Accused of Laundering $6 Billion," *The New York Times,* May 28, 2013, accessed June 8, 2013, http://www .nytimes.com/2013/05/29/nyregion/liberty-reserve-operators-accused-of -money-laundering.html?pagewanted=all&_r=0.
34. *The Buck Stops Here: Improving Anti-Money Laundering Practices,* US Senate Caucus on International Narcotics Control, April 2013, accessed

August 12, 2013, http://www.feinstein.senate.gov/public/index.cfm/files/serve /?File_id=311e974a-feb6-48e6-b302-0769f16185ee.

35. Celina B. Realuyo, "It's All About the Money: Advancing Anti-Money Laundering Efforts in the US and Mexico to Combat Transnational Organized Crime," Mexico Institute, Woodrow Wilson International Center for Scholars, May 2012, accessed August 12, 2013, http://www.wilsoncenter.org/sites/default /files/Realuyo_U.S.-Mexico_Money_Laundering_0.pdf.

36. "FACT SHEET: Overview of the Foreign Narcotics Kingpin Designation Act," Press Release, Office of the Press Secretary, The White House, April 15, 2009, accessed August 12, 2013, http://www.whitehouse.gov/the_press_office/Fact -Sheet-Overview-of-the-Foreign-Narcotics-Kingpin-Designation-Act.

37. Jon Matonis, "Department of Homeland Security to Scan Payment Cards at Borders and Airports," Forbes.com, November 7, 2012, accessed August 16, 2013, http://www.forbes.com/sites/jonmatonis/2012/11/07/department-of-home land-security-to-scan-payment-cards-at-borders-and-airports/.

38. Cynthia Merritt, "Crossing the Border: More Reason to Check Your Pockets," Portals and Rails (blog), Federal Reserve Bank of Atlanta, October 29, 2012, accessed August 16, 2013, http://portalsandrails.frbatlanta.org/2012/10/crossing -the-border-more-reason-to-check-your-pockets.html.

39. Ibid.

40. Matonis, "Department of Homeland Security to Scan Payment Cards at Borders and Airports."

41. Ken Ellingwood and Tracy Wilkinson, "Mexico seeks to fill drug war gap with focus on dirty money," *The Los Angeles Times,* November 27, 2011, accessed August 11, 2013, http://articles.latimes.com/2011/nov/27/world/la-fg-mexico -money-laundering-20111127/2.

42. Ibid.

43. Ibid.

44. Aruna Viswanatha and Brett Wolf, "DOJ targets banks, others in new money laundering offensive," Reuters, August 31, 2012, accessed August 11, 2013, http://www.reuters.com/article/2012/09/01/us-usa-moneylaundering-doj -idUSBRE87U11020120901,

45. Ibid.

46. Realuyo, "It's All About the Money."

47. *The Buck Stops Here.*

CHAPTER 9: TAKING MATTERS INTO THEIR OWN HANDS

1. Michael Garczyk, "Lacking Federal Manpower, Gov. Perry Sends Texas Rangers to Texas-Mexico Border," CNSNews.com, September 11, 2009, accessed October 19, 2013, http://cnsnews.com/news/article/lacking-federal-manpower-gov -perry-sends-texas-rangers-texas-mexico-border.

2. Shawna Shepherd, "Texas Gov. Rick Perry: Immigration is a 'federal responsibility,'" CNN.com, August 19, 2011, accessed October 19, 2013, http://politicalticker .blogs.cnn.com/2011/08/19/perry-immigration-is-a-federal-responsibility/.

3. Rick Perry, "Op-Ed: Federal government isn't offering proper toolkit," *Austin-American Statesman,* July 2, 2012, accessed October 19, 2013, http://www.rick perry.org/media-articles/op-ed-federal-government-isnt-offering-proper-tool-kit.

4. Telephone interview, March 3, 2013.

5. Ibid.

6. Melissa del Bosque, "Ag Commissioner Declares War on the Border," *The Texas Observer,* September 27, 2011, accessed June 1, 2013, http://www.texasobserver.org/gop-declares-war-on-the-border/.

7. Ellen Brisendine, "5 Tons of Narcotics and Counting," *The Cattleman,* September 2012, accessed June 1, 2013, http://thecattlemanmagazine.com/archives/2012/sept/operation-drawbridge.html.

8. Ibid.

9. "Texas Department of Agriculture Awards $225,000 to DPS for Operation Drawbridge Expansion," Press Release, Texas Department of Public Safety, October 11, 2012, accessed June 1, 2013 http://www.txdps.state.tx.us/director_staff/public_information/pr101112.htm.

10. Telephone interview, March 3, 2013.

11. "About BlueServo," BlueServo website, accessed June 4, 2013, http://www.blueservo.net/about.php.

12. Ibid.

13. "Krentz family honored with selection into Farming, Ranching Hall of Fame," *Douglas Dispatch,* April 19, 2008, accessed March 20, 2013, http://www.douglasdispatch.com/articles/2008/04/19/news/doc480a84d440a10680616836.txt.

14. J. D. Wallace, "Illegal Immigration Costly for Southeastern Arizona Ranchers," KOLD News 13, May 18, 2005, accessed March 20, 2013, http://www.tucsonnewsnow.com/Global/story.asp?S=3364733.

15. Paul Greenberg, "Death of a Rancher," *Jewish World Review,* April 29, 2010, accessed March 20, 2013, http://www.jewishworldreview.com/cols/greenberg042910.php3#.UUnjjKXQzy8.

16. Ibid.

17. "Murder of Arizona Rancher Roils Immigration Debate," FOX News, April 10, 2010, accessed March 20, 2013, http://www.foxnews.com/politics/2010/04/10/murder-arizona-rancher-roils-immigration-debate/?utm_source=feedburner&utm_medium=feed&utm_campaign=Feed%3A+foxnews%2Fpolitics+%28Text+-+Politics%29.

18. Curtis Prendergast, "Narratives in the News: The death of Robert Krentz," *The Sonoran Chronicle,* March 19, 2011, accessed March 20, 2013, http://sonoranchronicle.com/2011/03/19/narratives-in-the-news-the-death-of-robert-krentz/.

19. "SB 1070 Timeline," *The Arizona Republic,* April 22, 2011, accessed March 20, 2013, http://www.azcentral.com/arizonarepublic/news/articles/20110422sb1070timeline.html.

20. Arizona et al. v. The United States, No. 11-182, argued April 25, 2012, decided June 25, 2012, accessed March 20, 2013, http://www.supremecourt.gov/opinions/11pdf/11-182b5e1.pdf.

21. Daniel B. Wood, "Opinion polls show broad support for tough Arizona immigration law," *The Christian Science Monitor,* April 30, 2010, accessed March 20, 2013, http://www.csmonitor.com/USA/Society/2010/0430/Opinion-polls-show-broad-support-for-tough-Arizona-immigration-law.

22. Seth Freed Wessler, "What Ever Happened to SB 1070?" ColorLines.com, March 5, 2013, accessed March 20, 2013, http://colorlines.com/archives/2013/03/what_happened_to_sb_1070_the_anti-immigrant_tide_recedes_in_the_states.html.

23. "New border fence: Arizona plans its own 200-mile fence," *The Christian Science Monitor,* August 27, 2012, accessed March 20, 2013, http://www.csmoni

tor.com/USA/Latest-News-Wires/2012/0827/New-border-fence-Arizona -plans-its-own-200-mile-fence.

24. Ibid.

25. "Fundraising for Arizona border fence almost dried up," Associated Press, July 22, 2012, accessed March 20, 2013, http://www.azcentral.com/news /articles/20120722arizona-border-fence-fundraising-almost-dried-up.html.

26. "Donations for Ariz. border cause sit in treasury," *Arizona Daily Sun,* August 11, 2013, accessed August 20, 2013, http://azdailysun.com/news/state-and-regional /donations-for-ariz-border-cause-sit-in-treasury/article_747c5fe5-a986-5c77 -8b11-83ead3ddc2a9.html.

27. "Glenn Spencer," Intelligence Files, Southern Poverty Law Center, accessed July 29, 2013, http://www.splcenter.org/get-informed/intelligence-files/profiles/gle nn-spencer.

28. Stephen Lemons, "Glenn Spencer, Nativist Anti-Semite, To Lecture Arizona Senate Committee," *Phoenix New Times* (blog), March 4, 2011, accessed July 29, 2013, http://blogs.phoenixnewtimes.com/bastard/2011/03/glenn_spencer _nativist_and_ant.php.

29. Personal interview, July 25, 2013.

30. Casey Sanchez, "Glenn Spencer, More Hateful by the Day, Drones On," *Hate- watch,* Southern Poverty Law Center, January 14, 2009, accessed July 29, 2013, http://www.splcenter.org/blog/2009/01/14/glenn-spencer-more-hateful-by -the-day-drones-on/.

31. Personal interview, July 25, 2013.

32. Personal email from Glenn Spencer, dated August 30, 2013.

33. Dennis Wagner, "Minuteman's goal: To shame feds into action," *USA Today,* May 25, 2006, accessed June 4, 2013, http://usatoday30.usatoday.com/news /nation/2006-05-24-minuteman-goals_x.htm.

34. Ibid.

35. Ibid.

36. Max Blumenthal, "Vigilante Injustice," Salon.com, May 22, 2003, accessed June 4, 2013, http://www.salon.com/2003/05/22/vigilante_3/.

37. Steven M. Thomas, "The Minuteman Reconsidered," MinutemanProject .com, accessed June 4, 2013, http://minutemanproject.com/the-minuteman-re considered.

38. David Holthouse, "Minutemen, other Anti-Immigrant Militia Groups Stake Out Arizona Border," Southern Poverty Law Center Intelligence Report, Is- sue 118, Summer 2005, accessed June 4, 2013, http://www.splcenter.org /get-informed/intelligence-report/browse-all-issues/2005/summer/arizona -showdown#.Ua4rZJVYry8.

39. Sonya Geis, "Minuteman Project In Turmoil Over Financial Allegations," *The Washington Post,* March 13, 2007, accessed June 4, 2013, http://www.washing tonpost.com/wp-dyn/content/article/2007/03/12/AR2007031201297.html.

40. Brady McCombs, "AZ-based border Minuteman group calls it quits," *The Arizona Republic,* March 24, 2010, accessed June 4, 2013, http://azstarnet .com/news/local/border/az-based-border-minuteman-group-calls-it-quits /article_7d47c702-378b-11df-95cb-001cc4c03286.html.

41. Linda Bentley, "Minuteman Civil Defense Corps cancels muster, announces dissolution," SonoranNews.com, March 31, 2010, accessed June 4, 2013, http:// www.sonorannews.com/archives/2010/100331/ftpgMinuteman.html.

42. Nick Miroff, "Body count climbs in Texas," *The Washington Post,* May 17, 2013, accessed June 4, 2013, http://www.journalgazette.net/article/20130517 /NEWS03/305179946/1066/NEWS03.

43. "Mission," Humane Borders website, accessed June 5, 2013, http://www
    .humaneborders.org/mission/.
44. "OpenGIS Initiative," Humane Borders website, accessed June 5, 2013, http://
    www.humaneborders.org/ogis/.
45. Personal interview, August 1, 2013.
46. Ibid.
47. Ibid.

CHAPTER 10: THE BIG BUSINESS OF BORDER SECURITY

1. Todd Miller, "The Billion-Dollar Industry of Border Security," CBSNews.
   com, June 8, 2012, accessed April 26, 2013, http://www.cbsnews.com/8301
   -215_162-57449831/the-billion-dollar-industry-of-border-security/.
2. Adam Bruns, "Keeping it Real," *Site Selection,* October 2010, accessed May 26,
   2013, http://www.siteselection.com/ssinsider/snapshot/Keeping-it-real.cfm.
3. Todd Miller, "Follow the Money: The University of Arizona's Border War,"
   NACLA Report on the Americas, spring 2012.
4. "Justify Your Attendance," GovSec West website, accessed May 27, 2013, http://
   govsecinfo.com/events/govsec-west-2013/information/attend/justifyatten
   dance.aspx.
5. Brian Skoloff, "Border security expo begins amid fed spending cuts," Associated
   Press, March 12, 2013, accessed March 12, 2013, http://hosted2.ap.org/APDEF
   AULT/386c25518f464186bf7a2ac026580ce7/Article_2013-03-12-Border%20
   Security%20Expo/id-8c1e3a60662042c39bdaf47fc1959a84.
6. Personal interview, March 12, 2013.
7. Ibid.
8. Clare Seelke and Kristin Finklea, "U.S.-Mexican Security Cooperation: The
   Mérida Initiative and Beyond," Congressional Research Service, January 14,
   2013, accessed April 25, 2013, http://www.fas.org/sgp/crs/row/R41349.pdf.
9. Ibid.
10. Fiscal Year (FY) 2010 Homeland Security Grant Program (HSGP) Frequently
    Asked Questions (FAQs), 2010, accessed May 22, 2013, http://www.fema.gov
    /txt/government/grant/2010/fy10_hsgp_faq.txt.
11. "Secretary Napolitano Announces More Than $1.8 Billion in Fiscal Year 2010
    Preparedness Grants," Press Release, Office of the Press Secretary, US Depart-
    ment of Homeland Security, July 15, 2010, accessed May 22, 2013, http://www
    .dhs.gov/news/2010/07/15/secretary-napolitano-announces-more-18-billion
    -fiscal-year-2010-preparedness-grants.
12. Fiscal Year (FY) 2012 Homeland Security Grant Program (HSGP) Frequently
    Asked Questions (FAQs), 2012, accessed May 22, 2013, http://www.fema.gov
    /pdf/government/grant/2012/fy12_hsgp_faq.pdf.
13. Brady McCombs and Stephen Ceasar, "Border program has vague goals, lit-
    tle oversight," *Arizona Daily Star,* November 15, 2009, accessed May 22, 2013,
    http://azstarnet.com/news/local/border/border-program-has-vague-goals
    -little-oversight/article_1d28018f-800d-5610-a34d-d8a430c14192.html.
14. Stephen Ceasar and Brady McCombs, "Officers worked long shifts, accrued
    sizable pay," *Arizona Daily Star,* November 15, 2009, accessed May 22, 2013,
    http://azstarnet.com/news/local/border/officers-worked-long-shifts-accrued
    -sizable-pay/article_52873ce8-1e0f-52ee-851a-b9e5b6a4770c.html.
15. Ibid.
16. Curt Prendergrast, "Overtime pay turns sheriff's pay scale upside down,"
    Nogales International, April 26, 2013, accessed May 22, 2013, http://www.no

galesinternational.com/news/overtime-pay-turns-sheriff-s-pay-scale-upside
-down/article_f814ec32-ae87-11e2-b428-001a4bcf887a.html?mode=story.

17. Ibid.

18. Nathan Scharn, "Oceanside police pick up speed in the water," *San Diego Union-Tribune,* July 21, 2012, accessed May 22, 2013, http://www.utsandiego .com/news/2012/Jul/21/oceanside-police-pick-speed-water/?#article-copy.

19. Tim Leeds, "Sheriff's office puts Homeland Security trucks into use," *Havre Daily News,* September 24, 2010, accessed May 22, 2013, http://www.havre dailynews.com/cms/news/story-191649.html.

20. Julio Morales, "Imperial City Council approves purchase of incident command patrol unit," *Imperial Valley Press,* May 2, 2013, accessed May 22, 2013, http:// articles.ivpressonline.com/2013-05-02/imperial-city-council_38990980.

21. "About BORDERS," National Center for Border Security and Immigration, University of Arizona, accessed May 26, 2013, http://www.borders.arizona.edu /cms/about-borders.

22. Stew Magnuson, "DHS Centers of Excellence Spared from Budget Cuts," *National Defense,* April 2012, accessed May 26, 2013, http://www.national defensemagazine.org/archive/2012/April/Pages/DHSCentersofExcellence SparedfromBudgetCuts.aspx.

23. "About the Park," UA Tech Park, University of Arizona, accessed May 26, 2013, http://www.uatechpark.org/static/index.cfm?action=group&contentID=8.

24. Ibid.

25. Personal interview, August 12, 2013.

26. Ibid.

27. Ibid.

28. "About ALIS," ALIS corporate website, accessed May 26, 2013, http://www .alisinc.com/?q=content/about-alis.

29. Tom Barry, "Who Is Securing the Texas Border?" Research: Commentary, Center for Immigration Policy, March 12, 2012, accessed May 26, 2013, http://www .ciponline.org/research/entry/who-is-securing-texas-border.

30. Ibid.

31. Jeremy Schwartz, "DPS outsourced border security to private firm via no-bid contracts," *Austin American-Statesman,* March 15, 2012, accessed May 26, 2013, http://www.statesman.com/news/news/state-regional-govt-politics/dps -outsourced-border-security-to-private-firm-via/nRmFb/.

32. Jeremy Schwartz, "DPS improperly diverted money between contracts for border security firm, review finds," *Austin American-Statesman*, March 29, 2012, accessed May 26, 2013, http://www.statesman.com/news/news/local /dps-improperly-diverted-money-between-contracts-fo/nRmZn/.

CHAPTER 11: THE FORGOTTEN NORTHERN BORDER

1. Dee Camp, "Drug drops become 'epidemic,'" *The Omak-Okanogan County Chronicle,* March 29, 2006, accessed August 21, 2013, http://www.omakchroni cle.com/archives/db_stories.asp?story=20060329A01-1.

2. Yvonne Abraham, "Volunteers beginning watch near Canada line," *The Boston Globe,* October 4, 2005, accessed February 10, 2013, http://www.boston .com/news/local/vermont/articles/2005/10/04/volunteers_beginning_watch _near_canada_line/.

3. "Ahmed Ressam's Millenium Plot," PBS Frontline, accessed June 6, 2013, http:// www.pbs.org/wgbh/pages/frontline/shows/trail/inside/cron.html.

4. United States of America v. Mokhtar Haouari, US District Court, Southern District of New York, Case no. S400Cr.15, July 3, 2001.
5. "Ahmed Ressam's Millenium Plot," PBS Frontline.
6. Ibid.
7. Ibid.
8. United States of America v. Mokhtar Haouari.
9. "Ahmed Ressam's Millenium Plot," PBS Frontline.
10. United States of America v. Mokhtar Haouari.
11. "Ahmed Ressam's Millenium Plot," PBS Frontline.
12. Ibid.
13. Amy Forliti, "Mohammed Abdullah Warsame, Terror Suspect, Deported To Canada," *The Huffington Post,* October 8, 2010, accessed June 6, 2013, http://www.huffingtonpost.com/2010/10/08/mohammed-abdullah-warsame_n_756263.html.
14. "Two Defendants Sentenced to 26 and 14 Years in Prison for Conspiring to Provide Material Support to the LTTE, A Foreign Terrorist Organization," Press Release, US Attorney's Office, Eastern District of New York, January 22, 2010, accessed June 6, 2013, http://www.justice.gov/usao/nye/pr/2010/2010jan22b.html.
15. Stewart Bell, "'Reject violence,' jailed Tiger arms broker urges," *National Post,* September 29, 2011, accessed June 6, 2013, http://news.nationalpost.com/2011/09/29/drop-tigers-jailed-arms-broker-urges/.
16. Edwin Mora, "Canadian Border Bigger Terror Threat Than Mexican Border, Says Border Patrol Chief," CNSNews.com, May 18, 2011, accessed July 29, 2013, http://cnsnews.com/news/article/canadian-border-bigger-terror-threat-mexican-border-says-border-patrol-chief.
17. David Perera, "Americans form greatest percentage of known terrorists crossing U.S. border," *Fierce Homeland Security,* January 16, 2013, accessed July 29, 2013, http://www.fiercehomelandsecurity.com/story/americans-form-greatest-percentage-known-terrorists-crossing-us-border/2013-01-16.
18. Telephone interview, August 1, 2013.
19. Ibid.
20. "Drug bust in Michigan's Thumb exposes use of tiny airports by Canadian smugglers," *The Blade* (Associated Press), May 15, 2011, accessed August 4, 2013, http://www.toledoblade.com/local/2011/05/15/Drug-bust-in-Michigans-Thumb-exposes-use-of-tiny-airports-by-Canadian-smugglers.html.
21. Ibid.
22. *Northern Border Strategy,* US Department of Homeland Security, July 2012, accessed August 4, 2013, http://www.hsdl.org/?view&did=710991.
23. Ibid.
24. Mitchell Maddux, "French Canadian drug kingpin pleads guilty to trafficking marijuana," *The New York Post,* May 29, 2013, accessed August 4, 2013, http://www.nypost.com/p/news/local/brooklyn/french_canadian_drug_kingpin_pleads_yc0mujvl8BDyUPB31eVBvN.
25. *United States-Canada Joint Border Threat and Risk Assessment,* US Customs and Border Protection, Canada Border Services Agency, and the Royal Canadian Mounted Police, July 2010, accessed August 4, 2013, http://www.dhs.gov/xlibrary/assets/us-canada-jbtra.pdf.
26. Ibid.
27. "Under Siege: America's Northern Border," The Discovery Channel, aired on March 17, 2013.

28. Ibid.

29. "Reporting Requirements for Private Boat Operators in the Great Lakes Region," US Customs and Border Protection pamphlet, January 2008, accessed August 22, 2013, http://www.cbp.gov/linkhandler/cgov/travel/pleasure_boats /boats/pleasure_locations/great_lakes.ctt/great_lakes.pdf.

30. "Diver caught smuggling marijuana across U.S.-Canada border," FOXNews .com, August 21, 2013, accessed August 22, 2013, http://www.foxnews.com/us /2013/08/21/diver-caught-smuggling-marijuana-across-us-canada-border/.

31. Telephone interview, July 24, 2013.

32. Ibid.

33. Ibid.

34. "Meth Boom Montana," *Drugs, Inc.*, National Geographic Channel, aired December 9, 2012.

35. Ibid.

36. "Apprehension and Seizure Statistics—Fiscal Year 2012," US Border Patrol, April 2013, accessed August 9, 2013, http://www.cbp.gov/linkhandler/cgov /border_security/border_patrol/usbp_statistics/usbp_fy12_stats/appr_seiz _stats.ctt/appr_seiz_stats.pdf.

37. Telephone interview, August 1, 2013.

38. *Northern Border Strategy*, US Department of Homeland Security.

39. Thomas Walkom, "Stephen Harper's U.S. border deal does imperil Canadian sovereignty," *The Toronto Star*, August 1, 2013, accessed August 22, 2013, http://www.thestar.com/news/canada/2013/08/01/surprise_stephen_harpers _us_border_deal_does_imperil_canadian_sovereignty_walkom.html.

CHAPTER 12: CONCLUSIONS

1. "A Guide to S.744: Understanding the 2013 Senate Immigration Bill," Immigration Policy Center, July 10, 2013, accessed August 23, 2013, http://www .immigrationpolicy.org/special-reports/guide-s744-understanding-2013-sen ate-immigration-bill.

2. Adam Isacson, "Senate Bill Sets an Unmeetable Standard on Border Security," Washington Office on Latin America, April 22, 2013, accessed August 23, 2013, http://www.wola.org/commentary/senate_bill_sets_an_unmeetable _standard_on_border_security.

3. Ibid.

4. Ashley Parker, "Border Deal by 2 in G.O.P. Lifts Chances of Immigration Bill," *The New York Times*, June 21, 2013, accessed August 23, 2013, http://mobile .nytimes.com/2013/06/21/us/politics/2-gop-senators-reach-deal-on-border -security-plan.html.

5. Andrew Becker, "Border agency report reveals internal struggles with corruption," Center for Investigative Reporting, January 29, 2013, accessed August 9, 2013, http://cironline.org/reports/border-agency-report-reveals-internal -struggles-corruption-4126.

6. Ibid.

7. John Rosman, "Measurements Of Border Security Remain Opaque," Fronteras Desk, March 22, 2013, accessed August 23, 2013, http://www.fronteras desk.org/news/2013/mar/22/measurements-border-security-opaque -immigration/?utm_source=twitter.com&utm_medium=referral&utm_cam paign=fronteras-twitter.

8. Yasmin Tadjdeh, "DHS Struggles to Find Effective Measures for Border Security," *National Defense*, May 2013, accessed August 2013, http://www.nationaldefensemagazine.org/archive/2013/May/Pages/DHSStrugglestoFindEffectiveMeasuresforBorderSecurity.aspx.

9. "A Guide to S.744," Immigration Policy Center.

10. Christopher Sherman, "House Panel's GOP Members Tour Texas-Mexico Border," Associated Press, August 6, 2013.

11. Telephone interview, June 13, 2013.

12. Bob Ortega, "Border Security Faults May be Result of Poor Analysis," *The Arizona Republic*, July 20, 2013, accessed August 25, 2013, http://www.azcentral.com/news/politics/articles/20130715border-security-poor-analysis.html?nclick_check=1.

13. Ibid.

INDEX